DECISIONS

DECISIONS
An Engineering and Management Perspective

Gerard H. Gaynor

3M Director of Engineering, Retired
IEEE Life Fellow

Library of Congress Cataloging-in-Publication Data:

Gaynor, Gerard H.
  Decisions : an engineering and management perspective / Gerard H. Gaynor.
    pages cm
  ISBN 978-0-470-16759-5 (pbk.)
 1. Decision making.   2. Problem solving.   3. Management.   I. Title.
  HD30.23.G374 2015
  658.4'03–dc23

                                                              2014039299

Printed in the United States of America

10 9 8 7 6 5 4 3 2 1

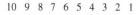

To my family, friends, and those who stir my imagination.

PREFACE

The history of failed projects, both large and small, provides well-documented evidence that there's much room for improvement. Research shows that less than 20 percent of projects meet requirements, schedule for implementation, and estimated cost. There are many reasons which crosscut the whole decision-making structure of organizations. At one end of the continuum is a lack of sufficient operations knowledge by executives at the decision-making level, and a lack of business perspective by the engineering and professional communities of the organization at the other. Approval of a major project that involves all organizational functions for its implementation, and consumes major organizational resources, requires one decision; the implementation of that decision may require thousands and often millions of decisions. Therein lies the dilemma.

A governing body approves a major project that is vital to the organization's sustainability, without a full understanding of the impact on the organization's operational functions and availability of the capabilities and effort required to implement the project successfully. The Board approves a major cost-reduction program, but the fulfillment of the decision becomes the responsibility of people who are not identified at the time of the decision. In essence, people who make the macro decision too often do not fully understand the scope and effort required to integrate the required competencies for fulfilling the decision's objectives; too often they are too far away from where the real work that takes place. Fulfilling the requirements of a decision involves getting into the nitty-gritty details and resolving the conflicting requirements that arise among the functional groups.

Industry's track record *of fulfilling* the three constraints of project management—meeting requirements, on-time delivery, and at estimated cost—has not garnered any awards; as a matter of fact, a realistic appraisal might record them as dismal. Some examples include such efforts as the Chrysler–Daimler-Benz merger that after many years ended in the purchase of Chrysler by Fiat; the collapse of General Motors and reconstruction under a government-financed program; Eastman Kodak's struggle to transition from traditional photography to digital; IBM and its missed personal computer market and then a rescue by Lou Gerstner; projects like the Big Dig in Boston and the New Denver Airport that involved many delays and cost overruns; Hewlett Packard's acquisition of Digital Equipment and a succession of reorganizations and chief executive officer (CEO) replacements; the 3-year delay in delivery of the Boeing Dreamliner; the dot.com debacle; managing the aftermath of Hurricane Katrina;

dealing with the earthquake and tsunami that struck northeast Japan and brought worldwide attention to the safety issues related to nuclear power; the problems associated with the start-up of the Affordable Care Act, and the thousands of other projects that fail to deliver the expected results on time and at cost. If you doubt that a problem exists, review your organization's project performance over the past five years.

Business press and management books, academic papers in journal and conferences, and other sources promoting management thought related to decision-making generally focus attention on the macro decision made at the executive levels of an organization, but seldom consider those thousands and often millions of decisions made after the macro decision sets the project in motion. These sources would lead us to believe that organizational boards, CEOs, and the highest level executives are the only ones who make decisions. The daily headlines tell the stories of the macro decision to invest billions of dollars in a new aircraft, to make the next round of staff cuts to improve financial performance, to merge or acquire an organization, or to implement the latest management panacea to guarantee unconditional success.

Decisions examines the issues required to stimulate new thinking for improving the decision-making processes to achieve higher project success rates by including implementation requirements in the executive decision-making process. Performance can be enhanced by understanding the actions and processes required to implement the decision, prior to making the macro decision. While that first macro decision initiates a project or some action, successful performance depends on how the organization manages the thousands and often millions of subsidiary decisions. *Decisions* considers what it takes to convert the macro decision into a positive outcome, to resolve the gap that exists between the macro and subsidiary decisions, to understand why so many decisions fail to meet expectations, to direct the mindset of the engineering community to focus on its relation to other organizational units, to perform diligently the up-front work required to meet objectives, to stop squandering valuable talent and resources, to urge engineers and other discipline professionals to take a more business-oriented approach in participating in the organization's decision-making process, and last but not least, to not only recognize the importance and role of communication in all decision-making processes, but to initiate appropriate communication processes.

Decisions also considers the critical decisions that need to be addressed in conjunction with preparations for making the macro decision. While the macro decision, made at the upper levels of management, begins the process of implementing some specific action, the preliminary effort seldom involves sufficient effort on what I refer to as the *up-front* work. The up-front work for approving an expenditure of resources includes developing the details of the *how* and *what* it will take to accomplish that which will be approved; this generally lacks the *specifics*. Those *specifics,* if not considered prior to approval of a project, frustrate the process of meeting requirements. As an example, many decisions involve the global economy, global participation, and global access to human and physical resources that add layers of complexity and are too often neglected. In the final analysis, a macro decision, which does not consider an implementation plan, leaves the organization to face those unintended consequences. But, these unintended consequences come about because of a lack of in-depth consideration of potential problems. We've all heard the comments; "Don't worry about it; we'll take care of it later." Those unintended consequences are not really unintended; they come about because of faulty assumptions and a lack of thinking at the time the macro decisions are made. This does not minimize the need for financial analysis.

From my experiences as an engineer and technology executive, all organizational decisions relate to some type of activity, and hopefully related to a specific project. Every activity that requires an allocation of human and physical resources involves identifying its purpose, scope, and benefits to the organization. Projects involve those identified by quantitative or qualitative measurements; the quantitative by some return on investment measure and the qualitative on providing some social benefit. Industry's track record of managing the three conditions for acceptable project management performance–satisfying requirements/objectives, delivering on schedule, and achieving estimated cost–has not garnered any performance accolades or awards. Research shows that industry needs a new mindset on project decision-making since less than 20 percent of projects meet the three conditions. You may question the 20 percent or argue that under no circumstances can the three conditions be met, but reflection on your organization's performance should convince you that there is room for significant improvement. Further, while some projects may meet the three conditions, the results often fail to contribute to the organization's bottom line: contributing to the bottom line is the final measure of performance.

Longitudinal studies have shown that too many projects fail to meet requirements with significant negative consequences. We can argue where the responsibilities for such poor performance should be assigned, but it's more important that we consider the issues and find ways to improve performance; it's all about across-the-board organizational leadership, spanning the continuum from executive levels to the discipline professionals.

I've structured *Decisions* to include topics that represent the greatest challenges to improved decision-making. Dealing with these challenges involves changing the mindset of engineering and its managers and convincing executive-level management to pursue the up-front work with greater diligence prior to making commitments. The process does not include more tools and techniques; it requires more thinking, in-depth thinking, and dedication to integrating the required resources.

Chapter 1: Confronting the Realities in Decision-Making provides some observations and perspectives on what it takes to convert macro decisions into useful results that not only meet the requirements, schedule, and estimated costs, but also have a positive impact on business performance. Decision-making at the executive level has changed within the past decades because many executives have limited time to spend on operations, so it's necessary to consider the business environment in which decisions are made. Executives now depend on reliable information from managers at all levels as well as the discipline specialists in all the related organizational functions. The history of failed projects teaches that somewhere in the past we began losing some management discipline as people interaction became more complex with a global economy.

Chapter 2: Managing the Organization explores these complexities involved in integrating the many functions and constituencies involved in providing information to reach a decision and the effort required to fulfill the commitments of the decision. While organizational functions work independently, their decisions impact others' performance. Decisions are not made in a vacuum; they're made by real people with different interests, biases, requirements, and levels of flexibility. This chapter considers the roles of executives, managers at all levels, project managers, and discipline specialists in reaching decisions. Who are the organization's executives, what are their responsibilities and to whom, and what are some of the common requirements expected from executives, managers, project managers, and discipline specialists.

Chapter 3: Decisions Have Consequences deals with specific types of decisions to provide some breadth of what decision-making involves. Yes, the world is more complex, and although information systems technology has not met the needs of the decision-makers, the inputs to the decisions have grown significantly. The economic environment does not mimic that of the past, except possibly in limited and specialized circumstances. Important decisions usually begin with a blank sheet of paper; rules of thumb do not apply. Knowledge and experience allow us to describe the known, the predictable, and the controllable issues within limits. Successful execution of any major decision depends on resolving the unknown, unpredictable, and uncontrollable issues and continually verifying the known, predictable, and controllable issues based on changing requirements and conditions. Chapter 3 spans the decision-making process and the sources for several types of decisions.

Chapter 4: Decisions and Project Scope focuses on projects that need approval by organizational boards, various executive and management committees at the operational and staff levels, and by engineers and other professional specialists. This chapter emphasizes the role of engineers and other discipline specialists and their part in the organization's management and directs attention to projects with various specific conditions: low impact to high impact, simple to complex, low cost to high cost, low risk to high risk, routine to innovative, current business to new business, current business to new game, decisions in functional units, and strategic to operational.

Chapter 5: Macro Decision to Implementation reviews the issues involved in executing these macro decisions that often involve a system of systems. The implementation of a "system of systems" macro decision brings together people not even remotely involved in developing the proposal, which led to the macro decision. If the macro decision involved investment in new plants and equipment, and required input from many organizational units, successful implementation will depend on the thousands or more decisions made by not only managers and specialists but also some key plant operators and technicians. If the macro decision involves developing a new-to-the-market product or service as an example, just about every organizational unit will be brought into the act. Chapter 5 considers the issues related to executing the decision from describing the problem to managing with a systems perspective.

Chapter 6: Making People Decisions focuses on the people decisions related to building and maintaining the competence of the organization's talent base for the sustainability of the organization. All decisions must eventually take into account the capability of the people responsible for implementing the decision. While some may appear to be trivial, on the surface, the consequences can damage an organization's reputation and destroy careers. It should not take years to determine that an employee has not met expectations; it does take courage to resolve situations related to inadequate performance. Some of the major issues involve energizing the HR department, hiring practices, evaluating performance, assessing employee potential, promotions, selecting team members, assigning work, transitioning from discipline specialist to management, and manager responsibility for building a technical succession plan.

Chapter 7: Developing Decision-Making Competencies presents the dilemmas organizations face developing decision-making capabilities. How do people learn to make decisions; fulfillment of those macro decisions becomes more dependent on decision-making competence of engineers and other discipline specialists and their managers; there are no 10 easy lessons. These are decisions that generally cannot be made by acting out some predetermined business model. We learn like we learn to master any other skill–through experience. Start with the small and somewhat inconsequential decisions, learn from the bad decisions, and practice, and learn that decision-making requires practice like any other skill. Chapter 7 focuses on approaches for developing decision-making capabilities of managers, engineers, and other discipline specialists.

Chapter 8: IBM Rochester, Minnesota: The Silverlake Project (Code Name) tells the story of how a group of engineers, programmers, and planners, totaling about 2,500, transformed themselves from a not-so-successful technologically driven laboratory into a customer-focused and market-driven organization. This transformation of IBM Rochester (IBMR) shows the role of decision-making at many levels in the IBM organization in meeting organizational expectations, creating a major change in organizational culture, and taking full advantage of the competencies of the available talent. The transformation began when Tom Furey, handpicked by IBM headquarters, and came to Rochester as manager of the IBMR Development Lab. This is a story of decision-making, which integrates the activities of the technology and marketing functions in making IBMR one of IBM's most successful businesses.

Chapter 9: Boeing and the 787 Dreamliner provides an excellent case study in decision-making that spans the continuum from the executive suite to the operational levels within Boeing, its outsourced partners, and to the factory floor. Boeing embarked on the design of a totally new aircraft based on (1) extensive use of reinforced composites as a substitute for aluminum; (2) not only extensive outsourcing to suppliers but also outsourcing to investment partners; (3) dependence on an extensive use of modeling and simulation of design, manufacturing, and assembly operations; and (4) reliance on high levels of precision in managing a major global supply chain. A program that was to be completed in half the time that it took to bring the Boeing 747 to the marketplace was bogged down by problems that delayed initial deliveries by more than 3 years and then grounded by various technical programs. This was a major undertaking with major changes not only in materials and design but also in production. It is truly a system of systems. My comments should not be considered as criticism of Boeing's executives, its managers, its engineers and other discipline professionals, or others responsible for implementation. There's no single reason why the delivery schedule of the first Dreamliner was extended on seven separate occasions.

Chapter 10: Communication in Decision-Making emphasizes the need for improving communication in managing the decision-making continuum from decision to execution. Improving communication is not some new twenty-first century phenomenon; Chester I. Barnard, an AT&T top executive, in 1938, considered communication as the central theme of management and the dominant factor in the structure of complex organizations. Lack of adequate and responsive communication plays a major role in the decision-making process, which in turn affects performance. Research shows that communication is a major contributor to performance. Research also has identified five requirements for effective and efficient communication—network transparency, knowledge codification, knowledge credibility, communication cost, and secrecy. Failure to solve problems is a result of poor communications and a lack of relevant and important information. Lack of adequate communication usually plays a major role in project failure. At the same time, adequate and appropriate communication does not guarantee project success. Nevertheless, communication drives decision-making and project execution. Chapter 10 focuses on the *communication* required to meet the requirements of the *decision to execution continuum;* it does not provide a guide for developing competencies in *communication.*

Chapter 11: Evaluating Decision-Making Performance provides a broad outline of the types of questions that may be asked in evaluating an organizations capability in making decisions. Not all decisions can be evaluated, time does not permit such actions, but successful and failed decisions of a cross-section of projects need to be evaluated to understand the variables that affect level of success or failure. Some answers are quantitative, others qualitative, but the qualitative should not be disregarded since they often tell as much as the quantitative, especially when dealing with people and departmental integration issues.

GERARD H. (GUS) GAYNOR

CONTENTS

Preface   xiii

1 CONFRONTING THE REALITIES IN DECISION-MAKING   1
History of Failed Projects   2
Organizational Discipline   5
Sources of Decision-Making Knowledge   7
Making Organizational Decisions   9
Key Points   11
Notes   12

2 MANAGING THE ORGANIZATION   13
Management Model   14
New Management Paradigm   15
Executives   17
Managers   19
Engineers and Other Discipline Specialists   24
Project Managers   25
Common Requirements for Executives, Managers, Engineers and
    Other Discipline Professionals, and Project Managers   28
Key Points   40
Notes   41

3 DECISIONS HAVE CONSEQUENCES   43
The Knowledge Chain   44
External Decision Drivers   46
Expanding Worldwide Operations   48
Dealing with Acquisitions and Mergers   49
Restructuring Organizations   52
Investing in New-to-the-Market Product/Services   55

Investing in New Technologies	57
Entering New Markets	59
Discontinuing a Product Line	60
Promoting Innovation and Entrepreneurship	61
Locating Business Operations	65
Key Points	66
Notes	67

4 DECISIONS AND PROJECT SCOPE — **69**

Organizational Decisions	70
Low Impact to High Impact	71
Simple to Complex	72
Low Cost to High Cost	74
Low Risk to High Risk	74
Upgrade to Innovative	76
Current Business to New Business Unit	77
Current Business Unit to a New Game	78
Decisions in Functional Units	79
Limited Scope to Expanded Scope	80
Strategic to Operational	81
Knockouts	82
Thinking Before Doing	83
Key Points	87
Note	88

5 MACRO DECISION TO IMPLEMENTATION — **89**

Executing the Decision	90
Using Tools and Techniques	91
Describing the Problem	94
Improving IT Project Performance	96
Advancing Project Management Practice	99
Managing Project Cycle Time	103
Managing with a Systems Perspective	109
Key Points	111
Notes	112

6 MAKING PEOPLE DECISIONS **113**

Energizing the Human Resource Department 114

Hiring Practices 116

Evaluating Employee Performance 120

Assessing Employee Potential 122

Promotions and Appointments 124

Selecting Team Members 126

Selecting the Right People 130

Assigning Work 131

Transitioning From Specialist to Manager 132

Salary Schedules 134

Continuing Education 134

Building a Succession Competence 136

Key Points 137

Notes 138

7 DEVELOPING DECISION-MAKING COMPETENCIES **139**

Decision Dilemmas 140

Learning to Make Decisions 144

Educating for Decision-Making 147

Dealing with Ambiguity 153

Executing the Deliverables 156

Key Points 162

Notes 163

8 IBM ROCHESTER, MINNESOTA: THE SILVERLAKE PROJECT **165**

Birth of IBMR Minnesota 166

Project Fort Knox 167

IBMR Faces Market Challenges 168

New Directions for IBM Rochester 168

Furey Asks the Hard Questions 169

Ambitious Goals 173

Market Launch 176

Lessons Learned 177

Key Points   184
Notes   185

9 BOEING AND THE 787 DREAMLINER   **187**
Dreamliner Scope and Expectations   188
Boeing—The Enterprise   189
The 787 Dreamliner Challenges   192
Commentary   198
Key Points   213
Notes   216

10 COMMUNICATION IN DECISION-MAKING   **219**
New-to-the-Market Product   221
What is Communication?   226
Types of Communication   228
Organizational Context   231
Barriers to Effective Communication   234
Ethical Issues in Communication   253
Eliminating the Communication Barriers   255
Key Points   258
Notes   259

11 EVALUATING DECISION-MAKING PERFORMANCE   **261**
People   262
Purposes   264
Processes   265
Strategic Thinking   266
Culture   267
Products and Services   268
Resources   270
Leadership   275
Innovation and Entrepreneurship   276
Organizational Readiness   278
Policies and Procedures   279
Employee Benefits   279
Downsizing   280

Going Global   281
Government Regulations   282
Offshore Operations   282
Integrating Organizational Units   283
General Governance Issues   284
Key Points   289
Notes   292

Index   **293**

1

CONFRONTING THE REALITIES IN DECISION-MAKING

Decisions: An Engineering and Management Perspective (Decisions) proposes that managing with a project perspective provides an opportunity to develop a discipline that enhances the decision-making process and a means for controlling those thousands of decisions before an objective becomes reality. In this context every action links to a specific project whether related to the Board of Directors, the Chief Executive Officer (CEO), and line and staff executives, managers at all levels, engineers and other discipline specialists in the organization's organizational units, and all support personnel. This applies to all activities whether performed within the organization or outsourced.

The business press and the management researches in academia publish volumes of information about the macro decisions made in the executive suites. Those decisions tend to be strategic, but with operational consequences. The literature on the conversion of those macro decisions into outcomes receives little if any attention. Execution of the macro decisions then becomes the domain of lower level managers and discipline specialists in research and development, marketing and sales, manufacturing, and the support functions.

Decisions: An Engineering and Management Perspective, First Edition. Gerard H. Gaynor.
© 2015 The Institute of Electrical and Electronics Engineers, Inc. Published 2015 by John Wiley & Sons, Inc.

Chapter 1 provides some observations, and perspectives on what it takes to convert macro decisions into useful results that not only meet the requirements, schedule, and estimated costs but also have a positive impact on business performance. Chapter 1 topics include

- History of Failed Projects
- Organizational Discipline
- Sources of Decision-Making Knowledge
- Making Organizational Decisions
- Key Points

HISTORY OF FAILED PROJECTS

The world of executive decision-makers has changed significantly in the past several decades. Fewer executives have long histories with their organization and tend to focus more on the financial and strategic and marketing issues rather than the technology issues that deal with operations. Executives also place greater emphasis on mergers and acquisitions, building the business, and the next quarter's results: they promote the organization's image. It's common to be critical about the emphasis and importance of achieving quarterly targets, but a word of caution, achieving the annual target requires achieving quarterly targets. As engineers, we know that delays in the initial stages of a project seldom are recovered. The days when the CEO was able to be engaged in product development or manufacturing or marketing with engineers and other discipline professionals and their managers seldom exist today: allocating a half day for visiting a research laboratory, reviewing some new major process improvement or being in a position to have first-hand information are at best very difficult to arrange.

The global workload no longer provides opportunities for executives to become actively involved in the realities of operational issues. CEOs and senior executives of major organizations in academia, government, industry, and the not-for-profit sector seldom have an opportunity to gain first-hand knowledge of organizational operations and functions by interacting with the people responsible for meeting those quarterly financial targets. Knowing requires more than reviewing bottom-line results from a report that too often, although unintentionally, obscures or distorts the facts of the issues under consideration. The executive paradigm focuses on delegation, and while delegation is essential, executive decisions now depend on information that has been screened through several levels of the organization and presents a new set of executive challenges. These comments are not made as criticism of the executive community, but to understand that in making those macro decisions, executives often lack a comprehensive understanding of the idiosyncrasies of the organization's operations, they do not understand the complexities involved with the implementation or choose to disregard them.

The environment in which executives operate has changed. We no longer live in an age where a person in the mail room becomes the CEO. Business now moves rapidly and doesn't allow for 20 or 25 years of experience to reach the top. These people, who made the move from the mail room to the executive suite, not only grew up with the organization, but also became the organization: they knew the organization from top to bottom; they didn't have to read about it. Further, they knew the people they worked for and with over many years. Executives and senior managers now operate under a different paradigm. Jack Welch, General Electric CEO retires with three top contenders as his replacement: Jeffery R. Immelt, James McNerney, and Robert Nardelli. Jeffery Immelt succeeds Jack Welch as General Electric CEO; James McNerney becomes the CEO of 3M for about 4 years, then becomes CEO of Boeing; Robert Nardelli joins Home Depot as CEO and after a not so successful performance becomes CEO of Chrysler, then part of Cerberus, and then is replaced by Sergio Marchionne of Fiat in April 2009 when Chrysler filed for Chapter 11 bankruptcy. Carly Fiorina became CEO of Hewlett Packard and after approximately 6 years departed because of a Board conflict, then explored a run for Senator from California and failed. Delta Airlines and Northwest received approval to merge both organizations, but questions continued if the executive levels of both organizations thoroughly understood what it takes to not only make a successful merger financially, but also, execute the merger effectively and efficiently and with minimum negative impact on customers.

The history of failed projects and unmet expectations continues to grow exponentially. It is difficult to identify projects that have met original requirements, time schedules, and projected costs. I'm not suggesting that achieving project success is a minor task. On the contrary, it is a very difficult task when we consider the human interaction required for success; it is a very difficult task when we pause to realize the need for integrating the many facets of a major project; it is a very difficult task when managers are not educated managerially and engineers and discipline specialists focus more on their disciplines than on the impact of their discipline on business performance. Very few in the technical and marketing communities realize that the business of engineering and marketing is business performance. Discipline competence, while absolutely essential, must be directed toward the broad needs of the business and the major component of that business involves a focus on sustaining business performance.

Research by Paul C. Nutt[1] shows that highly regarded managers often make bad decisions and the truth is that half of the organizational decisions fail.

Nutt's research includes detailed analysis of over 400 decisions to assess the decision-making practices, to account for the special situations confronted, and to measure success or failure. The findings show that failure usually stems from decision-maker actions and not from bad luck or situational limitations. Examples include the Firestone and Ford tire debacle in 2000, Eastman Kodak's late entrance into digital photography, the demise of the dot-coms, the inability of the US automobile industry to maintain its dominant position, the continued negative financial performance of the US Post Office, and the delivery issues with two major aircraft suppliers Boeing and Airbus. A study of the management decisions by federal, state, and local jurisdictions related to hurricane Katrina, the Big Dig in Boston, the Walter Reed Medical Center negligence related to returning veterans, the Challenger incident, delays and cost overruns in the construction of the Denver International Airport, the Deepwater Horizon incident in the Gulf of Mexico, and the waste generated in academia, government and industry at all levels certainly focuses our attention on the lack of executives to make timely decisions to prevent such disastrous and long-reaching outcomes.

Research by Heike Bruch and Sumantra Ghoshal[2] on the behavior of managers in well-known organizations shows some startling results based on measures of energy and focus. Their extensive research shows that 30 percent of managers were procrastinators (low energy, low focus), 20 percent were disengaged (low energy, high focus), and 40 percent were distracted (low focus, high energy), and only 10 percent were purposeful: purposeful being defined as highly energetic and highly focused. Such negative results definitely affect decision-making at all levels of the organization. You may question the results of the Bruch and Ghoshal research, but I ask you to reflect on the behavior of not only your managers, but also the executives, engineers, and the other discipline professionals.

Kathleen Eisenhardt[3] studied the speed at which managers make decisions. Eisenhardt concluded that slow decision-makers rely on planning and futuristic information while fast decision-makers gather real-time information and in essence *measure everything*. Eisenhardt's research shows that slow decision-makers take 12–18 months to reach a major decision, the fast decision-makers 2–3 months. Further, fast decision-makers use more information than slow decision-makers, develop more alternatives, and recognize conflict management as a critical element in making decisions. Of course, terms like more information, more alternatives, and how much conflict are all relative and will vary from project to project and organization to organization. We cannot predict the future, we can speculate, but too much speculation leads to paralysis. The research also revealed that fast decision-making is linked to strong performance; central decision-making is not faster; cognitive, emotional, political processes drive rapid decision-making; and operational decisions follow strategic decisions.

Aaron Shenhar and Dov Dvir[4] report the results of the Standish Group, Cooper, and their own research that includes a 15 year study of more than 600 projects. The Standish Group in 2000 found that only 28 percent of IT projects were successful and estimated that in 2003 the $382 billion spent on IT projects yielded $82 billion in total waste. One-third of all projects either failed or did not meet business requirements and had overruns of 200 and 300 percent. Cooper's studies on new product development showed that 46 percent of resources were allocated to projects that were cancelled or failed to deliver the expected returns. Over a 15-year period Shenhar and Dvir collected data on more than 600 projects in business, government, and the not-for-profit sector, in various countries, and found that about 85 percent of projects overran scheduled time by 70 percent and budget by 60 percent. A 1998 study by Bull Computer Corporation in the United Kingdom found that 75 percent of IT projects missed their deadlines, 55 percent were over budget, and 37 percent failed to meet project requirements.

In *Innovation by Design,* Gaynor[5] included a chapter on the *Innovation Prevention Department* and listed the 25 obstacles to promoting innovation. Those related to decision-making included rejecting new thinking of any kind, focusing on single issues, ignoring the blind spots, being insufficiently informed, keeping decision processes confidential, disregarding potential knockouts in the early stage of innovation, preventing rule breaking, and disregarding the constructive mavericks.

These few examples demonstrate how the lack of decision-making capability affects organizational performance. Somehow over the years many organizations have lost their management discipline. As I reviewed this research and considered my past personal experiences and how engineers view their role in the business enterprise, I raise the question: are engineers missing an opportunity to expand their base of operation and influence and take a proactive approach in the management of the business enterprise?

ORGANIZATIONAL DISCIPLINE

What has happened to the performance levels of managers, engineers, and other discipline specialists? Organizational cultures have changed significantly in the past several decades and have been driven by some form of entitlement. This began during the early 1980s and was followed by the dot-com era that began to make headway in 1997. It was the time when organizations introduced the idea of hiring bonuses in the search for engineers with advanced competence in specialized areas. It then became easy for moving from one organization to another and in the process gaining a financial benefit by distorting salary structures. There is no doubt that the dot-com era was one of high energy and opportunities for those who wished to pursue their vision of the future: it also introduced an era where the career path involved "making a quick buck" and retiring early. With the demise of the dot-com era many managers and discipline specialists became self-satisfied with their work environment and upper management never recognized what began to occur in the early 1980s. I'm not against advancing one's career; however, long-term careers require a discipline that involves making a contribution in each move.

By mid-1980 the management situation was best exemplified by an article "Broken Bonds" written by Amanda Bennett,[6] a writer for the Wall Street Journal, who presented a classical description of average mid-level managers. Realistically, the description fits managers, engineers and discipline specialists at all levels, and even applies to many executives whether in academia, government, or industry. Bennett says that most middle managers thought they had a contract with the corporation, and even though it was unwritten and unspoken, it was very specific. It said:

"Take care of business and we'll take care of you. You don't have to be a star; just be faithful, obedient, and moderately competent, and this will be your home for as long as you want to stay."

What a stinging indictment. It appears that leadership which requires sticking your neck out, being proactive, taking initiative, accepting risk, dealing with uncertainties, meeting commitments, basing decisions on fundamentally sound premises, understanding the business environment, and having the courage to deliver bad news was no longer a prerequisite for becoming a manager. From years of personal experience, I suggest that engineers and other discipline specialists succumbed to practice similar behaviors. At the same time, many organizations stopped filling the pipeline with new entrants, who will provide a base for not only managerial and executive talent, but also engineers and other specialized disciplines.

Someplace along the line executives, for many different reasons, allowed a lack of discipline to permeate the organization. James M. Kilts[7] in *Doing What Really Matters* cites a situation, when he became CEO of Gillette, a part of Procter & Gamble. Kilts asked the senior vice president of administration and human resources to present an overview of how Gillette was organized and their performance management system. As the senior vice president described the organization, Kilts asked about the categories used in evaluating manager performance. There were five categories: Does Not Meet Expectations, Needs Improvement, Meets Expectations, Exceeds Expectation, and Outstanding. When Kilts asked what the percentages were in each of the categories, the VP responded that 65 percent were in the Exceed Expectations and followed up by saying that's where most companies were at. So Kilts wondered how business results justified such ratings. Further, research on Gillette's 3000 worldwide managers showed 59 percent had been rated Exceed and 4 percent Outstanding, 34 percent received a Meets rating, and 3 percent a Needs Improvement or Inadequate rating. During this same period, Gillette's sales growth was zero, profit growth was zero, and earnings per share were up 4 percent. At the same time two-thirds of the worldwide group of 3000 managers were rated Exceeding Expectations and Outstanding.

This situation is not solely a problem within Gillette: it is not only a common business problem, but also a national problem affecting all segments of society. For some reason we have stopped making critical assessments of performance. There is a difference between a critical assessment and criticism. Critical assessment requires follow-up measures to improve performance. We have developed a culture that makes excuses for nonperformance and on too many occasions even rewards it. Every organization recognizes how that typical distribution curve has shifted to the right where more and more people exceed the requirements. Such actions do an injustice to the organization and the employees. Unfortunately, the future does not hold great prospects for change.

As our social culture moved from the Traditionalists (born pre-1945) to GEN Y (1980 to present), we moved toward greater entitlement, and new organizational cultures followed: both have influenced each other. The 1950s were governed by accountability; performance appraisals were more realistic; communication took place face-to-face; newly minted graduates recognized the need for experience; organizations were not involved in providing guidance on personal matters; mental-health days were unknown; meeting commitments was not a choice; and this list could continue. Slowly but surely, employees became more dependent on the organization. Historically, if unchecked, we could go back to the days where the company owned town, company owned schools and grocery stores, and the company was the provider of recreational and other personal needs. This is not to suggest that the 1950s represented some form of organizational utopia, definitely not, but to show the progression of the entitlement society.

SOURCES OF DECISION-MAKING KNOWLEDGE

Today's mega-organizations prevent executives from having hands-on knowledge, if for no other reason than a lack of adequate time: executives now depend almost entirely on delegation and trust, except on programs where their past experience allows them a level of comfort. This dependence on others, and often without even cursory knowledge of the topic under discussion, changes the managing model. Often not even those secondary and tertiary sources of information are totally knowledgeable about just what is involved in reaching a decision. As managing now involves integration of functions and disciplines, it becomes more difficult to negotiate the selection of an appropriate option. Time is a constraint. Executives face many challenges in allocating their time: consider the increase in governmental regulations at all levels, from the federal to the smallest village, and then add the international legal requirements.

Executives and managers in this twenty-first century face an almost impossible task to fully understand the issues being considered by their many organizational units, the idiosyncrasies' of the many market segments in which they operate, and the technologies used throughout those diverse product/service organizations. We know that the success of any decision requires linking the decision with an understanding of the difficulties associated with the implementation process. We know the competencies to make a macro decision to authorize some major investment differ from the competencies required to implement the decision. However, in the final analysis, implementation determines not only the future of the organization, but also the future of those who participate in the venture and finally society.

Executives now depend almost totally on other executives, managers at various levels in the organization, engineers, and other discipline specialists to provide major input to any major decision that crosscuts functions or disciplines; they require and depend on integrity and candor of the supporting managers, engineers, and discipline specialists to move the organization forward. Unfortunately integrity and candor are often in short supply; especially candor. As humans, in one way or another, we follow some identifiable philosophy of life. That philosophy defines attributes, and application of integrity is one of those attributes. Integrity is more than telling the truth. We speak of the integrity of a design. What does that mean? It means robustness which translates into everlasting. Practicing integrity allows our colleagues to know where we stand on issues and what to expect from us; it defines our value system. Candor begins by telling it like it is, but being cautious not to offend. When, as executives and managers, we fail to be candid in managing the activities of others, we begin to destroy careers. When, as engineers and other discipline specialists, we fail to deal with candor, we plant the first seeds of project failure.

The decision-makers of that first macro decision lose control once that decision has been passed on to subordinate levels of management for implementation. The world of managing has become more complex and as that complexity increases executive level management must find a way to move the macro decision to a successful conclusion which includes meeting three basic conditions—meeting requirements, schedule, and estimated cost—that requires an understanding of the implications on the implementation process.

MAKING ORGANIZATIONAL DECISIONS

A daily scan of the business press gives the impression that organizational boards, CEOs, and other high level executives are the only ones who make decisions. That's not quite the real world. Yes, they make the macro decision, but every macro decision usually requires hundreds, thousands, and sometimes millions of decisions, anyone of which can negatively affect the outcome.

There is no doubt that decision-making processes have become more complex at all organizations since the decision-makers now depend more on expertise which they do not possess and the dimensions have increased significantly: global competitiveness, technology advancements and complexities, and customer demands have introduced issues which in the past were not considered. No individual in today's organizational environment possesses all the knowledge required to make the appropriate decision. While one individual may make the final decision, that decision-maker depends on many sources besides his or her experiences and biases. While communication systems now allow for instantaneous contact across a global network, decision-making processes now involve greater consideration of the impact of cultural differences, language barriers, time constraints, business practices, political and economic situations, and working habits. While choices for action have increased significantly, these cultural differences add an element that cannot be disregarded.

There are no algorithms that guarantee the success of a decision. The algorithms can define the "a" to "b" to "n" but more is required than the sterile algorithm to reach a decision. The algorithm, if used, only provides part of the information. Developing a balance between rational decision-making must take into account human behavior as practiced in a particular culture. Depending solely on intuition can be as dangerous as depending solely on rational decision-making that fails to take into account the environment which will be affected by the decision. Decisions must take into account the human response to the decision and consequent behavior toward the decision must be considered in addition to the rationality of the decision. As noted previously, decision-making involves factual and value elements and the value elements may have an equal or higher priority. Those decisions have a significant impact on the organization's performance. In the final analysis decision-making requires judgment.

Figure 1.1 illustrates a simplified version of a typical organization with its many levels and functions that become the building block for groups of divisions, multiple groups per sector, and corporate. A typical division of an organization includes, Product Genesis, Distribution, and Services. Product Genesis includes research, development, and design. Distribution includes manufacturing, marketing and sales, physical distribution, and customer service. A group generally involves several divisions; a sector is comprised of several groups. Corporate

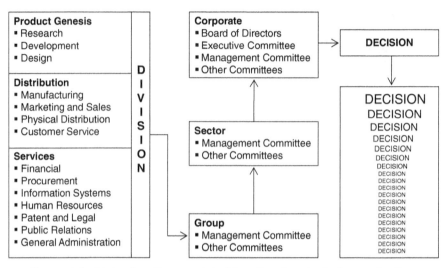

Figure 1.1. Major functions and decision flow in a typical organization.

includes all the groups. Divisions, groups, sectors, and corporate include various levels of services such as financial, procurement, information systems, human resources, patent and legal, public relations, and general administration. What each of these organizational units is called is immaterial; they are shown only to indicate a typical hierarchical organizational structure. A proposal for approval of an activity will go through a series of approvals by higher level authority and eventually lands at some corporate level for approval. That decision, as noted, then results in the multiplicity of decisions where any one of them can create delays, increase costs, and in some way, not only disappoint customers, but also force them to choose other suppliers.

Requests for a decision generally arise from the action of some organizational unit or individual. Decisions at the corporate level include (1) mergers and acquisitions; (2) approval of budgets and capital investments; (3) expansion into worldwide markets; (4) major investments in research, new product development, and innovation; (5) personnel issues; and (6) issues that have important organizational consequences.

The process for gaining approval at any of the management levels does not provide any difficulties if the organization describes the procedures and follows them. Here is an example: Assume that a request for funding a major investment in a new-to-the-market product arises at the division level and requires approval at some corporate level that could include an executive or management committee or the board of directors. Most organizations have established policies as to level of approval for new investments. Since the request comes from a division, elements of product genesis, distribution, and services as shown in

Figure 1.1 will be involved in preparing a proposal. The proposal will be fully vetted by the division management and subsequently move to the group and sector management. There could be several iterations, since the sector executive will most likely only be willing to present the proposal to the decision-makers if it meets the strategic directions of the organization and has a possibility for approval. The sector executive plays a key role since he/she has a more comprehensive picture of the organization's future directions. However, if the division and group executives communicate effectively with the sector executive and staff during the proposal preparation process, there should be no difficulty obtaining support. However, too often proposals are not socialized sufficiently to determine possible objections and then countering those objections in preparing the final proposal. Approval of the project is the first decision that launches the project. The execution of the project will be the responsibility of the division through its product genesis, distribution, and service functions. Success will require integration and timely performance of all the related division organizational units and their subunits. However, this one decision made at the executive levels for approval will now require thousands of decisions: some will require even more thought than the approval decision and of course others by rules of thumb. The process appears to be simple but unfortunately complications arise from participants with their biases and prejudices, unjustified personal likes and dislikes, and the naysayers more satisfied with maintaining the status quo.

KEY POINTS

- **Failed Projects**. Our personal experiences clearly demonstrate that failure to meet project requirements, schedule, cost, and business performance not only significantly reduce the return to the stakeholders, but also generate an environment that leads to lower expectations.
- **Sources of Decision-Making Knowledge.** Knowledge, experience, and capability no longer resides in one person. The era of Henry Ford as lone decision maker no longer exists. Success now requires integration of information from many sources and the major decision-making body of an organization may be dependent on information from the depths of the organization; that new employee, who may have just joined the organization.
- **Making Organizational Decisions**. Organizations require some form of decision-making process. Participants need to understand what's required and it should not depend on one's level in the organization. That may be too much to expect, but nevertheless essential. No single process will meet

all requirements and the greater the global reach, the greater the need for that process to be clearly defined.

- **Decision-making Capability**. Our daily experiences with decision-makers and decision processes can supplement the body of research that continues to show a shortage of managers, engineers, and other discipline specialists who possess adequate decision-making capability. I use decision-making capability instead of skills or competence, because decision-making capability includes a combination of competencies. These competencies include breadth of knowledge; the competence to think deeply about the issues at hand; the competence to think from a systems perspective; the competence to accept the responsibility for the decision; the competence to communicate clearly and concisely; the personal characteristics of focus, self-confidence, dedication, respect, courage and integrity; and the put-it-all-together competence. These competencies describe decision-making capability.

NOTES

1. Paul C. Nutt, "Expanding the search for alternatives during strategic decision-making," *The Academy of Management Executive*, 18(4): 13–28, 2004.
2. Heike Bruch and Sumantra Ghoshal "Beware the busy manager," *Harvard Business Review*, Reprint 8903, pp. 5–9.
3. Kathleen M. Eisenhardt, "Making fast strategic decision in high-velocity environments," *Academy of Management Journal*, 32(3): 543–576, 1989.
4. Aaron Shenhar and Dov Dvir, *Reinventing Project Management*, Boston, MA: Harvard Business School Press, 2007, pp. 5–7.
5. Gerard H. Gaynor, *Innovation by Design*, New York: American Management Association, 2002, pp. 220–242.
6. Amanda Bennett, "Broken bonds," *The Wall Street Journal,* December 8, 1989. p. R21.
7. James M. Kits, *Doing What Matters*, New York: Crown Publishing Group, 2007, pp. 5–14.

2

MANAGING THE ORGANIZATION

Managing an organization or organizational unit of any size requires an understanding of the complexities involved in organizational decision-making at the executive, management, and the professional discipline levels, across the organization. Few decisions can be made where a decision-maker can exclude the impact of a decision on other organizational units. Chapter 2 explores these complexities involved in integrating the many functions and constituencies involved in providing information to reach a decision, and the effort required to fulfill the commitments of the decision. While organizational functions work independently, their decisions impact other's performance. Chapter 2 topics include

- Management Model—what are the new requirements?
- New Management Paradigm.
- Executives—who are the organization's executives?
- Managers—developing the competence to execute decisions.
- Engineers and Other Discipline Specialists—integrating organizational disciplines.

Decisions: An Engineering and Management Perspective, First Edition. Gerard H. Gaynor.
© 2015 The Institute of Electrical and Electronics Engineers, Inc. Published 2015 by John Wiley & Sons, Inc.

- Project Managers—reaching agreement between supporting disciplines.
- Common Requirements for Executives, Managers, Project Managers, and Discipline Specialists.
- Key Points
- Notes

MANAGEMENT MODEL

Decision-making requires managing the organization's priorities; integrating its functional activities; communicating clearly at all levels; and improving overall organizational effectiveness and efficiency. Once a macro decision has been made, at the executive level, the execution of the decision becomes the domain of many different levels of management and numerous disciplines of professional specialists in the organization's functional units.

Figure 2.1 describes the principal organizational functions which will be used as the organizational model throughout this book. The functions, as shown in Figure 2.1, fit any organization whether that organization is classified as industry, government, or academia; working in the profit or not-for-profit sector; and whether the organization provides products or services. To simplify and at the same time accommodate the vast differences in organizational structure, the model divides all activities into three categories: creation, delivery, and administration. *Creation activities* include research, development, design, manufacturing, marketing, and information. You may argue that service organizations do not include manufacturing, but in reality they do; eventually those reports, models, and related support documents must be prepared in some physical form.

Delivery of products and services includes sales, physical distribution, and customer service. Successful organizations depend on sales of products and services and take on many different organizational structures depending on the industry and the history of the industry. Sales in the fast-food industry require different approaches than sales in the auto industry. Physical distribution includes all the activities from order entry to delivery to the customer and receiving

PRINCIPAL ORGANIZATIONAL FUNCTIONS		
Creation	**Delivery**	**Services**
Research	Sales	Financie
Development	Physical Distribution	Procurement
Design	Customer Service	Patent and Legal
Manufcturing		Human Resources
Marketing		Communications
Information		General Administration

Figure 2.1. Principal organizational functions.

payment. Customer service involves all activities required to satisfy and keep a customer. The functions listed under Administration involve every enterprise to greater or lesser degrees.

The organizational model of Figure 2.1 shows the complexity involved in successfully executing decisions. A decision at the executive level, to invest in a new-to-the-market product or service, will include all the functions shown in Figure 2.1 to lesser or greater degrees. Integrating the activities of these functions and making the thousands of independent, yet interdependent decisions, involved in project execution presents significant challenges. Integrating not only the decision processes of each function, but also the work activities and requirements of each professional discipline, requires due diligence prior to fulfilling the requirements of the executive decision.

NEW MANAGEMENT PARADIGM

Managing an organization in the twenty-first century can no longer be managed by twentieth century management policies and practices. The business practices, that guided Henry Ford in building the Ford Motor Company, and the strategic principles that guided Alfred P. Sloan in building General Motors Corporation, would prevent today's organizations from maintaining business viability. Today, the marketplace is the world, not the local community, state, or country; the transition has taken place slowly over the past 60 years. The United States no longer lives in a world with uninhabited markets; technological progress expands globally. This does not suggest that old principles no longer apply, but those management principles must be adapted to a new economic and social environment. New technologies have added more complexities. Information technologies now drive many decisions. While executives need some out-of-the-box thinking, they cannot disregard what's-in-the-box. Whether the more recent emphasis on big data will improve decision-making in the future remains to be seen.

In the 2008 No. 1 issue McKinsey Quarterly,[2] Gary Hamel, author of *The Future of Management* and Lowell Bryan author of *Mobilizing Minds,* which he co-authored with McKinsey partner Claudia Joyce, discussed innovative management. They call for *forward-looking executives* to look for a new management model. Hamel argues that the decades old practices of orthodox decision-making practices, organizational designs, and approaches to employee relations will undergo significant restructurings. Bryan and Claudia Joyce in *Mobilizing Minds* arrive at similar conclusions, but from a different perspective: the current management model, managing organizations based on hierarchical structure and labor and capital inputs, fails to emphasize collaboration and wealth creation by talented professionals (the knowledge workers) and adds unnecessary complexity. In both cases, the authors are asking executives to bring the same innovation energy to management innovation, as they now do in bringing innovative products and services to the marketplace. Hamel suggests that if you get the right people in the room, create the right incentives, eliminate the distractions, innovation can flourish. But, the minute you turn your back innovation dies.

Hamel notes that management was designed as a means for solving problems. In the days of Frederick Taylor, management involved replicating products and processes with greater efficiency. The current model involves getting people to serve the organization's goals. The future model should ask; how does management build organizations that encourage the gifts of creativity and passion and initiative? How does management build organizations that are nimble, that mobilize the imaginations of every employee, and that are engaging places of work? Whether that expectation has a chance of succeeding will be determined at some time in the future. Not everyone is passionate about the same issues. One may prefer to be dedicated totally to a profession another to a leisurely life on the beach. Bryan, on the other hand, focuses on the impact of technology and globalization on organizations; technology and globalization creating new opportunities, and companies struggling to take advantage of those opportunities.

The internet may have provided opportunities to change the way organizations plan, hire, motivate, organize, lead, and allocate resources. Hamel raises the issue of the impact on performance through technology management. But it appears that Hamel, like many academics and consultants; focus only on information technology which is a very narrow segment of technology, though vitally important. Information technology, although a great tool, is only a tool: it's a means to some end, not the end or the result. Too many technologies such as automation, communication, chemical, materials, and medical technologies are dismissed.

As part of this changing management paradigm, Hamel notes that the generation that has grown up on the internet and the web wants contributions to be judged simply on the merits of what one does, rather than on the basis of credentials, title, or providence. This is an old argument. Credentials, titles, birthright, and providence may play a role in rewarding employees, but we live in an imperfect world and have not found ways to differentiate levels of contribution. Who should receive the greatest merit, the person who originates the idea, the person who makes sense of the idea and develops it into a workable concept and provides a proof of concept, the person who put the proverbial meat on the bones, the inventor, the technical person or the marketing person, the innovator or entrepreneur, or the project manager who had the competence to put-it-all-together. Major tasks require an organization, a team, a task force, or some grouping of the required competencies, and while we can identify the individual contributions, the integrated contributions must meet expectations.

Bryan and Hamel also raise the issue of available talent. Talent appears to be what every organization seeks, but talent is not the issue. There's a market for talent and as long as you're willing to pay the price, it's probably available except in some very exclusive niches. The challenge involves organizing talent in such a way as to generate an income; more specifically generate a profit. The major issue involves integrating talent and technology as a catalyst to create value. A 3M Company CEO once remarked, "We achieve great things through average people." Having spent a major part of my career at 3M, I can attest to that statement. However, some of these average people were exceptional, with broad interest, high levels of insight, wide range of interests, and the capability of *putting-it-all-together.*

When it comes to reinventing management processes Hamel suggests that the vice president for human resources, the chief financial officer, and the director of planning should take the lead in reinventing management. Here is where I tend to question Bryan and Hamel's thesis; this was an interesting group of organizational executives to give responsibility for reinventing the organization; not a single individual with line or P&L responsibility. As an example: These staff groups are not generally known for their creative thinking that positively affects the organization's *bottom-line*; they're not exactly known for their innovation, they often are too far away from the action to understand the issues. They are not known for the freedom they would give employees to become innovators. I suggest that if an organization chooses to reinvent its management, it will be driven from middle and the bottom-up and not top-down: finance and HR may set goals, but they're not responsible for making something happen. The action takes place in the depths of the organization. The decision may come from the top, but it will be implemented through the efforts of the many suborganizational units. The reason that most organizational reengineering efforts fail to meet expectations is because they are driven top-down without supportive buy-in from the middle and the operational levels of the organization.

EXECUTIVES

The final performance evaluation, of an organization and its suborganizational units, stops at the highest level of assigned management responsibility. But the ability to meet expectations begins long before decisions are made. There is no doubt that at the time of decision many choices are made based on the available facts and the interpretation of incomplete information. If project approval would have to wait until all the facts were identified, no project would ever be developed. The time it would take to gather all the information, assess its usefulness, consider the alternatives, modify operating parameters, and reach an acceptable decision would delay implementation to the point where the project was no longer of value.

What groups of people make up an organizations' cadre of executives? Like the many levels of managers there are also levels of executives with different responsibilities and accountabilities. The list begins with the Chief Executive Officer (CEO); the immediate reports that might include the business sector or group executives; the staff executives for R&D, marketing, manufacturing, engineering, finance, human resources, and legal; and the executives of the many operational groups across the organization's global operations. These positions basically make up the senior executives of the organization. This group of executives is supported by the vice presidents of business divisions, geographical areas, managing directors of international subsidiaries, and functional directors in the operating divisions. Each of these executives plays a different role in meeting the organization's objectives. As an example: The issues that Mr. Toyoda, Toyota CEO, faced in February 2010 with the recall of millions of cars for safety problems are substantially different from those faced by a division vice president or the director of a functional group. The issues, that Alan Mulally faced when he departed Boeing to become CEO of Ford Motor Company in Dearborn, Michigan, were of greater magnitude and scope than those faced by any of his functional executives. His responsibility involved turning around a failing company that played a major role in the US economy. Top priorities included rationalizing business operations, shedding brands that no longer added value, and providing for a new lineup of products. Mulally has made great progress without government support. Were Messrs. Toyoda and Mulally the only executives or did those professional discipline specialists also play an executive role?

So, how do we describe this person we refer to as an *executive*? Trying to rationalize the many descriptions would not provide any benefit. An operational and practitioner description, not necessarily bound in theory, suggests that executives include the people who establish the mission, vision, and values of the organization and *execute* them with the support of *others*. The *others* include people in positions such as directors, several manager levels, the contributions of engineers and other discipline specialists, and all other participants. Organizations, as a general rule, fail to implement a consistent organizational pattern. Each of these categories immediately begins to proliferate to include senior executive in many variations, senior executive vice president, executive vice president, senior vice president, executive director, senior manager or executive manager, and the list could go on. Drucker[1] refers to *executives* as

> "... those knowledge workers, managers, or individual professionals who are expected by virtue of their position or their knowledge to make

decisions in the normal course of their work that have impact on the performance and results of the whole."

Peter Drucker raised the issue of the knowledge workers and suggests that in the modern organization, knowledge workers are *executives* by virtue of the fact that they contribute materially to the output of the organization. Knowledge workers make decisions; they do not just carry out orders given by others. By virtue of their knowledge, they are better equipped to make decisions in their sphere of knowledge than anyone else. Drucker cautions that knowledge work is not defined by quality or costs; it is defined by results. He provides the following example: Having many people involved on a particular market research effort may provide incremental insights, imagination, and quality that benefit the organization. But, think of the problems encountered with managing all the people interactions. The manager may be so occupied with the minutiae that little if any time is left for market research and the big decisions.

MANAGERS

After a major decision is made at the executive level, implementation of the decision transitions to various levels of managers. This group of managers, with their engineers and other discipline specialists and support people, play the major role that at this time includes resolving many unknown problems. These managers also take responsibility for decisions that they make within the limits of their authority. Some of these decisions may be minor and require little thought and others may be very complex. Some may be resolved through use of personal rules of thumb, and others may require extensive study.

So, who is a manager, what is the role of the manager and just what does it mean to manage? It's an accepted premise that managers get things done through others. However, I add a caveat to that premise; *managers do not manage people; they manage activities in which people participate.* This caveat should be made very clear to anyone who has responsibility for the actions of others, and especially when the management functions involve knowledge workers: those engineers and other discipline specialists. I'm always surprised; when the management research community speaks about managing people; how can one even think of managing professionals in any field, if you could, would that person be making the greatest contribution to the organization and at the same time enhancing some personal career directions. As one who has held major technical and executive positions over a lifetime, it is very evident to me that it is difficult, if not impossible to manage people, especially the knowledge workers. Perhaps, people who perform very menial jobs may be managed, but that approach seldom provides for reaching acceptable levels of performance. Command and control management usually doesn't work over long periods of time, yet may be used on occasion. When a crisis occurs someone must make the decision, someone must, so to speak, *give the order* or nothing will happen. The only place where people can be ordered to perform some task, with fear of some type of reprisal, is the military.

> Peter Drucker[3] in *The Essential Drucker* describes the function of management: "management is about human beings. Its task is to make people capable of joint performance, to make their strengths effective, and their weaknesses irrelevant. This is what organization is all about, and it is the reason that management is the critical determining factor."

Drucker suggests that "the one contribution a manager is uniquely expected to make is to give others vision and the ability to perform." In the final analysis it depends on how the managers view their responsibilities. A favorite story was told, at management meetings years ago, that provides an opportunity for managers to change how their workforce views the work in which they engage.

> The story relates the attitudes of three stonecutters who were asked what they were doing. The first replied: "I'm making a living." The second kept on working and replied: "I'm doing the best job of stonecutting in the entire country." The third one looked up with a visionary gleam in his eyes and said: "I'm building a cathedral."

While this anecdote relates to stonecutters, it also applies to how managers and employees in general view their responsibilities. The majority of managers would meet the requirements of the first and second stonecutters: doing their job and trying to be the best in their profession. Focusing on being the best stone cutter is commendable, but is it sufficient. Such an attitude loses sight of the fact, that while getting the work done efficiently and to acceptable standards of workmanship is essential, and involves making sure that the work effort complements the work of others, there also are responsibilities to the enterprise: the activities that focus on integration with other organizational units in building a successful future.

Henry Mintzberg[4] reminds us that:

> "No job is more vital to our society than that of the manager. It is the manager who determines whether our social institutions serve us well or whether they squander our talents and resources."

No proof is required to demonstrate that talent and resources are squandered in all organizations at significant cost to the organization and the employee. The sum total on any one day would provide significant resources to take advantage of other opportunities: the sum total represents lost opportunity costs. A management decision, to track the make-work activities, and both the mental and physical rework activities, would provide the motivation to begin finding ways to stop squandering talents and resources. Squandering talent not only has a negative impact on the organization's competitive position, but perhaps more importantly, on the future of its employees. Many careers are destroyed, because managers fail to make assignments that provide career growth opportunities.

Managing involves integrating purposes, people, and processes influenced by the availability of resources and a supportive organizational infrastructure. The management function can be described by the actions in which managers are expected to engage in, and meet requirements. I describe these management competencies to include seven major activities that often require simultaneous responses; they include general organizational administration, providing direction, demonstrating leadership, dealing with the people issues, taking action, resolving the high anxiety conflicts, and the focusing on the business.

Administration: Administrative work is probably the least satisfying part of any manager's job, nevertheless it requires attention. Policies, practices, and procedures must be followed; reports must be written; hiring, evaluating, assigning, and dismissing personnel requires attention; meetings need agendas; boss-imposed activities require attention; and those nondepartmental committee activities cannot be disregarded. While these activities are important, managers cannot be consumed by them. They may be painful to perform, so complete them judiciously instead of laboring about them.

Direction: Managers deliver on commitments, teach, coach, promote, strategize, and innovate. Managers integrate knowledge, skills, experience, attitudes, and personal characteristics into effective and efficient teams; manage organization's resources; communicate at all levels, monitor activities and actions, motivate through their own actions, analyze and synthesize information for cohesive action, negotiate issues for the benefit of the organization, and promote their operation to the organization. Managers also set the strategic direction within the limits of their resources and responsibilities.

Leadership: Taking the Lead: Leadership receives a great deal of visibility and discussion in the management and public press; it also includes many contradictions. Much of the leadership literature focuses on individuals who rise to greatness, because of some unexpected event. Here, we consider leadership that takes place every day, by technical professionals and their managers, in meeting organizational objectives. The argument then focuses on the differences between leading and managing. I suggest that leading and managing are two sides of the same coin; both support each other. Leading without managing for results or accomplishing some goal destroys motivation; managing without leading and providing direction leads to organizational stagnation. I prefer to focus on what I consider as *taking the lead*, because it involves not just doing what is assigned or what is asked for, but expects active participation in meeting the organizations purpose. So, taking the lead involves not only being the visionary, the pathfinder, the motivator, the coalition builder, but also the doer and the implementer. Those who take the lead build a sense of collegiality and trust, and a sense of excitement.

People: While people are an organization's greatest asset, they're also the manager's greatest challenge. With little and often any understanding of human behavior, managers tend to minimize the effort required to manage the activities of diverse personalities; people with different aspirations; people from different national cultures; people with different value systems; people with different competencies; and people who bring all their personal baggage with them that either supports or hinders the group performance in some way. Much of the manager's angst can be avoided by following a few principles: learn how to select the right people; invest in them through cross-disciplinary education and provide growth opportunities; tolerate mistakes; listen; and understand the impact of culture on performance.

Action: Managers are responsible for meeting the agreed upon objectives. While managers delegate many tasks, there are many that cannot be delegated: they do receive assistance from their staff and others, but responsibility and accountability rests with them. Managers have certain specific responsibilities some of which involve reviewing and understanding workloads; providing current and planned for future competencies; linking competencies to the workload; developing budgets and forecasts; focusing on the customer's needs; dealing with the unexpected; and managing the manager's work. In fulfilling these responsibilities, managers do not have all the necessary information to reach a decision, so they make decisions without all the facts. That's a given for anyone making a decision. There is a rule of thumb known as the Pareto principle, which states that 80 percent of the effect comes from 20 percent of the causes. The 80/20 rule applies to most decisions. Eighty percent of the information can be collected with 20 percent of effort. Decisions are not binary: they are not answered by a yes or no, or a true or false. Responses are mostly, a qualified *yes or no* and a qualified *true or false* with conditions attached. Applying the Pareto Principle requires experience and judgment: all information will not be available, judgment is required and it comes from experience, making mistakes and learning from them, and increasing the breadth of knowledge.

High Anxiety: Managers face high anxiety issues over which they have little or no control, but must engage in resolving them. These are the occasions that test not only a manager's competence, but the essence of character; these are the decisions associated with employee personal issues that consume time and a great deal of thought and angst. These high anxiety issues involve dealing with harassment and addiction of all types; being forced to discipline for serious infractions of policies; managing serious nonperformance issues; terminating an employee for nonperformance; or coping with the unexpected death of an employee during working hours. Working with the constructive mavericks and the host of innovators who need freedom to act, and are the lifeblood of the organization, creates anxious moments for many managers.

Business: The manager's responsibilities go beyond managing the activities as defined by some charter or the organization chart; not all requirements can be identified in writing. A manager cannot claim that the group fulfilled all of its obligations, but the project failed because of nonperformance in associated groups. If one group fails, all the involved groups fail. And it is here where manager's responsibilities go beyond the job description. Every manager has an unwritten responsibility to the organization. It takes courage to raise issues in other groups that may result in some level of nonperformance: but competent managers display high levels of courage, not as objectors, but as supportive contributors beyond their immediate assigned activities. In a paper at the First International Conference on Engineering Management[5] (1986) I stated that the "business of engineering is business performance." Doing the engineering or other professional work only is insufficient; engineering must make sure the project meets the business requirements. This statement led to a great amount of discussion, mostly negative. To me, engineering commitments and business commitments required approximately equal levels of attention. Engineering managers argued this was expecting too much from someone responsible for the technical work. Over the years I extended that description to include all organizational groups: "the business of any organizational group is business performance."

These seven activities comprise the principal responsibilities of most managers. Whether you agree with these seven issues or not, at one time or another, you'll find yourself in positions facing the issues described. Managers will face occasionally many of these actions simultaneously; times when several actions converge and require immediate attention. Demands are made on a manager's time from all directions; one may arise within the department only to be followed by one from some executive who insists on an immediate response, because of the alignment of a set of conditions that could have negative consequences. The manager has no alternative but to respond. In fulfilling the requirements of these seven actions, managers make many decisions related to their own activities and also validate the decisions of others by virtue of their agreement and acquiescence to the decisions of others. The decisions at this level determine to a great extent the success of any organization's activity.

ENGINEERS AND OTHER DISCIPLINE SPECIALISTS

While managers play a major role in an organization's success, they depend on the engineers and other discipline specialists to do the work of the organization; they are no longer specialists, but now need to develop a basic understanding of the breadth of the different disciplines involved in the organizational unit's decision-making. The engineers and other discipline specialists comprise the *brain trust* of the organization, when related to technology, marketing, manufacturing, and related disciplines. These knowledge workers, who like all other employees, bring those personal characteristics, those attitudes, those prior work experiences, their academic credentials, and their personal baggage to the workplace. While some may not be the most creative and innovative, they do possess the knowledge that can be applied to resolving the organization's problems and pursuing new opportunities. Some are creative and innovative; some are difficult to work with, others are accommodating; some are single minded, others pursue broad interests; some want immediate gratification; some seek continuous praise and recognition, others find casual praise objectionable and unprofessional; some need continuous attention from their manager, others prefer taking individual initiative; and the differences are never ending. Managers have the responsibility for integrating this vast knowledge and experience pool of engineers and other specialists into teams that focus on meeting organizational objectives.

Engineers and other discipline specialists include a broad range of talent from the self-educated technician to the advanced degree people including individuals involved in post doctorate level studies. Each brings their own experiences and predispositions to the decision-making table. The post doc would most likely not be able to perform the duties of the well-qualified technician and vice versa. However, each plays a role in the teams' success.

Most knowledge workers consider freedom as an essential requirement for fulfilling their organizational obligations. Yet, very few can function effectively with total freedom. Total freedom requires self-discipline. Total freedom requires working without full knowledge of the expectations. Here is an example that illustrates how people act when given total freedom.

At one time in my career I hired an experienced engineer who had a track record that included taking individual initiative, who by virtue of experiences demonstrated high levels of creativity, took a business perspective toward product development rather than a strictly technical approach, and met all the organization's requirements. I'll refer to him as Mike for purposes of this example. Mike joined the group, was accepted by his colleagues, was participative, demonstrated his creativity and ability to look beyond the technical issues, and quickly earned respect from his peers and younger engineers in the group. After roughly six months, Mike came to my office and asked me if I had a few minutes to talk. This wasn't particularly strange, because many of my people would ask for informal discussions on their projects; usually discussing some new technology or product idea; modifying work processes, schedules, or changing specifications; and occasionally on personal issues.

Mike came to my office and after the usual discussion of the local issues; I asked Mike what I could do for him. Mike said he was frustrated because he felt he was not able to express his creativity fully on the assigned projects. That comment appeared strange to me, because the major projects in which he participated required a great deal of personal initiative and creativity. Mike continued to emphasize the need for more freedom. We discussed the issue at some length and then I suggested to Mike that if he wishes, I'd reassign his workload to others, and for the next 90 days or so, he would be allowed to work on whatever caught his interest. We continued our discussion regarding operational and administrative issues and Mike left my office excited and elated over the fact that he was now free to expand his work effort wherever he chose.

Within about eight weeks, Mike returned to my office in search of an assignment. While he considered and thought through some ideas for potential exploration, he recognized the complexity of proposing a workable idea, developing it into a communicable concept, and demonstrating the idea's potential. A desire for total freedom sounds like the ideal work environment, but few people can accept total freedom; most cannot live in an environment of unknown expectations. Providing freedom does promote innovation, but it must be done with an operational and mental discipline to be effective. 3M Company provides a great example, where engineers and scientists and others are given 15 percent of their time to work on projects of their own liking. But that freedom only provides benefits to the organization if appropriate discipline is exercised: the 15 percent time allocation must focus on productive effort, even if it eventually fails to produce anything of value. Few people can work in an environment that grants total freedom where expectations are not defined.

PROJECT MANAGERS

Project managers play a major role in meeting organizational objectives, especially if the organizations promote the project approach throughout the whole organization; their work crosscuts organizational lines and disciplines. The principles of project management that began in the various engineering functions are slowly making their way into other organizational units. Their role involves more than engineering and more than practicing management principles.

Project managers require basic knowledge almost equivalent to that of organizational unit managers. In some cases even more, because of the diverse groups involved in implementing a project. They need to acquire staff; take requirements used for approval purposes and translate them in operational terms; understand procurement issues; have some background in contract law; know how to communicate effectively, not only with those directly involved with the project, but also with engineers and managers and other discipline specialists up and down the organization; and even knowing how to develop an environment that fosters tolerance in negotiating the many issues that arise in the work effort. At the same time project managers are expected to meet the project requirements, the projected time for completion, and the estimated cost.

Meeting the project requirements, schedule, and cost are the primary metrics used for measuring project performance. This project performance model is based on predictable events and a plan, which in the best of circumstances will require many changes during the project cycle. Too often these changes are not reflected in the daily operations. Another issue involves the ability to predict time for completion and cost. There is no doubt that on what I refer to as *handbook projects*, projects essentially involved with nothing new of consequence and lacking any innovation, that schedule and cost should be determined accurately within guidelines, pending any major catastrophe. But, when we face projects with significant unknown and unpredictable, and uncontrollable factors, we're providing our best calculated estimate: we have no reference point. But, are these three factors— requirements, cost, and schedule—sufficient?

Aaron J. Shenhar and Dov Dvir,[6] in *Reinventing Project Management*, present some new metrics for consideration when making major project investments. They classify these measures as efficiency, impact on customer, impact on team, business and direct success, and preparation for the future.

1. **Efficiency:** Including meeting schedule, budget, yield, and other appropriate efficiency factors based on the organization's needs
2. **Impact on the customer:** Meeting requirements and specifications, benefit to the customer, extent of use, customer satisfaction and loyalty, brand name recognition
3. **Impact on the team:** Considering team satisfaction, team morale, skill development, team members growth, team member retention
4. **Business and direct success:** Recognizing the importance of sales, profits, market share, return on investment and return on equity, cash flow, service quality, cycle time, organizational measures, regulatory approval
5. **Preparation for future:** Promoting new technologies, new markets, new product lines, new core competencies, new organizational capabilities

Shenhar and Dvir consider project management as a dynamic process. Even though the usual triple efficiency constraints of time, schedule, and performance may require primary focus, other metrics need to be considered. The authors note that the simple model that focuses only on the efficiency constraints is decoupled from the environment and business needs.

The question is which of the five metrics are the most important for a specific project? Initially, the triple efficiency constraints of time, schedule, and performance will be the top priority for just about every project. Managers have been educated to meet the efficiency constraints. Meeting *the triple efficiency constraints* and losing *customer satisfaction* and loyalty by pursuing the original plan, where some elements are no longer of value to the customer, may lead not only the project manager's eventual downfall, but the organization's poor performance. It may be more important to focus on the *business and direct success* elements recognizing that costs may be overrun and delivery schedules moved to a future date, because of changes in the economy, pursuit of different business strategies, recognition of new technologies, or changes in customers' requirements. Any long-term project, 3 years or more, has the possibility of being affected by such conditions. Competent project managers recognize these operational sensitivities and manage them based on the latest information available. At times, they may need the courage to inform the organization's executives, that even though a major investment has already been made, the project should be written off as a loss.

Most projects involve some form of matrix organization. So, who has the responsibility? Who is accountable for results? Where does the functional responsibility take precedence over that of the project manager? The problems begin with selection of the project manager. If the project involves multiple disciplines, it's essential to select a project manager with some multidisciplinary experience. This does not suggest that this person possesses all the knowledge required to meet the requirements. It does mean that this person has an understanding of the various fields of interest involved. There is a tendency to appoint newly minted MBA graduates as project managers. However, managers need to ask, "What knowledge, experiences, and other required competencies does the newly minted MBA bring to this project management position." Success requires a combination of academic credentials, plus knowledge related to the project's scope and experience. Project management is a discipline that determines organizational success or failure, so organizations need to recognize that a cadre of qualified project managers must be available.

Organizations need to grow their project managers. Developing project managers begins with an assignment in an organizational unit on a relatively small project. This can be followed with assigning greater project responsibility within the same organizational unit. It can be followed by a project in an associated operation, and on to another organizational unit for developing greater breadth of experience. Making several moves with an opportunity to manage different types of projects and acquiring new knowledge and skills allows the person to become a competent project manager capable of taking on major assignments.

COMMON REQUIREMENTS FOR EXECUTIVES, MANAGERS, ENGINEERS AND OTHER DISCIPLINE PROFESSIONALS, AND PROJECT MANAGERS

Executives, managers, project managers and the engineers and other discipline specialists bring to the organization certain competencies to meet the organization's requirements. These vary by degree depending on position in the organization's hierarchy. While the decisions made by this group vary primarily in scope, collectively they determine organizational success. These common requirements include

1. Vision or Purpose
2. Leadership
3. Innovation
4. Introducing Change
5. Literacy
6. Managing with Projects
7. Rationalizing the Silos
8. Implementing Decisions
9. Single-Issue Management
10. Appointing Managers
11. Selecting Project Team Members
12. Rewarding Performance
13. Return on Investment

Vision or Purpose

Providing a vision is not the sole purview of the executives. The product engineers or marketers need a vision or mental image of what they expect from their work effort. The concept of organizational vision often appears to be just what it says, a vision endorsed by a visionary without any possibility of implementation. Developing an organizational vision is Act 1. Implementing or executing the vision involves Acts 2 through N: it's about meeting commitments, it's about sticking your neck out, and above all, it's about looking at the organization's activities through a wide-angle lens. It is not about promoting some lofty or audacious goal that will never be accomplished, it is about performance. Vision statements to be useful must be accompanied by an implementation plan and the sources of the resources identified to fulfill the vision. While it's important for an organization to consider its vision of the future, it might be well to consider the vision for the short term as well. As we look at the world economy beginning 2008, any long-term vision would not have provided guidance: 2008 required a short-term vision. This is not to negate the need to promote an organizational vision, but to put the concept of visioning in perspective. Visions must be achievable, if they're to serve their purpose. At the suborganizational levels, I prefer to approach every activity with defining its *purpose*. Why does the organization, the project, or the activity exist? Why are we doing this? What are the benefits? What is the downside if we don't do it? Is this the best use of our resources? Does it support the organization's purpose, vision, and strategic directions?

Leadership

Leadership studies and research usually focus at the highest levels; Winston Churchill and Franklin Delano Roosevelt during World War II; Jack Welch as General Electric CEO; Lou Gerstner rebuilding IBM; Dr. Martin Luther King during the civil rights movement; Rudolph Giuliani after the September 11, 2001 attacks on the World Trade center; Carly Fiorina attempting to merge successfully Hewlett Packard and Compaq into a homogeneous innovative organization; and others in significant executive positions with high levels of responsibility. In the meantime the academic and business press devotes an excessive amount of space in describing the leaders' responsibility of providing a *vision* for the organization and arguing the difference between leading and managing. In our current international economic environment, we continually hear about a lack of leadership; political, economic, financial, industry, and academia. Leadership occurs in all segments and at different levels of importance of the organization; it is not limited to the executive suites and takes on totally different dimensions.

Research studies give us an opportunity to recognize the inconsistencies in just what it means to be focused on developing organizational leaders. A Center for Creative Leadership[7] survey of 750 executives yielded the following results in response to questions about the importance of leadership in their organizations.

- Developing leaders most important—78 percent
- Executives involved in leadership development—90 percent
- Most important—people skills followed by personal characteristics and strategic and process management skills
- Communication—less than 42 percent have communicated a leadership strategy
- HR support—49 percent have an HR program to support a leadership program

These statistics can be viewed as encouraging or very discouraging, depending on the frame of reference. Are 90 percent of the executives *involved* in leadership development; it depends on the meaning of *involved*. There's a significant difference in voicing and encouraging leadership, establishing a formal program that includes education and opportunities for practice, and personal involvement as an active participant. It's obvious that executives will support leadership development, they have no choice, but there's a significant difference between supporting leadership and becoming actively involved.

Leadership involves more than *keeping the store open*. Leaders are often classified as visionary, strategic, managerial, and organizational, but such a classification loses sight of the fact that leadership involves each of these, although at different times and perhaps in different combinations. Leaders do not vision, strategize, manage, or organize as independent issues: they integrate these activities into one to provide direction for the present and sustainability of the future. Certainly, one could function in the capacity as a visionary or a strategist, but that's professional competency. Leadership allows executives to influence the organization not only by words but more importantly by their actions. Risk-aversive executives will not provide the essential cadres of risk takers that every organization needs for survival. There are many leadership models and the research of Edward E. Lawler III,[8] and Bruch and Ghoshal[9] provide two different approaches to deliver what we call leadership.

Lawler's research involves four styles of leadership: Laissez-faire, Authoritarian, Human Relations, and Participative. Laissez-faire managers, as the name implies, are basically passive, avoid risk taking, have little impact on the organization, operate *ad hoc*, and promote the status quo. Authoritarian managers make decisions without input from others usually, tend to threaten employees for performance, and manage with a command and control mentality. We also need to keep in mind though that situations might occur when command and control may be essential; a burning building is not the time to attempt to reach consensus. Human relations managers go to extremes to focus on people issues, tend to justify nonperformance, and generally disregard issues other than those relating to person. Participative managers encourage input from others and use it in decision-making, involve members of the group beyond their immediate interests, and are good motivators. However, participative managers must guard against unrealistic expectations achieved from consensus building.

The research of Bruch and Ghoshal classified managers they studied as Procrastinators, Disengaged, Distracted, and Purposeful. These descriptions can be found in Chapter 1. Like all research, these categorizations tend to identify the extremes. It's difficult to argue against promoting good human relations values, an authoritarian approach may be necessary at times, and one cannot argue against participative management. Those in the work force have firsthand knowledge about working with the procrastinators, the disengaged, and the distracted and understand the perils both in the short and long term. In the final analysis, leaders adapt to different circumstances and environments, create a shared meaning and mindset, motivate, treat people with dignity and respect, maintain a moral compass, and at the same time meet the organization's expectations. Bennis and Thomas[10] suggest that leadership skills are gained through profound experiences. They refer to these profound experiences as *life-defining moments*. I suggest that as managers and engineers and other discipline specialists experience these *self-defining moments* and learn from them, they become purposeful managers. Being a leader or as I prefer to think about people willing to *take the lead*; this where managers position themselves and become the pathfinders, the visionaries, the coalition builders, the doers, and the supporters, the promoters, the implementers, and at the same time avoid micromanaging. Managers look to their staffs for ideas, but must also inject their own.

Innovation

Innovation cannot be relegated to any group in an organization, it requires organization-wide involvement. From my perspective innovation includes more than the organization's technical community; it includes the total organization. Innovation involves executives, managers of all types and descriptions, and the engineers and other discipline specialists, which Drucker referred to as the *organization's executives; the people* who by virtue of their work have an impact on performance. While most product and service innovation begins in the depths of the organization, the organizational innovation spirit must come from executives; they establish the organizational culture that allows innovation to take place. This group of *executives* does have opportunities to innovate and promote a culture that fosters innovation, (1) in their own sphere of influence, management, and (2) by conveying what they have witnessed or heard during meetings with their peers in other organizations. Innovation must involve more than novel organizational realignments and product and service improvements: its focus must be on new-to-the-market products and services.

In situation (1), *working in their own sphere of influence*, innovation involves accepting and promoting the appropriate levels of risk in reaching a decision. Risk-aversive *executives* cannot foster innovation, except perhaps minor incremental innovation: they seldom invest in the breakthrough. If nothing new originates from the executive levels, why should anyone else care? While executives have a responsibility to provide the direction, or a vision if you prefer, they must also participate, at least in building a culture that fosters innovation. They must be able to demonstrate, through their actions, that innovation will be rewarded. In situation (2), *disseminating information from colleagues and executive level experiences*, the *executives* who travel extensively come in contact with colleagues and are provided with countless opportunities to gain new information of value to others in the organization; this is independent of their background, and they only need to be observers and translate those observations into meaningful content to those who have the power to act on them. In organizations, where ideas flow from the *executives* involved in technology, marketing, and manufacturing, and on other issues and not by command, but as information, those organizational members under the right circumstances can move the organization forward. There's a mutual respect among those who make the decision and those who implement the decision.

Organizations also need to define *innovation*; the word is used so loosely today in conversation and in the media, that just about anything that is known can be classed as an innovation. As an example, every new cellphone that comes to the marketplace speaks about its innovations, but unless we consider the smallest of changes or improvements, innovation cannot be identified. Using a piece of string instead of a rubber band is not an innovation. In *Innovation by Design* I defined innovation as invention plus commercialization or implementation.

INNOVATION = Invention + Commercialization or Implementation

There must be an invention and that invention must be either commercialized or implemented in some manner to provide added value. No commercialization or implementation, no innovation!

Introducing Change

People fall into three basic categories, when it relates to change: those who cannot live with change, those who accept change and can live with it, and those who cannot live without change. Those who cannot live with change not only detest change, but are often repulsed by it: why can't it be like it has been in the past. If it isn't broken, why fix it. It's working OK, why mess up a good thing. The questions do remain, if *it isn't* broken and has been around for a long time, it might be a good idea to take a good look under the hood: is it really working and will it meet tomorrow's requirements. Those who accept change have been there before, it's probably not as bad as everyone thinks, so why get too excited as long as there's no serious negative impact. Those who can't live without change make a purposeful contribution to the organization as long as change is not done solely for the sake of change.

Introducing change creates levels of discomfort and anxiety. It makes little difference whether the change involves a new CEO, a change of the immediate manager, a change in the organization's structure, or a change in a common business administrative routine. Such changes seem to affect the complete organization. Talk at the water coolers abounds. But much of the anxiety can be avoided if people are prepared for the change and the change-makers follow through. There are changes that are not foreseen, such as the initial downsizing of organizations, but once a few organizations made the decision to downsize, it should have been obvious that other organizations would follow. The same situation occurred with outsourcing: right or wrong, effective or ineffective, outsourcing became the order of the day. Introducing new technologies or entering new markets brings selected people together who give greater consideration to the impact on their specific organizational unit or themselves personally, thus in essence resisting change. People tend to resist change, especially if an organization is more than meeting its targets. A sense of complacency and self-satisfaction begins to take hold and everyone becomes comfortable. The management discipline that built the organization, now gives way to a more leisurely attitude and a lack of organizational discipline. Change provides opportunities: eliminate change, you destroy initiative and eventually the organization.

Literacy

First, let's recognize that no one can be literate in all phases of an organization's fields of interest or in all its administrative functions. Certainly, knowledge of management principles and experience in the management function is essential. Knowledge of the organization, its vision, its mission, its value proposition, and its strategic direction need to be mastered: these issues set the organization's priorities. While executives, managers, engineers and other discipline specialists, and project managers may bring broad-based knowledge and experience to the job, that knowledge and experience include only some of the requirements. There was a time when executives did understand their technologies, their markets, their key customers. They actively participated in those businesses from their inception, but they didn't participate in a global economy and operations in many parts of the world. Many built those businesses from day one and intimately knew the workings of their markets and technologies. Life was much simpler. They didn't need focus groups because they could contact a few key industry people by telephone or in person, not only for product opinions, but also for performing product tests. Executives were then literate for their times. Their dependence on knowledge from others was far less. That situation is quite different from today's marketer starting from the bottom of the learning curve, without any knowledge of the industry or the market or the customers' needs.

Literacy in the global sense extends beyond having knowledge in the language of one's country of origin. There is no doubt that English is used throughout the world in business transactions, but at many different proficiency levels. International literacy requires recognizing the quality of what's being communicated; misinterpretations occur by all parties concerned. Having spent many years as an industry Foreign Service employee in Europe and extensive travel to

Asia, I learned how many times it may be necessary to ask a question in order to fully understand the response to a question or statement. It was necessary for me to speak more slowly and structuring questions and responses in simpler terms. One sure way was to ask for a response to a question or proposition and then confirm by having someone repeat their response. In many situations, understanding only comes about after considerable discussion: it may take several tries and it's necessary to understand that the confusion comes from both parties.

Managing with Projects. Project management, as a discipline, began in the construction, engineering, and defense industries. It began with Henri Fayol's management principles, Henry Gantt's development of the Gantt chart for planning projects, and supported by Frederick Winslow Taylor's theories on scientific management. Also Mary, Parker Follett who defined management as: "management is the art of getting things done through others." Please note that Follett used the word *art* instead of *means*. Since those days, project management principles have evolved, and countless software programs exist to support the management of projects. In spite of the advances in project planning tools and techniques, studies on the success rate of meeting project requirements, schedule, and cost show dismal performance: 85 percent of projects overran scheduled time by 70 percent and budget by 60 percent. (See details in Chapter 1, Aaron Shenhar and Dov Dvir.) Management can argue about these statistics and rationalize circumstances that caused such poor results, but it's time to take a serious look at how organizations manage their projects. The problems begin with the decision to proceed with an unrealistic time schedule, no resolution of the knockouts, insufficient staff with the required knowledge and experience, failure to monitor performance based on the premises of the approved proposal, professional specialists in all related disciplines changing designs without communicating those changes to all who need to know. You know this, what do you do about it.

Most organizations fail to estimate project cost and schedule within acceptable percentage rates at an appalling cost to the organization; misuse of resources and both physical and mental rework. They fail to put together a realistic schedule. They fail because they haven't been taught how to do it. These two elements set the stage for failure. Ask the typical technical person, engineers, and scientists from all disciplines to estimate the cost and time to implement a project and the reply will be a sigh. Ask a marketer to estimate the potential sales volume for a new product and the guessing game begins. Yet both of these groups of specialists are capable of learning the process. Unfortunately it's necessary to start at the bottom of the learning curve. Another issue that arises in our current social milieu is that nonperformance is easily excused. It's time that *executives* give due consideration as to why projects fail to meet expectations.

Rationalizing the Silos. Most organizations operate with functional silos with various levels of destruction; they are destructive because they limit inter-disciplinary and inter-functional communication. Functional silos need to be brought under control. Silos often create organizational frustration for its members, because a "no entrance sign" greets the entrant. With so much education channeled toward specialization, engineers do engineering and then in narrow segments of a specific discipline, scientists do science in the same way, marketers do the work of marketing, and so on. Each function lives in its own silo and rejects entrants from those multidisciplinary invaders. Engineers and the other discipline specialists need to explore each other's silos and learn how those other silos function, how they affect performance, and what impact they have on organizational performance. More employees should leave those cubicles and search those other silos that might inspire them to work more cooperatively, because of an understanding of each other's areas of interest.

The greatest difficulties arise when they are required to share their people with project teams. The level to which silos negatively influence cooperation depends on how silos are rewarded. Management does have a choice and if silos fail to cooperate there are options; (1) notice of what will occur if changes aren't made, (2) a change in management, (3) termination of the manager if necessary, and (4) a forced change in organizational culture. However, the easiest way to breakdown the silo effect is to begin assigning managers to the silos that operate from a total business perspective, rather than solely a functional one.

Implementing the Decision. The approved project was prepared by various functional managers, with the support of their engineers and other discipline specialists in the related functions, which are now charged with the responsibility to produce results: to do what they said they'd do. The work begins. If the project involved the introduction of a new product, all the functions such as engineering, marketing, and manufacturing begin reviewing what was agreed to in the approved project. Reservations begin to surface about certain data that were considered during the lengthy pre-approval stage, and now after review, often require significant reassessment of the original assumptions. Assumptions that were made prior to approval, on further detailed review, appear to have lost some of their validity. This becomes the first intervention in post-approval of the requirements.

While project success largely depends on the engineers and other discipline specialists who have the required competencies and capabilities, the final responsibility for performance rests with the competence of the managers involved in integrating all activities, and negotiating the necessary compromises to accomplish the objectives of the project statement. Usually more than one department has responsibility for a new product project or a major product upgrade. At a minimum, engineering, production, and marketing would be involved. While organizations use the project management approach to activities that involve multiple functions, little evidence exists where the project manager is not bombarded by various functional managers and assigned coordinators. Functional managers assign the personnel and often create operational difficulties for their own people, because the assigned people feel a greater alignment and loyalty to the project manager.

Single-Issue Management. Executives need to be cautious about proposing organization-wide programs that often fail to meet expectations or become an implementation burden. Institutionalizing programs such as quality; continuous improvement; reengineering the organization; the learning organization; knowledge management (KM); and Six Sigma need to be approached with a considerable amount of judgment. As an example, it's difficult to argue against the benefit that these programs should afford an organization. But during the days of Philip Crosby, W. Edwards Deming, and Joseph Juran, obsession with quality led to what I call *playing games* with a serious issue. Much of the quality reporting resulted in distorted reports. The issue became the *quality program*, not the program results: as an example, when organizations began counting the number of quality circles they developed rather than the accomplishments of those quality circles. It's difficult to argue against KM as a discipline, but we haven't seen much of it. The idea was to find a way to codify the organization's knowledge base and use it in managing the organization. KM wasn't going to be accomplished by appointing a learning officer: it would take a lot of work and would require neutralizing the organization's functional silos that stored all the knowledge. The idea was popularized and hyped to the point where interest slowly decreased. When management of technology (MOT) was introduced, organizations began appointing Chief Technology Officers (CTO). In many situations the research vice president became the CTO. It's difficult to argue against Six Sigma in its many forms. But, when Six Sigma is applied to research and development, it might be a good time to revisit the appropriateness of the program and determine where the principles may be applied. The difficulty arises when such programs become some executive's or manager's passion without full realization of consequences within the organization. Too often such programs begin without even a full understanding of how they should be implemented.

In recent years organizations depend more and more on policies, procedures, and processes (3Ps) to guide the organization's actions. This is not an argument against the 3Ps, but a call for use of judgment in applying them. It often appears that *judgment* has been relegated to the trash bin. This is evident from the simplest decision to be made by a grocery clerk to the upper management levels.

This dependence on the 3Ps came about as organizations adopted the principles of *internalizing* just about everything. Nirvana arrived when the concept of the way of doing something was internalized. It became gospel. The 3Ps and other single-issue management practices often referred to as *flavor of the day*, seldom meet expectations. Executives decry lack of innovation without realizing that innovation does not occur when using the 3Ps. This is not to suggest that some level of 3P activity is not essential, but it must be guided by judgment. All of these single-issue approaches have merit, begin with good intentions, until someone decides to apply a measure of performance and then the games begin to distort their merit.

Appointing Managers

Anecdotal evidence shows that the process for selecting first-level managers leaves much to be desired. A vacancy occurs, a replacement is needed. Some manager looks over the organization, decides to interview several specialists who could fill the position, deliberates the pros and cons of each candidate and makes the selection. This is the abridged version. However, seldom does the new manager have an opportunity to understand the details of the assignment such as purpose of the group; expectations from the group; changes that might need to be made; competencies within the group; interaction with other organizational units; specific areas of responsibility and accountability; annual budget; communication protocols, current problems that need to be corrected; and the list can go on and on. Friday 3:00 P.M. arrives, everybody meets in a conference room and the current manager introduces the new manager. The new manager receives congratulations from the group and everyone departs. The usual buzz begins as to why the person was selected, but 5:00 P.M. is approaching and everyone departs for the weekend. The newly minted manager has the weekend to get into a new mental state. Monday morning arrives; the new appointee embarks on a new career. This may be oversimplification, but not too far from the truth.

A general view suggests that far too often, the new manager brings the old job into the new office. Many years ago there was a cartoon that displayed this action. It showed an engineer as the newly minted manager bringing his drafting board into his new office and setting up an alternative workspace based on his past position. There is no doubt that the transition may be difficult, but that old job is not the job in the new position; the new position involves gaining a general understanding of all the related specialties, see the linkage among the various specialties, and integrate those specialties into a whole before making any decisions. Managers are not expected to be specialists, they're integrators; they manage activities and lead.

Selecting Project Team Members

For many years great emphasis has been placed on teams and team building. Organizations send their employees to team building programs: they climb mountains; they run the rapids; and they bear their souls in behavioral modification sessions; all for the purpose of getting to know each other, and then function as a team. Peter Senge[11] describes the team as a collection of experienced people from different functions and areas of expertise. Senge suggest that a sense of cohesiveness is necessary yet cohesiveness seldom exists. Too often the major issues are never raised, disagreement can be squelched in many different ways, and going against the majority way of thinking can be considered as an act of disobedience. I do not suggest that teams are not required, but team building does not begin when a project is approved. My personal experience is that a well-managed organizational unit should be able to put together a competent team at any time. Team development requires continuous attention by determining how people work together, finding the pressure points, and developing a culture where people have no fear of expressing their feelings, but doing so respectfully. However, we should not expect Nirvana. People bring all their baggage with them to the team, and if any one single attribute is important, it's tolerance; tolerance of others' behaviors.

Rewarding Performance

Over the years organizations have become risk averse to rewarding for performance. The idea of annual increases somehow now dominates most compensation programs. Less and less is required for more and greater rewards, more compliments, more thank you notes, and personal attention. Grade inflation that once dominated the elementary school activities progressed to universities and the world of multinational organizations. Lead people became supervisors, supervisors became managers, and managers became directors, and directors became executive directors. All doing the same jobs that they did prior to this fictitious advancement. Is that the way to reward performance? One would think that such practices only lead to further concessions on performance. A *Wall Street Journal*[12] article, "Business Owners Try to Motivate Employees," discusses the problems organizations face as the recession lingers and the impact on increasing employee stress levels. The suggested solutions, for relieving the employee stress, appear to be tactics that create future problems. In this Wall Street article, the owner of a leadership consulting firm, suggests that, "You've got to think outside the money box when it comes to motivating your employees in this economic environment." The solution, upgrading their job titles to director or manager because it makes their resumes "more robust." This is from an organization that promotes leadership. Another owner started employee venting sessions and ended up preparing a breakfast of waffles, bacon, and coffee every Wednesday.

Managements should recognize the senselessness of such actions, as described in The Wall Street Journal. The organization's management team should recognize that knowledge workers are professionals, and should be treated as professionals. While much of the research will show that recognition by peers and management rates high on the recognition scale, that recognition must be purposeful, justified, and well deserved. In the final analysis, job satisfaction depends on working on challenging projects that provide career growth and a sense of accomplishment supported by an across-the-board support for providing the required resources.

Return on Investment

The decision to invest or not to invest organizational resources includes more than considering the financial justification. An acceptable return on investment (ROI) may or may not tell the whole story: *executives* need to look beyond the figures and determine the credibility of the data used to develop the ROI; the information used to develop the ROI must be analyzed for its validity and importance. However, too often decision-makers fail to ask the simplest of questions: the what, why, who, when, where, and how. Consider the following examples: one referring to engineers and another to a marketing group.

An engineering manager and a colleague from manufacturing presented a proposal for a sizeable investment with a very acceptable ROI. The project focused on building a new manufacturing site, with the latest technologies that provided significant savings. But, not everyone on the approving body seemed to be convinced. What did the proposers fail to answer adequately? Will the new manufacturing technology reduce the current waste levels you're experiencing? Have you considered the additional costs associated with warehousing due to the new location? Do the new technologies provide a platform for future expansion in relation to other potential products? The responses to these questions were vague and inconclusive. The group was asked to rework its proposal.

A marketing manager was presenting a proposal for an improved product with new capabilities. That ROI more than met the organization's ROI requirements. However, a look at the pricing showed that the new product with the added features, that benefited buyers significantly, was being sold for less than the old product. A further investigation found that sales projections were unrealistic and the presenter could not provide a suitable answer regarding the source of new customers. It's not difficult to meet ROI requirements as organizations establish fixed or virtual thresholds that must be met. Establish minimal ROI requirements and project planners will meet them; it's far more important to know what factors are included in the ROI, than the ROI figure.

KEY POINTS

Executives. Executives operate from a position of power. They have opportunities to accomplish what others cannot. They make the major decisions whether strategic or operational. While Peter Drucker considers knowledge workers as executives, the hierarchy of organizational executives needs to listen, but to listen, they must know these knowledge workers not from reports, but through personal interaction. We no longer live in the era of Frederick Taylor, who focused on efficiency in an era of expanding manufacturing operations. While academics like Hamel and Bryan call for a new management paradigm, that new paradigm requires focus on integration of the functional units without losing the necessary freedom with discipline, and a focus beyond the immediate demand of Wall Street. That new paradigm must focus on productivity of the knowledge worker, which in many organizations exceeds 50 percent of total employment. We need a new Taylor to consider the work methods of today's knowledge workers.

Managers. The implementation of those executive level decisions involves doing the *real work* of the organization. This does not suggest that executives do not work, but they do a different type of work. *Real work* can be described as the effort required to move the product out the door and to the customer. The many levels of managers in the organization's functional units take on this responsibility. However, the studies of Edward E. Lawler III and Bruch and Ghoshal about manager performance pose some serious problems regarding how few managers practice some form of participative management and demonstrate high levels of energy and focus. However, these situations can be resolved by appropriate actions from the organization's executives. Managers must develop a mindset that goes beyond the need to fulfill their limited responsibilities; they need to recognize that they're part of the enterprise system.

Engineers and Other Discipline Specialists. The engineers and other discipline specialists include a broad range of talent from self-educated technicians to those with post doctorate level credentials. Managing the discipline specialists involves (1) understanding their competencies and capabilities, (2) providing work challenges that meet the organizational needs and the needs of the discipline specialists, (3) offering appropriate levels of freedom with discipline, and (4) including managers with the necessary competencies to integrate and develop future organizational needs.

Project Managers. Organizations cannot function without qualified project managers. They are one of the most, if not the most, important group of managers except for the general functional managers who depend on the performance of project managers for meeting requirements. Project managers in R&D, product development, manufacturing, and marketing, at any organizational level hold the future of the organization in their hands. In essence they are generalists with both multidisciplinary knowledge and experience as required for the project. The project manager, for the construction of the Denver International Airport, required totally different competencies than the project manager for Apples iPhone or iPad. However, as Shenhar and Dvir note, project management involves a dynamic process, and project success must not be measured solely on business success, but also on customer impact, impact on the team, and preparation for the future.

Common Requirements. Executives, managers, engineers and other discipline specialists, and project managers share a group of common skills and competencies, but at different levels. They include organizational leadership, fostering innovation, introducing change, becoming literate in a breadth of issues related to the organization, managing projects, bringing the silos under control, implementing decisions, eliminating single-issue management, appointing managers, selecting project team members, rewarding performance, and realistic use of ROI. Collectively, meeting these requirements determines organizational success, and each involves a continuum of decisions from relatively simple to very complex.

NOTES

1. Peter F. Drucker, *The Essential Drucker*, New York: HarperCollins, 2001, p. 10.
2. Gary Hamel and Lowell Bryan, McKinsey Quarterly, Innovative Management; A Conversation with Gary Hamel and Lowell Bryan, 2008, No. 1.
3. Peter F. Drucker, *The Essential Drucker*, New York: HarperCollins, 2001, pp. 10–13.
4. Henry Mintzberg, "The manager's job: folklore and fact," *Harvard Business Review*, March–April 1990, Reprint 90210.
5. Gerard H. (Gus) Gaynor, "Engineering and engineering management: a model for improved business performance," First international Conference on Engineering Management, Washington, DC, September 1986.
6. Aaron J. Shenhar and Dov Dvir, *Reinventing Project Management*, Boston, MA: Harvard Business School Press, 2007, pp. 26–29.

7. Peter Haapaniemi, "Leading indicators: the development of executive leadership," Center for Creative Leadership, *Chief Executive Magazine*, October 2002, p.S1(2).

8. Edward E. Lawler III. *Motivation in Work Organizations*, San Francisco, CA: Jossey Bass, 1994, pp. 219–232.

9. Bruch and Ghoshal, Ibid, 5–11.

10. Warren G. Bennis and Robert J. Thomas, *Geeks and Geezers: How Era, Values, and Defining Moments Shape Leaders*, Boston, MA: Harvard Business School Press, 2003.

11. Peter Senge, *The Fifth Discipline*, New York: Doubleday (Currency), 1990, p. 24.

12. Sarah E. Needleman, "Business owners try to motivate employees," *The Wall Street Journal*, 14 January 2110, p. B5.

3

DECISIONS HAVE CONSEQUENCES

Inputs to decision-making have expanded over the years to the point where top-level decision-makers depend on input from many levels within the organization. Yes, the world is more complex and although information systems technology has not met the needs of the decision-makers, the inputs to the decisions have grown significantly. The future social and economic environment will not mimic that of the past, except possibly in the short term. As investment managers warn, past performance is no indicator of future performance. In essence, every major decision begins with a blank sheet of paper. Knowledge and experience allow us to describe the known, the predictable, and the controllable within limits, but describing and understanding the unknowns, the unpredictable, and the uncontrollable factors, comes through subsequent experimentation and research and at times through trial and error methods. Successful execution of any major decision depends on resolving the unknown, unpredictable, and uncontrollable issues and continually verifying the known, predictable, and controllable based on changing requirements and conditions. Delaying a decision, until all unknown, unpredictable, and uncontrollable factors are resolved, would never lead to a decision; there would always be one more issue to resolve. So, at the time of decision, many issues lack definition and clarity.

Decisions: An Engineering and Management Perspective, First Edition. Gerard H. Gaynor.
© 2015 The Institute of Electrical and Electronics Engineers, Inc. Published 2015 by John Wiley & Sons, Inc.

Inputs to the decision-making process come from many sources with varying levels of knowledge and experience. Chapter 3 topics include

- The Knowledge Chain
- External Decision Drivers
- Expanding Worldwide Operations
- Dealing with Acquisitions or Mergers
- Restructuring Organizations
- Investing in New-to-the-Market Products/Services
- Investing in New Technologies
- Entering New Markets
- Discontinuing a Product Line
- Promoting Innovation and Entrepreneurship
- Locating Business Operations
- Key Points
- Notes

THE KNOWLEDGE CHAIN

Decision-making requires trust and intellectual discipline and rigor from all who provide input and participate in the process. Obviously, dealing with decisions, where the proposal's purpose has not been adequately documented for the particular situation, presents serious degrees of risk. Figure 3.1 compares Responsibility for Decision with Knowledge for Decision: unfortunately in most cases the two take diverse paths. Executive and upper level managers generally lack first-hand knowledge of the requirements and solutions for making the macro decisions. Knowledge for reaching the decision lies at various levels and with specialists from many disciplines not involved in making the major/macro decision. Figure 3.1 also illustrates the dual paths of *decision responsibility* and *knowledge to reach the decision*, and shows the progression from Other Contributors to Discipline Specialists, to Managers at All Levels, Executives in All Areas, Staff Executives, Chief Executive Officer, and the Board of Directors. Obviously, not all decisions will reach the Board of Directors level. While the Board of Directors and Chief Executive Officer are well defined, the remaining positions cover many different configurations.

- Staff Executives—finance, human resources, procurement, patent and legal, information public relations, administration

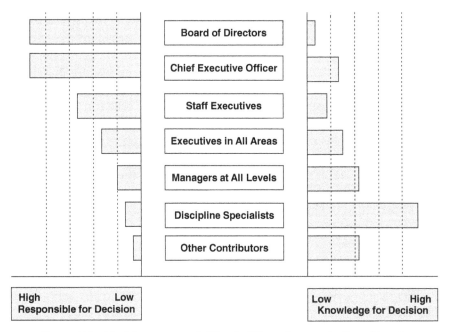

Figure 3.1. Decision responsibility at different organizational levels.

- Executives in All Areas—this group involves all those identified as CEOs, and executives, as sector, group, and division vice presidents; the functional vice presidents in groups like research and development, engineering, design, marketing, sales, manufacturing, logistics, and other operational functional areas of expertise
- Managers at All Levels—within all operations and staff groups, but further divided into specialties such as mechanical, electrical, computer, civil, logistics, engineering; scientists in all specialties like materials technology, chemicals in all its forms; physicists in optics, fluid mechanics, statics, dynamics, heat transfer, thermodynamics; marketing and sales of many different types; product/service distribution from order entry to delivery, customer satisfaction, and reorder; and all the administrative support functions like finance and accounting, information services, human resources, procurement, patent and legal, and all the related administration functions and their subcategories
- Discipline Specialists—as noted in section on Managers at All Levels, but with further subdivisions into specialties and subspecialties
- Other contributors—anybody either within or outside the immediate organization capable of making a contribution of some sort to the

decision—build relations with people in the service groups regardless of their level in the organization—value input from customers and suppliers

Here we face a disconnect between decision-makers making decisions at the highest organizational levels with information gathered primarily from the department managers and discipline specialists, where each can influence with their own biases, as well as considering the benefits that might accrue to them personally or to their organizational unit. People, who work on the project or activity of any significance, provide the information and make decisions that guide the top-level decision-makers. That information is not infallible; it's based on knowledge, experience, and judgment: it's also based on biases and personal preferences. This situation exists whether the action requiring a decision originates from the bottom or top of the organization. The level, to which this inverse relation exists, between those responsible for the decision and those with knowledge related to the decision, determines the potential for successful implementation.

CEOs and organizational boards and major committees really approve what others have considered in depth and within the scope of the organization's fields of interest. The information in the proposal, massaged by many managers and specialists from many disciplines, comes to the decision-makers who may have minimum first-hand knowledge or experience in the complexities involved in the implementation. Obviously they are not approving the details. This does not suggest that those making the decision are totally disconnected from the knowledge base that justifies bringing the proposal forward: the difficulty arises if the decision-makers fail to have sufficient knowledge to ask the questions that reveal the inconsistencies and potential problems in fulfilling the requirements as specified in the proposal. There's a succession of decision points along the decision continuum from discipline specialists to various management levels, and ultimately to the highest required decision level, so trust and a demonstrated and successful track record in meeting expectations gives decision-makers confidence in meeting the expectations.

EXTERNAL DECISION DRIVERS

Decision-makers must also be guided by competitive forces that may govern their particular industry, government rules and regulations from the local to national to international requirements that impose restrictions on operations, the economy from local to national to international, and the changes in social mores and structure. The US auto industry, once the world leader in the automotive industry, found itself with excessive losses of market share, multi-billion dollar financial losses, and one downsizing followed by another. Management decisions, related to providing what are now insurmountable costs for employee benefits have come to haunt the US auto manufacturers. Millions of dollars were spent on automation that did not pay off as expected. Car designs were usually more of the same. Granted that the automobile industry changed over the last 50 years and became more complicated not only technologically, but also in marketing, finance, and other operating functions. There was a time when there was a standard and deluxe Chevrolet. Now all the different models with their personalized variations create new orders of complexity.

While we like to recall with nostalgia the days of the Ford Model T and the first automobile assembly line, in 2006 the Ford Motor Co. was amassing billion dollar losses and continued downsizing. Every downsizing became a prelude to another downsizing. Every new CEO brought in a choice solution. But where are the "car guys" who really know the car business. The Financial Times described Ford as:

"A combination of incompetent management, chaotic product development"

Ineffective cost control plunged Ford into a record $12.6 billion loss in 2006. William Clay Ford Jr., great grandson of Henry Ford, is Ford's Executive Chairman and Alan Mulally, a former Boeing executive, now functions as President and CEO. Cost cutting alone will not change an inbred organization into a leader in its industry and it doesn't take a major study to reach that conclusion. What we can infer from what appears in the business press is that over the years there have been a series of very poor decisions starting at the very top of the organization. There were financial decisions, acquisition decisions, design decisions, marketing decisions, and structural decisions whose long-term impact on the business was not addressed. Who really made the decisions that led to this situation? Did the CEO and the Board of Directors make the decision or did they only ratify the decisions made by other managers and discipline specialists? Unless the decision-makers really have knowledge of what they're approving or rejecting, they're really only ratifying the decisions of others. They may ask the questions, may ask questions in depth, but they will not be privy to all the minute details that could scuttle a project. Fortunately, William Clay Ford, recruited Alan Mulally a former Boeing manufacturing executive, and now appears to be resolving the problems: he focused on solving the systemic problems. Mulally and his team built Ford into a formidable and profitable competitor without federal government involvement.

It may be a good idea to declare a moratorium on the use of PowerPoint presentations (formerly transparencies or foils) that have created a barrier to effective communication; communication that is open, forthright, and honest. PowerPoint is a great invention, but credibility can be a problem. I had a major surprise as chair of an international project review committee when I asked an engineering director to "put away the PowerPoints and suggested that we should just discuss the projects with key managers and specialists. Just put up the list of your major projects and tell us about them." The groans were audible. The uneasiness of the managers and specialists attending the meeting was evident. As I glanced around the room at times, the body language showed that not everyone would second the director's comments. I knew I'd have to engage the whole group diplomatically in order to leave with an understanding of the status of the major projects. The purpose of the review was not to put the director on the spot, but to identify the problems, determine if the projects required additional resources, identify problems to bring the resources of the whole organization to resolve issues in a timely manner, and to focus on those knockouts that may need attention.

EXPANDING WORLDWIDE OPERATIONS

A decision to expand an organization's business worldwide undoubtedly involves dealing with uncertainties and accepting various degrees of risk. Obviously, such actions should be guided by the organization's strategic directions and may take years to accomplish. Organizations expand into worldwide operations in different ways. There is no foolproof model. While the US auto makers had a presence around the world, US car models found it difficult to gain acceptance in overseas markets. So Ford, General Motors, and Chrysler took the acquisition route. That is quite different from the acquisition approach taken by such companies as Hewlett Packard, IBM, 3M, Eastman Kodak, Fuji, and Caterpillar. These companies grew their worldwide operations over a period of many years and in some cases decades. Little by little they expanded their product lines across the world through acquisitions and mergers that added value to their current product lines.

Building a worldwide organization involves more than making an arrangement for selling an organization's products. The process involves developing totally new organizations over a period of time and integrating their activities to gain major operational benefits. The foreign-service contingent asked to build those new organizations faces many challenges. They're working in different cultures and they need to balance adapting totally to the new culture with their ability to influence it. Eventually some concessions can be accommodated by both sides for the benefit of both groups. The major decision often involves determining how many foreign-service people are required in offshore operations. A basic fact remains; the natives must run the organization. Seldom does an organization have even one foreign-service employee, at the executive level, who speaks the language fluently and could interact with foreign governing bodies.

The macro decision made at an executive level to begin to enter into the worldwide economy has a steep learning curve. The history of becoming worldwide tells of the countless sad stories of the wrong people being sent to work in a new environment. Sending the best and brightest may not be the answer. From my personal experience, I found the ideal candidates come from the proactive opportunity finders who have the ability to dig into the nitty-gritty details, accommodate the needs of the culture and at the same time influence it, and the ability to limit the interference from the organization's headquarters.

The foreign-service engineers and the other discipline specialists play a major role in the success equation. Engineers usually become involved in transfer of technologies, rationalization of various standards, bringing products in compliance with the nation's requirements, safety and environmental issues, and that host of problems associated with reconciling the cultural differences. By cultural differences I mean very simply how people work. Many US managers would not admit this, but too often use the ready, fire, aim approach. Not every culture believes in this approach. Some cultures are much more thoughtful about how they approach a problem. My experience in Europe and Japan brought this situation to the forefront. Engineers in the UK, Germany, and Italy work very differently. Including Japan in this triumvirate brings another totally different dimension. UK engineers seemed to have been restricted to a great extent in demonstrating personal initiative. It might be difficult for a non-degreed person to receive consideration of an idea that might be of great promise. German engineers may be accused of extreme precision to an extent that the approach increases costs. Italian engineers, probably the most creative of all these groups, bring an artful design to its products. Want a design review; go to Japan to see how meticulously they go through each dimension and consider it in relation to all related dimensions. This is just sampling of differences to demonstrate that working in a new culture requires knowledge of that culture and how it responds to other culture.

DEALING WITH ACQUISITIONS AND MERGERS

The success rate for merging or acquiring organizations has been at best very disappointing. Fast Company[1] reports that technology giants have bought 144 companies with very few breakout products since 2004: Google acquired 44, Yahoo 36, Facebook 2, Amazon 17, and Microsoft 45. General Motors attempted to unravel its acquisitions made over the past two decades with mixed results. Chrysler for the second time is attempting to restructure under the Fiat brand. The specific reasons for buying these organizations were based on how executives viewed the advantages in pursuing their strategic direction at the time of decision. There is not much point in speculating on the decision processes used in reaching these decisions. However, significant organizational resources were used to reach these decisions.

What can be done to improve the process for reaching such decisions that have an impact, in both the short and long term, not only on the organizations involved in the acquisition or merger, but also on all the stakeholders? The potential difficulties in merging and acquiring organizations too often tend to be minimized, in spite of the due diligence associated with the various required actions. The Daimler-Benz AG's $36 billion buyout of Chrysler Corporation in 1998 provides an excellent example of the difficulties of not only physically merging two organizational cultures, but blending the totally different personalities of those left to govern. As noted by Vlasic and Stertz[2], Schrempp considered the creation of DaimlerChrysler as the greatest of experiment in cross-cultural combinations, and the new benchmark for international deals on an epic scale; he hailed the merger as "a merger of equals, a merger of growth, and a merger of unprecedented strength." Within 4 years DaimlerChrysler stock no longer appeared on the S&P 500; the merger was anything but the merger of equals; and the benefits to be achieved from economies of scale, integration of production methods, and reductions in labor never reached expectations. By the time the recession began in 2008, Chrysler was ready for bankruptcy, but was acquired by Fiat. Why did the merger of equals fail?

Professor Sydney Finkelstein[3] suggests that the merger failed because of a clash of cultures and mismanagement. Culture clash often extends negotiations or destroys a merger or acquisition. Here are a few reasons

- At the senior management level, there was a meeting of the minds, they focused on the key issues, their command of English was impeccable
- The Post-Merger Integration Team spent millions on cultural sensitivity workshops, but the business practices and management principles remained the same
- Mercedes was perceived as the *special brand*, Chrysler was the *blue collar* relation
- Distrust and dislike ran deep with different wage structures, corporate hierarchies, and values
- The Chrysler image as one of American excess, its brand value based on assertiveness and risk taking within a cost-controlled environment: in contrast Mercedes-Benz extolled disciplined German engineering and uncompromising quality
- The culture clash appeared to exist as much between products as among employees
- Distribution and retail largely remained separate

- Some Chrysler products were overpriced for European consumers when compared to the competition
- Different product development philosophies hampered joint purchasing and manufacturing efforts

    Mismanagement stifled any progress. A review of the Daimler-Chrysler "merger of equals" facts forces the question: how could two intelligent people, Jurgen Schrempp and Robert Eaton make such a mess of what was hailed as merger of equals.

- Daimler-Benz remained committed to its credo; *quality at any cost* while Chrysler focused on *price-targeted vehicles*
- The *merger of equals* statement loses its significance when Schrempp lets the world know that he always considered Chrysler to be a subsidiary of DaimlerChrysler
- Daimler-Benz was the major shareholder from day one and had the majority seats on the Supervisory Board, yet there were two parallel management structures under co-CEOs in different headquarters and in different locations
- The co-CEOs failed to follow a coordinated approach in determining Chrysler's fate—some key Chrysler executives departed for Ford and GM, German pressure stifled the American dynamism, Eaton went weeks without talking to Schrempp
- Schrempp concludes there's no way of bringing Daimler-Benz and Chrysler together because of a lack of key Chrysler executives
- Chrysler bled cash waiting for Daimler's next move that came much too late
- People at the Auburn Hills Chrysler facility observed that Bob Eaton was detached and lost the passion to run Chrysler even while Schrempp was urging him to act like the *co-chairman*
- The *merger of equals* did not achieve the predicted synergy of savings and a *profitable automotive production* capability was never achieved

The failure of the DaimlerChrysler *merger of equals* could have been predicted—the culture clash and potential mismanagement issues were visible at the beginning of negotiations. Did either Daimler or Chrysler management have a clear vision as to what this *merger of equals* would look like? Evidently much information and analysis was missed in the due diligence process or management chose to disregard the warning signs. The failure to meld the two cultures reminds me of a situation where a US vice president of manufacturing decided to appoint a German as a plant manager for a Southern Italy operation in order to bring some management discipline to the uncooperative Italians. The plant manager lasted less than 6 months, and everyone except the vice president of manufacturing knew such an appointment was bound to fail. The vice president had absolutely no understanding of what's required to bring two cultures together and work in harmony.

The potential culture clash between Chrysler and Daimler-Benz should have been a major issue that required consideration before the *merger of equals* took place and not after signing the legal documents. This culture clash was predictable. While it was predictable, a group of managers and engineers and other discipline professionals evidently failed to engage in the process. While cultures ascribe success and failure to the top-level executives, they have little control over what occurs in the depths of the organization. It appears, on too many occasions, that managers have abdicated their responsibility in managing the affairs of the organization. They're minding the store, so to speak, but not doing much to look beyond their immediate responsibilities and become proactive participants in the organization. While much of failure can be squarely placed on Schrempp and Eaton, there were a countless number of managers on both sides, who failed to fulfill their responsibilities as managers and discipline specialists.

The mismanagement issues generated a situation that's difficult to comprehend. Under most circumstance, someone would have taken the reins and governed, perhaps to the dismay and anxiety of both Daimler and Chrysler. No one took on the leadership role. The *merger of equals* was based on reconciling *quality at any cost* with *price-targeted vehicles*; identifying Daimler as owner of Chrysler as subsidiary was not defined; making Daimler responsible for DaimlerChrysler operations, and establishing an organization with co-CEOs militated against a possible successful merger. The co-CEOs neglected to define responsibility for performance; including a sufficient number of Chrysler executives in the management process, and developing business strategies to take advantage of the synergies gained from integrating the best of both organizations. Someplace along the negotiations continuum, both Schrempp, Eaton, and their teams of lawyers and finance people failed to ask the right questions, discover the relevant and perhaps troubling data, listen to the dissonant voices with seriousness, and communicate with all who would eventually be required to implement the decision.

RESTRUCTURING ORGANIZATIONS

Why raise the topic of restructuring organizations in a book on decision-making directed to the technical community? The answer is quite simple. Regardless of from what angle we may view restructuring; the decisions have a significant impact on the technical community as well as all other employees. The technical community participated in the decisions that led to the need for reorganization.

Every organizational restructuring involves countless decisions. Those decisions have an impact, in one way or another on every organizational unit; on every individual in the organization; on every functional unit; on the future financial position; on relations with customers and suppliers; and touch every activity in the organization looking at the organization as a system. The business press abounds with stories of restructuring for any number of reasons. Most restructurings lead to another restructuring and then another restructuring. Eastman Kodak, as an example, has pursued many organizational changes since the birth of digital photography, failed to develop a workable business model, and eventually filed for Chapter 11 bankruptcy. The US auto industry faced similar restructurings, yet until recently never resolved the basic problems hindering the successful pursuit of business. Carly Fiorina becomes CEO of HP in 1999, projects double-digit revenue growth that fails to materialize. The supposed reason, a once innovative organization became overly bureaucratic, innovation seemed to be lacking, and the product mix could not justify the double-digit growth projections. Restructuring for greater effectiveness and efficiency, mainly, created frustration and confusion. While Ms. Fiorina won the battle to merge HP and Digital Equipment, it put her on the road to eventual termination. There is no doubt that restructuring will occur in an economic downturn, as witnessed in 2008 and 2010, but too often the restructuring is driven by the finance department with no responsibility for implementation. Most restructuring involves reducing costs, rather than implementing a program that includes cost reduction and business development.

There are legitimate reasons for restructuring an organization when the need arises. The need arises when it appears that the current organizational structure no longer meets the needs of the organization and the business environment, but reorganization involves both major and minor consequences. People generally prefer stability and anything that changes that stability creates various levels of anxiety. The few who cannot live without change drive the organization; hopefully there are a sufficient number. A manager of a small group, implementing changes in assignments or attempts to consolidate certain operations to develop a critical mass, can create disruptions that go beyond the immediate organizational unit.

Management methods changed after World War I, but took on significant added influence after World War II. Henri Fayol in 1910 and Alfred P. Sloan in 1920 provided organizational models when businesses were primarily involved in manufacturing and related operations. The French industrialist, Fayol, used a model that included functions such as manufacturing, engineering, selling, and so on. Alfred P. Sloan organized General Motors (GM) into individual divisions based on Fayol's functional organization model, but expanded the model where each GM division (Chevrolet, Oldsmobile, Buick, and Cadillac) operated as an autonomous business unit, with their own management and with profit-and-loss

(P&L) responsibility. Under this model GM corporate made major capital decisions, it set policy, made senior management appointments, set standards of performance. In essence, the GM divisions had P&L responsibility under the control of GM management: a type of federal decentralization model. That model worked well for manufacturing facilities, but does it fit all organizations in today's service economy? It may or may not.

The Sloan model may or may not fit a multiproduct, multitechnology, and multimarket organization. 3M operates much like the Sloan model in spite of its many divisions, technologies, markets and diverse global operations. Divisions have P&L responsibility; freedom to operate within 3M policies and procedures, but corporate owns technologies, information, manufacturing facilities, all capital, and staff activities such as human resources, finance, patent and legal, and the other administrative functions. However, organizational design lives in the eyes of the beholder; the CEO and the executive officers. There is no optimum model for a large organization and attempts to define a universal model have failed. Organizing by teams, projects, centralized, decentralized, and other approaches as panaceas usually ends in some form of matrix.

I suggest that structure may not be as important as the policies and procedures that guide the structure. Policies that prevent freedom of expression are bound to fail any organizational design: don't expect innovation. Procedures that restrict freedom of operation unnecessarily are bound to fail any organizational design; don't expect innovation. In the final analysis, the informal organization and those white spaces on the organization chart define the organization. A more appropriate approach to organizational design may require focusing on how people communicate. In the final analysis avoid the biases and prejudices; evaluate the reasons and objectives for restructuring; understand the scope of the impact on various organizational units; recognize that productivity will be affected negatively for some time; find a solution to the problems; make provisions for those who might depart because of being bypassed for a particular position; use judgment in the implementation. There are no algorithms to guide the process; make sure that managers are knowledgeable about the issues. These are major decision points that impact all segments of the organization. Don't lose sight of Henry Mintzberg's[4] admonition that

> "No job is more vital to our society than that of the manager. It is the manager who determines whether our social institutions serve us well or whether they squander our talents and resources."

Keep in mind that restructuring of any organization does not come about through democratic means: those decisions come from the executive suite and managers with various levels of input and biases.

INVESTING IN NEW-TO-THE-MARKET PRODUCTS/SERVICES

Investing in new-to-the-market product or service probably involves a greater amount of specialized input and expertise from engineers and other discipline specialists and the functional managers: it also involves added levels of risk, because for the many unknowns that must be resolved successfully, those knock-out issues must be resolved. Investing in a new-to-the-market product involves the complete organization: it is not an R&D decision. As a matter of fact R&D may not be the major player. Here's a somewhat typical example recognizing that any single effort to introduce a new product will not be duplicated.

The process begins with someone or some group suggesting a potential opportunity and the idea could come from any participant in the organization. While new products usually are initiated by the discipline specialists in marketing or in the technology and the related functions of research and engineering, no single group can take ownership: ideas are not dependent on knowledge alone, but stem from powers of observation and the competence to think and synthesize information from many sources. Even CEOs, because of their exposure to nontraditional or personal information sources, have an opportunity to put two and two together and propose new products.

Introducing new products and services requires a process that must be designed to meet the needs of the organization. There is no one size that fits all except in very general terms. The process must begin with open discussion. To be successful, the dissonant as well as the supportive voices must be brought forward; however, all attempts must be made to avoid biases and unsupported comments. Someone must formulate the idea in such a way that allows discussing the idea and this effort falls on the person who generated the idea. Just tossing out an idea and hoping someone will grab it doesn't add much to the organization's bottom line. Ideas are cheap; developing the idea into a business concept requires the involvement of all the related organizational functions. According to Theodore Levitt[5]

"The trouble with much creativity today is that many of the people with the ideas have the peculiar notion that their jobs are finished when they suggest them: that it is up to somebody else to work out the dirty details and then implement the proposals. Typically the more creative the man, the less responsibility he takes for the action."

It takes time and effort to take an idea and massage it to the point where it can be discussed with some possibility of reaching a preliminary conclusion.

This process may best be accomplished by informal *ad hoc* discussions with colleagues.

The process of transitioning an idea into a product or service requires an appropriate design that fits the needs of the organization. It can be divided into three broad phases: Phase 1, Determining Idea Viability; Phase 2, Project Development; and Phase 3, Project Execution.

Phase 1—Determining Idea Viability—The objective is to capture the idea and bring to bear the resources that can determine the viability of the idea in relation to the organization's fields of interest and the resources and capabilities of its infrastructure. A further objective is to develop the idea into a *business concept*. Since the organization is dealing with a new-to-the-market product, all the related functions need to be involved in the process. The extent and time of involvement will depend on the specific needs to bring the idea to the marketplace. This is primarily a responsibility of engineers and other discipline specialists with support from their immediate management.

Developing a *business concept* is an interdisciplinary activity. Marketing ideas cannot be approved without the involvement of research, development, engineering, manufacturing, legal and patent, and all the other functions: product requirements must be agreed to at the inception rather than at the time of market launch. The technology-related functions cannot operate independently without full participation from their colleagues in the related functions. Waiting to determine production requirements when a product is ready to go into production will only cause delays. The developed business concept provides the basis for establishing a project.

Phase 2—Project Development—Assuming that the *business concept* has been agreed to, a formal project plan must be developed to bring the concept to the marketplace. It's easy to say, just follow basic project management principles, and think all will be well. As noted previously, project performance statistics do not justify such a conclusion. Most projects fail to meet expectations because of a lack of dedication to what I refer to as the *up-front work*, the due diligence, the work to define all requirements in all functions; describe the availability of the various competencies and levels required; review and update the requirements; integrate the design work with the needs of other organizational functions; meet all government requirements; identify the difficulties and inconsistencies in the supply chain; put together a viable business plan that justifies the investment; gain approval of the investment from the required authority. The process is obviously more complex than described, but fulfilling these broad requirements as related to those of a specific project establishes the minimum requirements.

Phase 3—Project Execution—All the project planning and preparation often fails to guarantee acceptable performance as to meeting requirements, schedules, and cost. As noted previously, the track record on effective project execution leaves something to be desired. Project execution lives in the world of the specialists and their support people from all functions: the CEO and executive staff, while ultimately accountable, do not participate in those thousands of decisions required to bring a project to a successful conclusion. Success depends on project leadership; integration of thousands of decisions any one of which can delay or scuttle a project; available competence in all disciplines and functions; an information system with sufficient capability to support the project; not only competent management and supervision but proactive management and supervision; and approval of the project based on available facts and the judgments made in relation to those facts.

Much has been written about why projects fail or fail to meet expectations. Part of the difficulty arises from the initial premises that an accurate estimate of costs and schedule can be made before the design is completed. I use the word *design* to include not only the design of the product or service, but the *design* required for all functional contributors whether related to the technology functions, the marketing and distribution functions, and all those supportive administrative functions. The new product or service requires an approved design. A marketing plan requires an approved design. The new production process requires an approved design. The communication process requires an approved design. However, the best detailed designs do not guarantee success without adequate supervision. As a general statement, many organizations, over the past two decades, have lowered their performance standards. Refer to comments already made regarding Gillette, HP, the auto companies, and even IBM. Much of this has occurred because managements failed to impose sufficient discipline regarding performance. Too many employees *exceed requirements* with no impact on the organization's business that could be measured quantitatively or qualitatively. In the process, some new management principles suggested that managers should set the goals and let the troops do the job, otherwise they were micromanaging. There's a fine line between managers participating and managers micromanaging. However, we need to distinguish between micromanaging and providing guidance. Everybody can't begin at zero on the learning curve and make the same mistakes.

INVESTING IN NEW TECHNOLOGIES

Investing in the development and application of new technologies probably creates the greatest challenge in the decision process, since relatively few executives and their board members are technically oriented, and the decision involves dealing with high levels of uncertainty and risk. It's difficult to make any decision without adequate knowledge, but the process becomes more complex when related to investments in new technologies. The majority of those in the decision stream find themselves being totally dependent on either managers or engineers and other discipline specialists to provide the information to reach the decision. In essence, they ratify the decisions of knowledgeable in the field of interest. They must have the ultimate levels of trust in their support personnel in order to reach a positive decision.

Personal prejudices and misinformation also complicate the decision-making process. As an example, an engineering department of a Fortune 500 Company had made proposals for computerizing certain manufacturing processes. The proposal was always vetoed by an engineering vice president before it could progress up the ladder for approval. The vice president, who had little or no understanding of computer control systems, had a close relationship with an executive in another Fortune 500 Company, which had undergone major and costly negative experiences in attempting to implement similar technologies, accorded more credibility to his colleague than to his own engineering staff. He never really understood the nuances and the differences in scope between the experiences of his colleague and the approaches proposed by his engineering staff. However, his staff engineers continued to send proposals with further justification and arguments as to why the proposal needed to be approved. It required several proposals over a period of almost 2 years before the vice president of Engineering reluctantly gave his approval. A committed group of engineers knew what the future required and persisted until the project was approved. Such situations are not unusual. All of us become skeptical when a proposal is presented for approval, where we lack the fundamental knowledge required to understand the underlying principles, and must make the decision. That applies to any organizational function and any professional discipline.

What do I mean by new technologies? The answer depends on the organization and where it operates in the realm of technologies that dominate its industry. New technology must be viewed in the context in which it will be applied. A new very sophisticated computer chip may be routine for one organization and a major source of frustration for another. A pneumatic controller may be new technology for one who only understands electronic controllers and vice versa. Nanotechnology may be a new technology for someone who just learned about it, but routine for the person involved with it since its first publications in engineering and scientific journals. A mechanical cam system may be new technology for the electronics engineer. All the electronic toys may appear to be mysterious to the uninitiated in the communication technologies. These are examples of new technologies, but at a very elementary level.

Investment in developing new technologies requires acceptance of high levels of risk: there is no guarantee that the investment will end with an acceptable return on the investment. DuPont provides an excellent example for investing significant resources in the development of basic polymers. The investigation took many years of tireless work filled with minor successes and major disappointments, before the results could be developed into marketable products.

The design and construction of a semiconductor plant may exceed a billion dollars before the first product leaves the factory floor to a designated customer. The amount of high risk investment in the medical area, both for devices and medicines of various types, very quickly reaches millions of dollars. Or consider the billions invested in bringing Boeing's 787 Dreamliner or the Airbus 380 to the marketplace. Bringing a new computer system to the marketplace may include anywhere from 2,000 to 4,000 engineers, scientists, programmers, marketers, and support people working for 3–5 years. Each of these projects comes with a high level of risk. Not all organizations have the billions or millions to invest in new technologies. One-hundred thousand dollars could be a major investment for a small organization and may afford even higher levels of risk than the billions spent by Fortune 500 companies. These decisions will be made with the primary income coming from the discipline specialists and their managers.

ENTERING NEW MARKETS

A decision to enter a new market with an existing product or a new market with a new product raises issues related to the organization's resources, its infrastructure, rationalizing the impact on current products or services, managing potential conflicts and redundancies, and related discontinuities. But such a decision made at the top executive levels does not take into account the many implementation decisions. The macro decision was most likely based on positive financial results. Such decisions are usually justified by marketing studies that define certain business opportunities, but minimize the uncertainties and risks involved

Questions will be asked by those responsible for implementing the project. What are the risks to the organization by investing in new markets? How does this decision affect my operations? What are the alternatives? While it's the responsibility of the executives at various levels to separate the facts from the opinions and fluff, which may be easier said than done, we're dealing with human beings and someone or some group is bound to have their ox gored.

Entering a new market with a current or modified product need not be accompanied by insurmountable problems, but also involves more than making a cursory decision without adequate reflection and study. Assemble the facts and the required resources; face those facts realistically taking into account the unknown future; eliminate the prejudices, biases, and pet-project phenomena; and the process can be implemented. Entering a new market area with a new product raises considerably more and different questions. 3M's Post-it Notes provide a good example of failure and success. The failure, 3M's marketing department did not consider the product, market worthy. There may have been many reasons to be negative especially if the marketers could only think of how 3M products are sold. In this case, the marketers had data, knowledge, perhaps some information, but lacked conventional wisdom that comes from practice. To take a positive stance on Post-it Notes, they would have had to divorce themselves from traditional marketing study approaches and how the company sells its products. Like many innovative products nobody asks for them. No one asked for Post-it Notes. Give me one, let me touch, feel, and use it, and I'll buy it. While traditional market study approaches provide valuable information when dealing with evolutionary products, those same approaches are ineffective when dealing with revolutionary of really new-to-the-market products. Like many new products, Post-it Notes was not an easy sell. It is well known at 3M that usually all major new product successes are killed at least three times by management. Proving management wrong may be the driving force behind those involved in pursuing ideas that materialize into major contributions to 3M's successes.

DISCONTINUING A PRODUCT LINE

One would think that making a decision to obsolete a product or line of products would be a relatively simple process based on facts. In such situations annual sales figures begin to erode, customer complaints about the product not meeting current requirements continue to increase, and perhaps there's no longer anything to get excited about. There just wasn't a champion to fight the issue in the executive suite. Every day that sales brochure looks exactly the same. Same faces and the same problems provide little enthusiasm and inspiration. This may occur from a lack of investment in upgrading the product line over the years which could have prevented this situation, nevertheless it exists. There is no choice at the present time, but to find a way to discontinue the product line. There are those few customers who swear by the product and the discussion focuses on how to maintain their loyalty. If we drop the proposed product we'll lose their other business. The product line may also have been conceived by the current CEO or other executive, at some time in the past, and the decision is not made on considering the facts, but not bruising egos. Arguments will be made as to how discontinuing the product will affect costs of other products because of synergies in manufacturing or sales. Even though the decision may be made through rational analysis and judgment, the ultimate consequences cannot be identified. Eventually a decision will be made to eliminate the product or product line, but in the meantime the issue will be revisited with every new piece of information vying for or against discontinuing.

Discontinuing a product line involves more than the financial and sales departments: such an action has consequences for just about all other organizational units. Some of the questions that must be asked but are often disregarded include

- What are the real consequences on customer relations? Identify them, in writing.
- What are the financial write-offs? The total write-offs without any rationalization to reduce the amount.
- What is the phase-out timeline? Developing the timeline requires competencies in understanding what it takes to discontinue a product line.
- How do we dispose of current inventory? There are always those who try to rationalize the value of inventory for future products. Beware of those decisions.
- Are there saleable or reusable assets? That old tooling is most likely of little value if any. Don't tie the hands of a future designer to try and salvage junk.
- What is the impact on all organizational units, one by one? Are redundancies identified and costs associated with those redundancies part of the cost of discontinuing the product line?
- Who is assigned responsibility, not a group but who? Identify the person capable of removing this product line with the least disruption to the organization.

If there are no current plans for replacing the product line with a new product line, what happened? Did the organization fall asleep? Will the organization wake up? Crunch time arrives and a flurry of programs will be proposed for immediate implementation. The panic button is pushed and continues to be pushed every day.

PROMOTING INNOVATION AND ENTREPRENEURSHIP

For several decades beginning with the Peters and Waterman book, *In Search of Excellence*, books, articles, and commentary on the need for more innovation and entrepreneurship have dominated the academic and business press. Federal Government agencies have also proposed various documents promoting innovation. But, organizations that were considered to be innovative continue to be innovative to a greater or lesser degree and those noninnovative organizations continue to be devoid of any innovation. Innovation requires innovators and innovators do not grow on trees. We can't pull the innovation switch and expect results in the next quarter. Actions by the US Congress will not provide innovation because innovation requires more than policy statements without understanding what innovation involves. Too many of these policy documents conclude that innovations come from research. Innovation does not come from research; it comes from putting mostly the known into new configurations that provide some useful benefits. Proponents of more innovation call for increased R&D spending by industry and government. Academia, government, and industry struggle to various degrees to translate ideas into innovations that not only provide for economic growth, but also provide some tangential social benefit. Those many articles that present *innovations of the year* too often describe substitute products with new bells and whistles that involved considerable effort and talent to bring to the marketplace. These *innovations of the year* while interesting and in some cases exciting do not provide significant economic value, if any. I recall from former reading that someone made a profound statement; innovation is born of personal initiative, but lives in the marketplace. So, innovation involves invention and either commercialization or implementation.

Stated simply, INNOVATION = INVENTION + COMMERCIALIZATION or IMPLEMENTATION: no commercialization or implementation, no innovation. Obviously, invention stems from ideas, but ideas are not innovations, they're ideas probably unscripted and lacking any system description. Promoting innovation not only requires innovators, but a culture that supports them. Innovators bring together a certain set of skills such as communication, a certain type of leadership, and some project management skills; they bring personal characteristics and attitudes that allow them to face the challenges for creating change: and they bring broad-based useful knowledge and experience gained by a heuristic approach from years of experience. While ideas for new products and services, new production processes, new marketing and sales approaches, new improved administrative routines, and innovations throughout all organizational units and affiliations with customers and vendors may come from anyone in the organization, implementation will reside with the engineers and other discipline specialists and their support groups. Executives may provide an idea, but subsequent activities that might lead to an innovation will reside with the discipline specialists and their immediate managers.

Innovators face a long list of organizational challenges. This list includes resistance to change, rejection of new thinking, lack of focus on the system issues, disregard for eliminating the blind spots, uninformed managers, lack of tolerance for constructive mavericks (those who think differently), total focus on short term, institutionalized traditions, inflexible hiring practices, indecisive decision-makers, ineffective bureaucracy, nonsupportive infrastructure, rigid organizational structure, rigid rules, politics and decision-making, and more. The challenges come from all parts of the organization and from all levels. While all of these challenges seldom challenge any one innovator, any one of them can create delays and unnecessary obstruction and kill the innovation spirit. The presence of naysayers requires adequate consideration by innovators. Innovators are focused and that intense focus can lead to disregarding constructive negative information that can lead to taking the wrong path.

Expanding the Innovation Horizon,[6] The *IBM Global CEO Study 2006* enabled 765 CEOs to share their views on innovation. The research identified 10 top obstacles to innovation segregating them as internal and external.

Internal Obstacles to Innovation

- Unsupportive culture and climate
- Limited funding for investment
- Workforce issues
- Process immaturity
- Inflexible physical and IT infrastructure
- Insufficient access to information

External Obstacles to Innovation

- Government and other legal restrictions
- Economic uncertainty
- Inadequate enabling technologies
- Workforce issues arising externally

All the *Internal Obstacles to Innovation* cited by the CEOs are under their control: have they abdicated their responsibilities, have they delegated these activities to others, has their role as CEO changed so significantly that they operate in the external world more than the internal world of their organization. It's interesting that culture, funding, workforce, infrastructure, and information somehow have escaped their interest.

The study also identified the most significant sources of ideas, the precursors to innovation. The results are in percentage; employees ~43; business partners ~38; customers ~37; consultants ~22; competitors ~20; associations, tradeshows, conference, boards ~18; internal sales and service units ~17; internal R&D ~17: and academia ~13. The split between internally and externally generated ideas appeared to be fairly even. Multiple items could be selected so that the total does not reach 100.

Gaynor[7] in *Innovation by Design* identified what it takes to make innovation happen, what it takes to make innovation thrive, and what not to do.

Making innovation happen

- Assess performance while it can be affected
- Develop an awareness for accountability for results
- Understand where people come from—not everyone has the drive
- Determine the organization's fitness for innovation

- Select the right people
- Provide time for constructive thinking and doing follow-up
- Encourage exploration of new approaches
- Promote freedom with discipline
- Develop interpersonal skills
- Set stretch targets
- Promote collegiality
- Delineate organizational, departmental, and project goals
- Invest in the future—people and other resources
- Develop open communication without retribution
- Find an adequate innovation metric
- Educate employees about the business
- Eliminate status symbols that affect performance

Innovation thrives when

- Freedom is allowed but with discipline
- Intellectual property is available to all
- Responsibility and accountability are defined but with multidisciplinary collaboration
- A formal but not rigid process exists for introducing new products and services
- When specific objectives and measurement criteria are established
- When the work adds value to fulfilling the organization's strategy
- When staff are educated to meet the workload needs
- A realistic reward system is in place
- When innovators meet the skills, characteristics, attitudes, and knowledge to satisfy the requirements for the potential innovation

What not to do

- Give short shrift to new ideas
- Reward uniformity in thinking
- Penalize the risk takers
- Prevent bootlegging of resources
- Manage solely by the numbers
- Practice the one-size-fits-all principle
- Interpret policies and practices to the letter of the law
- Micromanage

- Discourage departures from the norm
- Limit resources
- Eliminate dissonance
- Limit divergent thinking

$$INNOVATION = INVENTION + COMMERIALIZATION \ or$$
$$IMPLEMENTATION$$

LOCATING BUSINESS OPERATIONS

Location of facilities whether for new office buildings, research centers, manufacturing operations, or other facilities probably are more sensitive to bias and emotion than most other decisions. Too often such property searches become just that, property searches. They often disregard the infrastructure required to support the operations. While elaborate descriptions of the ideal site are prepared and due diligence applied by those responsible for the search, an arbitrary decision by some board, committee, or executive can totally disregard the recommendations. Such decisions eventually require making compromises and the resolution of those compromises becomes the responsibility of those involved in operations. Selecting the appropriate site should be based on meeting a set of requirements depending on needs, not personal preferences without justification. Another factor that often arises is that practices of the home office tend to dictate design and materials of construction. The mother house has specifications that call for specific materials and traditional designs, but often those materials of construction may not be suitable or economically available in the new geographical area under consideration.

While locating a new facility of any kind may not be an everyday occurrence, it has long-term consequences. The process involves more than just locating a piece of property on which to construct a facility for some organizational operation. The issues involve evaluating the availability of local services such as water- and energy-related resources of all types; availability of employees with the appropriate competencies; accessible transportation for employees, shipping, etc.; environmental regulations that might affect operations; taxation policies; acceptance by the community; and similar requirements. While the development of industrial parks has somewhat simplified the process, those same parks may not be the most appropriate location; it may be the easiest in which to begin an operation, but totally inappropriate for any long-term planning. So, finding the site that best meets the needs of an organization usually requires people knowledgeable about the facility requirements, skilled in the business of analyzing the many issues and reaching a decision or rating several selected sites for management's consideration. Management, by disregarding the recommendation or the results of a search committee, sends the message to the organization that squandering resources is acceptable. Such actions militate against proposing management programs to improve organizational effectiveness and often lead to cynicism. Management may have reasons for rejecting the results or the recommendation, but the reasons cannot be capricious or without clarification. The problems become more difficult as organizations move operations outside their home country. In the final analysis, location decisions become an engineering responsibility with cooperation of the financial group.

KEY POINTS

- Successful project execution depends on making decisions with consideration of the unknown, the unpredictable, and uncontrollable.
- Decision-making involves those responsible for making the decision and those who possess the knowledge to make the decision meaningful: reaching the appropriate decision depends on the levels of trust.
- Homegrown executives, with few exceptions, have an advantage over the imported executives. In the final analysis success depends on selecting employees to meet specific requirements. Reading resumes is not a substitute for first-hand knowledge.
- The most critical issue in the decision-making process includes the courage to ask the difficult questions without alienating the other participants. It's easy to say "lay all the issues on the table" for open discussion but difficult to gain active participation.
- External industry and economic factors often drive both short- and long-term performance to a greater extent than internal actions.
- A decision at the executive level to enter the worldwide economy involves more than selling products: it involves an understanding of those new cultures and how to work within them successfully.
- Acquisitions and mergers have not yielded the expected breakthroughs. The plan for integrating the organizations into a new whole must be developed before the merger or acquisition and not after.
- Decisions to restructure an organization must include a purpose and motive and must be supplemented with the action plan and metrics to determine level of performance.

- Decisions related to locating business operations of any type should be on data related to site requirements professional analyses of and not by personal preferences that disregard the facts.
- Investing in new-to-the-market products or services involves significant levels of risk: the process requires more than a plan; it involves careful attention to execution.
- Investing in technologies involves managers who make the decisions and the engineers and discipline specialists with the knowledge: integrity requires managers to listen and the professional specialists to meet expectations.
- Entering new markets with either current or new products challenges the best and brightest of an organization's talent base: management must be willing to accept well-intentioned failure.
- Removing products that no longer meet performance targets creates a decision-making dilemma: the answer, what are the consequences on customer relations?
- A decision related to developing an innovative organization is simple; yes simple: develop an organizational infrastructure and culture that supports the innovators.

NOTES

1. Farhad Manjoo, "How to sell or not to sell," *Fast Company*, December 2009–January 2010, p. 50.
2. Bill Vlasic and Bradley A. Stertz, *Taken for Ride; How Daimler-Benz Drove Off with Chrysler*, New York: McGraw-Hill, 2000, p. 281.
3. Sydney Finkelstein, "The Daimler Chrysler merger," Tuck school of Business at Dartmouth, No. 1.
4. Henry Mintzberg, "The manager's job: folklore and fact," *Harvard Business Review*, Reprint 90210, p.12.
5. Theodore Levitt, *The Marketing Mode,* New York: McGraw-Hill, 1969, pp. 155–170.
6. The Global CEO Study 2006, *Expanding the Innovation Horizon*, IBM Global Business Services, pp. 29–33.
7. Gerard H. Gaynor, *Innovation by Design*, New York: American Management Association, 2002, pp. 221–242.

4

DECISIONS AND PROJECT SCOPE

In a short span of 100 years, the world moved from an agrarian society to an industrial society, to the birth of the information society, and more recently, to the communications society. Aviation progressed from Charles Lindberg's crossing of the Atlantic to development of the Boeing 787 Dreamliner and the Airbus 380. Wireless communication transitioned from the telegraph, to the crystal set, to the radio, to television, and to sophisticated communication technologies with unimaginable capabilities. The ballpoint pen moved from a luxury item to a giveaway. Film photography was replaced by digital. In that same period, decision processes became more complex than in the past, and now as we're into the second decade of the this twenty-first century, we find segments of industry, government, and academia struggling to make decisions that provide an adequate return on investment in human capital. All of these accomplishments occurred through multiple decisions that spanned a continuum from the very simple to the very complex.

Countless numbers of projects within any organization are completed in less than 10 hours and require minimum amount of thought: they are often repetitive, well known, and documented and can be completed by standard operating procedures that depend on experience and rules of thumb. However, these

Decisions: An Engineering and Management Perspective, First Edition. Gerard H. Gaynor.
© 2015 The Institute of Electrical and Electronics Engineers, Inc. Published 2015 by John Wiley & Sons, Inc.

projects represent a minor although important segment of any organization's project list. Chapter 4 focuses on projects that need approval by organizational boards, various executive and management committees at the operational and staff levels and by engineers and other professional specialists. Chapter 4 topics include

- Organizational Decisions
- Low Impact to High Impact
- Simple to Complex
- Low Cost to High Cost
- Low Risk to High Risk
- Upgrade to Innovative
- Current Business to New Business Unit
- Current Business Unit to a New Game
- Decisions in Functional Units
- Limited Scope to Expanded Scope
- Strategic to Operational
- Knockouts
- Thinking Before Doing
- Key Points
- Notes

ORGANIZATIONAL DECISIONS

Organizational decisions span a continuum from the very simple, yet important, to the very complex that determine the sustainability of the organization: no single decision-making design meets the requirements for reaching all decisions and every organization is trapped in its own organizational procedures and customs. Yes, some simple approaches such as, (1) describing the issue and the expectations, (2) gathering the facts, (3) creating the various scenarios, (4) evaluating scenarios against expectations, resources, and so on, and (5) making the decision, laying down the basics, but are insufficient. The principal issue involves understanding what is meant by gathering sufficient factual information. What may be required varies according to project scope, level of risk, organizational policies and procedures, and individual and group preferences. However, all the facts will not be known at the time any organization makes the decision to go forward with a project, regardless of scope.

When investment decisions, for any purpose, require approval by a board or executive committee, greater scrutiny and diligence guides the process, than if the decision was made at the functional levels. These higher level decisions usually affect the total organization: they have a significantly higher level of impact on the future of the organization's sustainability. Assuming that the decision-making process at the highest level met all the requirements, execution fails not because of the inappropriateness of the decision, but because of the thousands of decisions required to implement the decision. The 3-year delay in launching Boeing's 787 Dreamliner, followed by a grounding of the fleet for almost 4 months, occurred not because of the original decision made by Boeing's board, but from difficulties in executing what the board approved: execution of those thousands and possibly millions of decisions required to launch the first test flight. Whether the potential critical issues were vetted fully or possibly totally disregarded for any number of reasons is left to those who eventually write the history of the 787 Dreamliner.

Too often board decisions of this type fail to take into account the implementation details of the decision. This does not suggest that board decisions totally disregard implementation, but that insufficient thought is given to identifying the potential knockouts: knockouts include those unresolved issues that if not identified early in a project generate unintended consequences. Anyone who has ever been involved in a major project understands the executive focus of shortening project schedules that usually end in extending the project schedule. On long-term projects, no one possesses the crystal ball that defines future events: the unknown, the unpredictable, the uncontrolled, and the unexpected. These schemas apply equally to industry, government, academia, and the not-for-profit sector. The situation becomes further exacerbated by overpromising and underperforming.

Overpromising and underperforming comes about because of lack of due diligence regarding the up-front work on the part of executives, managers, and engineers. There are no guarantees that any amount of thinking will identify all potential issues that could setback progress. But, referring again to the 787 Dreamliner, the communication problems in working in multiple languages and different cultures were evidently disregarded or given a, "don't worry about it, we'll work it out when the time comes," and all will be well. The breakdown of the supply chain could have been avoided if the issues had been fully vetted and accommodations made to avoid the breakdown.

LOW IMPACT TO HIGH IMPACT

Within any organization, many people make very many *low impact* decisions. In other words, the low impact decisions will not significantly affect the organization's performance metrics, the bottom line or immediate stakeholders. Such decisions usually include those made in relation to administrative matters;

routine decisions in functional groups like human resources, research, development, procurement, marketing, manufacturing, sales; and other organizational functions. Managers, especially senior managers, make these decisions quickly without taking time to do an analysis of the consequences of the decision. Senior engineers, likewise make many decisions without great deliberation. Experienced decision-makers usually have their own set of what's known as *rules of thumb*. The expression "rules of thumb" simply provides a method that comes from practice or experience. These decisions may be made "off the cuff" so-to-speak, without much thought, but must be grounded in established fundamentals. Seldom will they require any financial justification: they must be completed for many different reasons. Keep in mind that one person's rule of thumb may be another person's road to unemployment. But, how does the neophyte manager or engineer or other discipline specialist cope in such a situation? Decision-making is basically a learning-from-experience process with the help of learning some basic principles. Developing the competence begins with learning from these early experiences. Mistakes will be made, but unfortunately one does not learn to make decisions by reading a book or listening to a professor or some consultant pontificate about the process. Two points must come together; (1) learning how to accept failure and learn from it and (2) the organization must be able to live with what I refer to as "well-intentioned failure."

At the high impact end of the decision continuum, using *rules of thumb* or making *off-the-cuff* decisions can have disastrous effects on organizational performance. The following are examples of high impact decisions.

- Decision to disregard critical project implementation issues
- Decision to use unproven technologies on a major new project without exploring potential impact on business impact
- Decision to pursue a new-to-the-market product
- Decision to use tools and techniques that do not apply to the product or service to be offered
- Decision to eliminate the educational and training programs required for future organizational sustainability
- Decision to invest in research, development, manufacturing, marketing, and information systems
- Decision to promote mergers and acquisitions

SIMPLE TO COMPLEX

The simple to complex continuum involves the same organizational units and the same people. As an example, a team involved in the design and construction of a major piece of production equipment costing millions of dollars is asked to improve the delivery by several months. If the project is on schedule this should be a relatively simple decision. However, it depends on the level of integrity that has been demonstrated during prior project reviews. We are all familiar with projects that are on schedule until the last month or two, and at the next project review, the project is months behind schedule. Such a decision may involve reviewing many details and contacting many groups for their projections, but the process is straightforward: it only requires due diligence and a return to facing facts. Under such circumstances, a sense of integrity must be reintroduced to the team.

Simplicity and complexity are in the eyes of the observer. What is simple to one person may be relatively complex to another, and this difference depends on breadth of knowledge and experience and the context in which it is viewed. Knowledge alone is insufficient. Here are examples of what types of decision might be classified as simple.

- Selecting components or subassemblies in the conduct of a design
- Making daily decisions in any professional field where knowledge is the most important factor
- Preparing project plans in a single professional discipline
- Reaching a decision within a team on promoting a new project
- Doing a search in any aspect of the business; engineering, marketing, manufacturing, sales, information technology, administration, and others
- Participating in a brain-storming session that leads to a decision
- Preparing designs in any area for evaluation
- Taking the initiative to speak to your immediate supervisor

The following examples involve much greater levels of complexity, but bear in mind that all decisions depend on the context in which they are viewed; what may be a complex decision depends on the experience and educational background of the decision-maker.

- Selecting a project team for a major project
- Recommending a colleague for a significant promotion
- Accepting a reassignment that involves a significant change in responsibilities
- Becoming the champion for an innovation
- Moving part of an organization to some foreign location
- Becoming a foreign service employee in a major organization
- Introducing change within a major organizational department

LOW COST TO HIGH COST

Decisions involve a continuum from low cost transactions to high cost trans-actions and at all levels in between. What is defined as low cost and high cost depends on the context in which the decision is made. Low cost decisions may involve any number of the issues considered in this classification process. Low cost does not necessarily imply low impact or a simple decision. A decision for a limited cost project could be complex. Likewise, a decision for a mod-erate or limited project cost could have significant impact. An out-of-tolerance manufacturing process, as an example, can have a severely negative impact on a manufacturing line's output. A relatively insignificant change could generate significant amounts of scrap. Yet the cost of reaching the decision to resolve the issue would be minimal: just knowledge, understanding, and a systems view of the parameters that affect product quality.

The decision to recall a product from the market presents a very different problem, a very costly decision. In recent times, we have seen recalls for auto-mobile malfunctions, defective tires and toys, dangerous computer batteries, medical devices, contaminated food, and others. Organizations often have no choice but to implement a recall, but the costs of implementing such an action often involve accepting significant costs; as an example, a recall of millions of automobiles for safety issues. That decision not only involves the supplier, but the customers who are then required to schedule an appointment in order to repair the problem. Disregarding action to resolve the issues would not be a very appropriate way to build brand or customer satisfaction. While recall of automobiles may generate dissatisfaction, the recall of implanted medical devices creates the added risks to human life by requiring additional surgical procedures.

LOW RISK TO HIGH RISK

What may be a low risk decision in one organization may be a high risk decision in another organization. At the same time, organizations often spend a great deal of time obsessing about the potential risk of a decision when identifying and describing the knockouts. So, what are knockouts? Knockouts are any issues whether related to technology, products, markets, or any other condition that preclude the project from being a success. The level of risk depends on the context in which the decision is made. Comparisons of decision processes from a group of organizations provide little benefit since the limiting conditions are never the same. General Motors invested billions in automation in a system of systems project and the benefits received did not meet expectations unless those expectations were very low. First, recognize that it is impossible to evaluate risk without carefully investigating the subsystems, assemblies, and components and evaluating the risk associated with each. The construction of the Denver International Airport provides an excellent example.

What were the risks associated with the development of the Denver International Airport? The project was perceived as a typical and very complex design and construction project. Most of the project was routine, fortified by well-established design and engineering principles; it was complex in terms of meeting the requirements of many different constituencies; but it failed to meet requirements when it made the decision to include an automatic baggage handling system. As Shenhar[1] points out, that while the project, as a system of systems may have been considered as routine and complex, it involved the automatic baggage handling system that was not routine but very complex, high risk, required invention and innovation, and involved an assembly that could and did create those unintended consequences. The designers of the automatic baggage handling system evidently failed to determine the cut-off point where automation fails to deliver the expected benefit. A visit to an airport check-in counter for several hours and viewing the range and sizes of the baggage that enter the system in a random sequence demonstrates the scope of the problem. While this may have been done, the complexities were evidently underestimated.

Shenhar has developed a Diamond Model as shown in Figure 4.1 to assess benefits and risks associated with a specific component of a project. Figure 4.1 considers the relations among technology, novelty, pace, and complexity. The

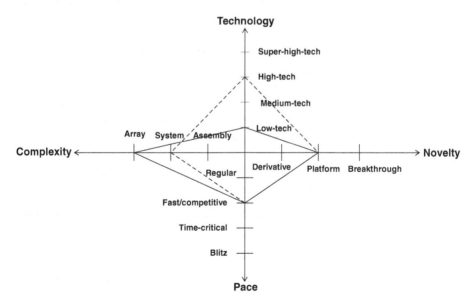

Figure 4.1. Diamond diagram of the Denver International Airport project.

gradations along each of the axes depend on the organization. Each organization will define its technologies differently: the definition in an organization where polymers play a major role in performance may be quite different than an organization involved in semiconductors. What may be considered a breakthrough in one organization may be a derivative in another. The same applies for the pace and complexity axes. The notations on the axes provide for flexibility: other variables relevant to the project can be used as will be shown later in this chapter.

Shenhar shows that the Denver Airport project, Figure 4.1, was conceived as a major construction project. This is shown by the solid lines. A closer analysis of the individual parts of the project would have shown the limiting conditions. The limiting conditions are shown by the dotted line. The limiting factors were not the construction of the Denver Airport but the baggage handling system. Why this was not realized at the time of project approval is difficult to understand. However, by considering the project as a typical although complex construction project, engineers failed to adequately identify the knockouts.

UPGRADE TO INNOVATIVE

There are many decisions related to product or service upgrading made in a single day as contrasted to the few decisions that may involve some aspect of innovation. Those upgrading decisions take place in all organizational functions and many without a great deal of thought. Of course, there's a continuum here and as the decisions approach the innovative end of the continuum they are no longer improvement decisions. Replacing a component may be a routine decision. Reorganizing a research or marketing team probably rests at midpoint of this continuum. Introducing a new manufacturing process may be an upgrade but could also move further toward the innovative depending on its scope and introduction of new unproven processes and technologies. Introducing those software upgrades, usually suggest improved performance, but often involve unexpected implementation problems and considerable user frustration. As noted few software projects meet the three project requirements; fulfilling specifications, delivering on schedule, and meeting the cost targets.

Innovation comes in many sizes and shapes. Every organization promotes its innovations, but most focus on improvement rather than breakthrough innovation. Our current emphasis on innovation, where just about any minor change is considered as innovative, really denigrates the concept of innovation. The concept innovation too often becomes intermingled with ideas and invention. Ideas are ideas and inventions are inventions. But innovation involves either commercialization or implementation of an invention that was preceded by an idea. Game-changing and disruptive innovations are difficult to identify.

Increasing the research budget does not necessarily increase innovation. And, innovation is not just about technology or marketing new products. It must encompass the complete organization from top to bottom. Decision-makers must understand what the concept of innovation involves. Innovation is not about generating ideas: it involves invention plus implementation or commercialization; no implementation or commercialization, no innovation. The annual lists of innovations that business and other publications compile, that add bells and whistles to already known products, are not innovations that expand the economy: in many cases they provide improved substitute products. This is not to say that they may not increase sales or provide customers some benefit, but they're obvious extensions of current products whether related to technology or marketing. They're really not new-to-the-market or breakthrough products: most qualify as product enhancements. Once Apple introduced the iPhone, all subsequent versions do not qualify as innovations; they are expected improvements. The same applies for the iPod and the iPad.

CURRENT BUSINESS TO NEW BUSINESS UNIT

The strategic and operational decision processes in a current business unit eventually develop some processes, methodologies, or models to guide the decision-making process. Building a new business unit, internally within an organization or as an entrepreneurial venture outside the organization, requires starting with a blank sheet of paper. Starting something new most likely will not become successful using current acceptable methodologies. The decision by the 3M marketing group to conclude that Post-it Notes had no future was not only flawed, but also demonstrated that standardized, accepted, and best marketing practices cannot be used in all cases. Virtual marketing may work, but it may not work under circumstances, where the best approach to sell the product requires the opportunity to touch, smell, or feel the product. New-to-the-market innovative products require innovative marketing approaches.

Operating business units often face problems because processes, methodologies, and models that guide decision processes have been institutionalized to the point they become untouchable. While a decision to institutionalize decision processes offers some benefits, those benefits become counterproductive when they no longer meet the new requirements of the new business unit. The same applies to institutionalizing any process, model, methodology regardless of its purpose and benefits.

As an example, imagine you've been given an opportunity to develop a new business unit within your organization. This assignment will most likely come with a broad description of the new business unit, but with minimum details, reasons for its implementation, an outline of the basic objectives, but most likely without an implementation plan. Management concluded that this new business unit would accrue significant future benefits by spinning it off into a new business unit. Since no plan was attached to this assignment, you'll be responsible for developing the business plan, getting it approved, building the team to fulfill the objectives, and taking on the leadership role for this major challenge. Obviously, the strategic and operational processes and models from the current organization are available for consideration, but only for consideration. The major question, do they fit the needs of the new business opportunity?

CURRENT BUSINESS UNIT TO A NEW GAME

World competition for markets; increases in manufacturing efficiency and effectiveness; and now expanded interest in technology research, development, and innovation globally, have created significant new challenges for all organizations. In essence, this situation presents management, the equivalent of a New Game. So, what is a New Game? A New Game involves any event generated either internally or externally that forces an organization to reflect seriously on its future. The current worldwide economic situation presents a New Game. A New Game operation would also include a major departure from an organization's fields of interest; competing in a new industry sector; managing a major turnaround of a business unit that has been underperforming for many years and requires major surgery; integrating two or more major business units with a new strategic business unit; implementing a major employee reduction program based on required competencies; reorganizing global manufacturing operations; introducing a leading-edge but unproven technology; reorganizing a global sales organization; and similar projects. These are both macro and subsidiary decisions that require not only thousands but often millions of implementation decisions that will be made by people who had absolutely no input to the macro decision.

In the early 1960s few organizations thought about going global, some did and over the years took their business operations closer to the customer, where products could be tailored to local needs and manufacturing sources no longer required shipment solely from the headquarters country. This was the beginning of a New Game in business operations. These decisions were made with considerable discussion, often acrimonious, and with considerable dissatisfaction by many senior executives. Yet today, many of those same organizations depend on foreign sales for more than 50 percent of their revenue, having made major investments in manufacturing facilities and office campuses. The New Game presents additional complications in evaluating risk; identifying critical cost factors; developing realistic schedules that accommodate unknown problems; dealing with new complex interactions between global organizational units; being sufficiently perceptive to changing world requirements; arbitrating the many related issues that can have an impact on meeting expectations; and working within many different political systems. The New Game can determine the rise or fall of an organization, but the organization will fail under the too-watchful eyes of the CEO and executives, who will be offering advice and expecting results more quickly than realistically possible. New Games require hands-on involvement, rather than virtual management by the CEO, senior executives, managers, supervisors, and discipline specialists: they need to become involved and provide freedom with discipline and that's quite different from giving orders and micromanaging. Decisions, related to what I refer to as an organization's need to depart from its Current Business to some face some New Game grow exponentially in number and complexity from those decisions required in a current business unit or a new spin-off business unit.

DECISIONS IN FUNCTIONAL UNITS

The decisions made within a single functional unit can create problems that span the spectrum of problems in other organizational units. However, just what does a decision by a single function or discipline involve? Is the engineering function a single or multiple-functional organizational unit? It can be both single and multiple. While one person may eventually make the decision, input from others will most likely be required. Relatively few decisions involve the input from only one person. Decisions as simple as selecting a mechanical or electrical component, deciding on the rationale for developing a market study, planning the review of the organization's operations, and deciding whether or not to file a patent application usually requires input from more than one person or one organizational function.

A decision to select or design a component part for an assembly does not necessarily require input from others, but it could depend on the organization's size, structure, principles, values, and its culture that spans a continuum from flexible and disciplined to rigid and punitive. The same is true for developing a market study, planning a review, or filing a patent application. The involvement by other than the principal investigator depends on the organization's infrastructure. Every additional person or group involved in the decision process multiplies the difficulties in reaching a decision. However, engineers and other discipline specialists that work at the bench level as specialists will most likely make the single-function or single-discipline decisions.

The level of conflict in reaching a decision depends on the level of homogeneity in the function, the flexibility of the participants, and the competencies of the group leader. Here too, it depends on how we define a single function. An engineering department that includes mechanical, electrical, chemical, industrial, and perhaps other disciplines, even though consolidated in a single group is multifunctional and multidisciplinary. Each discipline negotiates to further its advantages. As an example, consider the development of an automated assembly line: engineers from all the disciplines negotiate to determine the best combination of technologies from the disciplines of mechanical, electrical, instrumentation, control systems, pneumatics, automation, and robotics. Reaching the appropriate design decisions, to provide the expected reliability and performance of the automated system, depends on negotiating tradeoffs of one technology over another. Engineering will not make those decisions alone. The manufacturing group responsible for the production emanating from that assembly line must also enter into the decision process: it will be responsible for the maintenance, meeting production schedules, and making provisions for improved or new product processes.

LIMITED SCOPE TO EXPANDED SCOPE

There are projects, then there are projects, and seldom does one project duplicate another. The Limited Scope to Expanded Scope continuum considers a current product or process modification at one end of the continuum, to a new-to-the-market product with its new process at the other end of the continuum. For our purposes, consider a service equivalent to a product. Every new service possesses some aspects of a product. It depends on our definition of product. A product is usually tangible and is a result of a work effort of some type. Most services also include something tangible and represent the results of a work effort. A consultant's report is a result of a special type of work effort. A data processing service provides data and an analysis of that data—result of a work effort. The work effort of the organizational administrative functions, normally referred to as services, provides a tangible output. Looking at products and services from these perspectives brings both into congruence.

Product modifications fall into the Limited Scope project class: risk and uncertainty do not present a major problem and investment of resources is usually limited. Obviously, the level of risk and uncertainty depends upon the product and the scope of the modifications. There is a difference between minor product modifications in the auto industry compared to changes involved in modifying the recipe for canned tomato soup. The annual upgrading in the auto industry usually involves many small changes, so the totality of those changes creates higher levels of risk and uncertainty than a slight change of the recipe for canned or frozen tomato soup.

At the other end of the continuum, we find the risks and uncertainties associated with introducing that new-to-the-market product. Keep in mind that this is a new-to-the-market product. The marketplace has yet to see this product. As we look at the development of this new-to-the-market product, it has no history in the marketplace. It only has market potential and business growth potential that resides between the covers of a report or proposal. That report contains human judgments integrated into what appears to be a growth opportunity. So all of the functions from research, development, production, marketing, sales, legal, all the support services and all of the levels of management from the CEO and possibly the Board of Directors down to the first level employees somehow play a role and have an impact on this project.

STRATEGIC TO OPERATIONAL

The strategic to operational continuum like the other continuums provides for a wide range of possibilities. A simple strategic decision often creates significant operational challenges while a major change in strategic direction may have limited impact on operations. A strategic decision, without consideration of the operational consequences, provides a slim chance of implementation; a major operational decision, without considering its relation to the organization's strategic direction, prevents the organization from fulfilling its intended strategy. Integrating operational decision-making with the organization's strategic directions provides the opportunity to achieve optimum results. Both are essential. As noted previously, the strategic decision while the most important, may be the easiest to make since the thousand and more decisions required to fulfill the requirements, receive little if any attention at the time the strategic decision is made.

As an example, for many years Toyota Motor Corp.'s Lexus promoted its cars as an alternative to Europe's Mercedes and BMW. However, as the Wall Street Journal points out, Lexus now wants to become a brand associated with luxury products: Lexus now wants to see the name Lexus mentioned in the same breath as Louis Vuitton, Prada, and Gucci. That's a change in strategic direction. To accomplish this recognition as a luxury car, Lexus introduced several models costing over $70,000. As the Journal points out, Lexus has an ultra-conservative culture; while Mercedes and BMW sponsor lavish parties when they launch a new model. Lexus dealers must be satisfied with inviting potential customers to a cheese and wine party. The question remains, will Lexus change its marketing culture? Over time, there is little doubt that it will. An organization finds it difficult to bypass the culture of the industry in which it operates. This is truly a strategic decision for Lexus. As the article points out Lexus proposes entering a new game and they'll have to play by the rules of the new game, if they wish to succeed.

As you consider this attempt by Lexus to be associated with peers in the luxury products class, think of all the operational decisions required to make this strategy a reality. The process begins with design of a new class of vehicles, fortified by the efforts from various departments in development and engineering;

the many functional units related to production; all the functions related to marketing, sales, and distribution; and those many administrative functions that too often are minimized or totally disregarded. With such a major change in direction, the whole organization while not necessarily being turned upside down will go through some rationalization of its culture and its values.

KNOCKOUTS

This chapter has considered the spectrum of decisions in a way where organizations, because of the many differences, imposed directly or indirectly by organizational and industry requirements, can gain an appreciation for the decisions that are consistent with the size, scope, and needs of the organization. Figure 4.2 shows the continuums in graphic form related to Boeing's 787 Dreamliner and 3M's Post-it Notes.

There is little doubt that Boeing's 787 Dreamliner received executive approval because of the high impact on its future business performance. The Dreamliner involves a complex arrangement of subsystems and became high risk when Boeing decided to outsource the design and production of major assemblies and function essentially in assembly mode. At the same time Boeing was transitioning from use of aluminum to composite materials. Referring to Figure 4.2, (B for Boeing and M for 3M) the Boeing Dreamliner positions marked with a "B" was High Impact; Complex, High Cost and Risk, High Innovation, not exactly a New Business in aviation, but technologically a New Game, and of course, Expanded Scope, and certainly Strategic. The strategic decision to go ahead with the 787 Dreamliner presented overriding operational challenges.

Contrast 3M's Post-it Notes, marked with an "M," with Boeing's 787 Dreamliner as shown in Figure 4.2. Post-it Notes involves Moderate Impact, Complex

	1	2	3	4	5	6	7	8	9	
Low Impact							M		B	High Impact
Simple							M		B	Complex
Low Cost			M						B	High Cost
Low Risk		M							B	High Risk
Improvement								B	M	Innovative
Current Business Unit							B		M	New Business
Current Business Unit					M	B				New Game
Limited Scope						M			B	Expanded Scope
Operational									B	Strategic

Figure 4.2. Comparison of Boeing 787 Dreamliner and 3M Post-it Notes. "B" represents Boeing 787 Dreamliner and "M" 3M Post-it Notes.

but complex from a materials requirements, relatively moderate Cost and Risk, highly Innovative, a New Business, somewhat of a New Game, Expanded Scope, and Strategic. As the project progressed, it was expanded to include all types of additional office products based on the 3M technology platforms and market requirements. Post-it Notes was a New Game and brought 3M into the office products business.

THINKING BEFORE DOING

Successful projects require doing what I refer to as the up-front work. We have all seen the various cartoons that suggest Ready, Fire, Aim. Many projects begin with those caveats with the idea that "We'll find a way to meet the schedule." Has management ever asked you within weeks of a project approval, "have you ordered the tooling?" or some similar question?" Not an uncommon situation that has a parallel in all disciplines. Has management coerced you into accepting a project schedule that was unrealistic? Has management asked you to participate in a project without clearly defined requirements? These are common requests that usually yield a result something less than acceptable.

Decisions emphasizes that decision-making related to project implementation requires consideration of context and the specific issues involved. One approach does not fit all projects. Let's look at two very dissimilar projects, (1) destruction of a production facility during a hurricane, tornado, or any other catastrophic event, and (2) investment in introducing a new product to the marketplace.

If a production facility is destroyed, the recovery options are limited; (1) replace the facility with the current or new design, but the timetable may not be acceptable, (2) find temporary outside sources, (3) find permanent outside sources, (4) possibly exit the related part of the business portfolio, and (5) other possible options depending on the products or services of the business. Any decision would involve a rapid analysis of the impact on the business based on the possible options. Impact on the business would probably most likely be very serious; complexity will range from moderate to exceedingly complex; and the risk will be substantial, but can be evaluated based on the return on investment recognizing the many factors that will play a role in the decision-making process. To fix the problem innovation across all functions and disciplines will be required to fill the gap of the destroyed facility. The level of effort depends if the decision involves replacement "as was" or considers potential future business needs and opportunities. Success will depend on operational leadership and include all organizational functions. The decision as to how to handle the catastrophic event will be quite different if the plant provides basic components for many products, is a single-source plant for many products, produces a single product, or any combination of activities. But the decision goes beyond crunching the numbers to select the appropriate alternative and solely depending on the numbers.

The General Motors Hydra-Matic plant in Livonia, Michigan was destroyed by fire in August 1953. This was probably the worst industrial fire in American history. Within 15–20 minutes the production facility that cost $80 million and included 1.5 million square feet was completely destroyed. Sparks emanating from an outside contractor using an oxyacetylene cutting torch ignited a conveyor dip pan. GM was producing Hydromantic transmissions within 9 weeks after the date of the fire. GM leased a vacant Kaizer Frazer plant at Willow Run just outside of Detroit, Michigan. Keep in mind this was 1953, prior to our information age. We probably couldn't make such a turnaround with present day information systems capability and its related technologies. We'd depend too much on modeling and algorithms instead of thinking and using judgment. Such decisions require more than knowledge, they require experience and judgment. The GM Hydromantic tragedy became a wake-up call to management on the impact of uncontained fires. This example demonstrates the need for insisting on engineering integrity in the design of any system. Fire protection, beyond the traditional means and based on the specific process, must be included as part of the design. It's difficult to understand how GM engineers and their managers could disregard the potential hazard of a plant dealing with volatile materials in a continuous assembly line.

To delve into the thinking process consider a project where the investment involves a new product entry with a total estimated investment of over $500 million: $500 million includes the remainder of the research and product development, manufacturing, marketing and sales, customer service, and all the functions involved in bringing a new product to the marketplace. Even in a very large organization, this project could have a high impact on operations, and if not, the following question must be asked, "Why are they doing this?" Obviously there could be projects that would be mandatory without necessarily being concerned by the return on the investment.

Based on available facts, experience, and judgment and using the continuum of options as shown in Figure 4.3 we might conclude that impact would lie between 8 and 9; complexity at 5–6; cost at 6–7; risk at 8–9; innovation at 7–8; new business at 7–8; new game at 4–5; scope at 7–8; and 8–9 for strategic, but with significant demands on operational discipline.

The emphasis now is on execution and that's an operations issue. So let's look at the possible knockouts.

- Lack of timely availability of all competencies in all disciplines and functions—R&D, engineering, production, marketing, sales, logistics, distribution, and administration and at the time required

	1	2	3	4	5	6	7	8	9	
Low Impact								▓		High Impact
Simple					▓	▓				Complex
Low Cost						▓	▓			High Cost
Low Risk								▓		High Risk
Routine							▓	▓		Innovative
Current Business Unit							▓	▓		New Business
Current Business Unit			▓	▓						New Game
Limited Scope							▓	▓		Expanded Scope
Operational									▓	Strategic

Figure 4.3. Proposed $500,000 new project.

- Introducing new technologies in product design without verification of status—experimental, with reservations, demonstrated in special situations, proven, a gamble
- Introducing new technologies in manufacturing processes—scale-up time and cost; complexity; logistics; education of operators, process engineers, maintenance staff
- Marketing—what kind of product, new-to-the-market or major upgrade; identifying market potential; competitiveness across international regions; first-hand industry knowledge; market introduction protocol
- Sales organization fit—does product need a new sales force or new product distribution channel; level of new major investment to promote product
- Customer service—focusing only on post sales activities; customer service begins with understanding customer requirements and ends with fully meeting the requirements and commitments; training customer service agents to go beyond the obvious
- Lack of patent protection—component, material, device, or other patents that add value and protection in the marketplace; processes either patented or held as confidential that provide competitive advantage; protecting the organization's brand
- Disregarding the need to manage the three components of cycle time: Total Time—such as system imposed, boss imposed time, monochromatic and polychromatic time; Timing—introducing the product to the marketplace at the most beneficial time, neither too early nor too late for market acceptance; Cycle Duration—time from concept to commercialization
- Economic conditions—appropriate for the current year and unknown for many years in the future; lack of market for some high priced goods and demographic changes may require change in business strategy

- Organization—lack of organizational discipline, oversight, and involvement in post-decision activities; too much micromanagement but too little hands-on management interaction
- Disregarding the content and context in the approved decision—using the approval of a project to begin reengineering a project without returning to the decision-making body for approval; not delivering what was promised

Each of these examples, in one way or another, creates difficulties in the decision-making process. Lack of timely availability of all competencies in all disciplines and functions during a project, provides a good example of where project problems begin. While every project requires general knowledge, it requires knowledge and experience and work-ready competencies of the many key people on the project: the specific competencies required to meet the project's requirements. Building a project team begins long before project approval. Learning the discipline knowledge when assigned to a project hardly meets requirements. Is this an impossible request? It should not be a problem, if organizations executed all those recommendations listed in the performance appraisals that too often are disregarded. If the situation exists, at least recognize the competence inadequacies at the beginning of the project, find substitute approaches, and eliminate the grief as the project moves forward.

As a second example, consider customer service, it doesn't begin at product launch. Anecdotal evidence shows that customer service requires an upgrade not only with a new-to-the-market product, but also for those upgraded products that provide new capabilities. As previously noted, customer service begins with understanding of customer requirements and ends when the customer's requirements are met, and the cycle begins again for the next improvement or new product. Customer service too often receives the same treatment as maintenance: cursory, it can be pushed off into the future and too often with grim consequences.

Here is a personal anecdote related to customer service which is not uncommon. Recently I experienced a problem with my wireless router when connecting a new computer. After having gone through four different technicians in almost 4 hours, I was becoming frustrated because each one, for some reason or another, was attempting to discredit my modem, or router, and even my laptop. I suggested that I uninstall the current router program and then reinstall it from my original CD. The fourth technician agreed; the other three disregarded my suggestion. It's interesting that the technicians weren't familiar with such a solution. I uninstalled, reinstalled the program, and within less than 10 minutes the system was operational. That's not what I would call acceptable customer service.

A third example involves the three issues of cycle time: Total time, Timing, and Cycle Duration: three interactive issues that need resolution. There is little doubt that considerable time is wasted in all organizations: the internet and all the information toys have exacerbated the situation. Too many people continue to work below their salary levels, and industry has yet to learn how to boost the productivity of their knowledge workers who now, in many organizations, exceed well over 50 to 75 percent of total employees. The impact of such actions not only involves costs, but more importantly brings employees down to their lowest level of performance. These examples provide management's challenges and require development of appropriate actions.

These knockouts can be identified and dealt with by people with breadth of knowledge and experience without excessive studies, since most of the information, except in very unusual situations, should be available to an organization during the proposal development phase. Problems are created when known facts are disregarded because of a lack of competence in understanding the basics of project management. Major projects today require management systems thinking: the Boeing 787 Dreamliner involves a system of systems, propulsion, composites, communications, aerodynamics, pneumatics, electrical, and more. In reality, any single component in any of these subsystems can ground the aircraft.

These are just a sampling of the possible knockouts associated with any project. Each of these issues can be evaluated well before making major investments. Just being sensitive to them can enhance project performance. These issues constitute the *indirect issues* that constitute the up-front work. While you may argue that these issues are thoroughly analyzed, but we find that too often occur in sufficient depth: sufficient depth does not imply making extensive use of extensive resources: it involves having knowledge and experience related to the organization, the industry, and the competition.

How can we easily appraise a project and determine its risk and viability for success? Shenhar's simple graphical tool, as shown in Figure 4.1, allows for a quick evaluation. Any single project involves components, assemblies, systems, and arrays. The decision about the choice or design of a component does not usually present a major problem. However, the decision about a particular assembly brings in many different constituencies to the decision process. Few decisions involve a single discipline such as electrical or mechanical engineering: each of these involves many discipline subdivisions. Most major projects comprise a system of systems. Many of the subsystems do not create any significant levels of risk. The difficulty rests in identifying the subsystems where difficulties in implementation can be envisioned.

KEY POINTS

- Organizational decisions span a continuum from the very simple to the very complex and all determine in some way the sustainability of the organization.

- No single decision-making process will satisfy all decisions and organizations must guard against being trapped in organizational policies and procedures.
- Decisions that may be made by executive level management do not necessarily receive greater scrutiny. Decisions at the executive level tend to limit consideration of the decision requirements after approval.
- Organizational decisions involve three critical areas: Operations, Governance, and Growth and each involve some level of strategy.
- The schema presented for considering variations and complexities in the decision process provide a means for quickly determining the most critical issues on the many continuums shown in Figures 4.1, 4.2, and 4.3.
- Shenhar's Diamond Model that relates technology, novelty, pace, and complexity provides a simple way for evaluating a project and the related decisions.
- Shenhar's diamond can be modified to replace the coordinates to Impact and Risk on the vertical coordinate and Innovation and Complexity on the horizontal coordinate. This adaptation provides a visual that allows for a quick and easy way to evaluate the project and related issues.
- Decisions made within a single functional unit must take into consideration the impact on other functions.
- Decisions made by innovators often release a barrage of criticism from the naysayers and skeptics. Fortunately, innovators tend to ignore such negativity and go on to pursue their objectives.
- Organizations operate with a talent base with narrow and specialized competencies that limit not only organizational opportunities, but also individual opportunities. Professional specialists and their managers need to focus on the business.
- Successful projects require doing the up-front work: that up-front work involves understanding all the aspects and interrelationships on the project; the various risks related to technology, manufacturing, and marketing and sales; and concern for the undefined, uncontrollable, and unpredictable issues.
- Resolving the project knockouts requires breadth of knowledge and experience in related technologies and business requirements, insight to anticipate potential problems, and the ability to resolve them in a timely manner.

NOTE

1. Aaron J. Shenhar and Dov Dvir, *Reinventing Project Management*, Boston, MA: Harvard Business School Press, 2007, pp. 15–16.

5

MACRO DECISION TO IMPLEMENTATION

Decisions are made in relation to taking advantage of opportunities that become visible or resolving problems that somehow limit the organization in meeting its expectations. As noted previously *Decisions* focuses on the countless decisions that must be made after that macro decision was approved at some executive level. The implementation of the macro decision brings together people not even remotely involved in developing the proposal, which led to the macro decision. If the macro decision involved the investment in new plant and equipment and required input from many organizational units, successful implementation will depend on the thousands or more decisions made by not only managers and specialists, but also some key plant operators and technicians. If the macro decision involves developing a new-to-the-market product or service or both, just about every organizational unit will be brought into the act. Chapter 5 topics include

- Executing the Decision
- Using Tools and Techniques
- Describing the Problem

Decisions: An Engineering and Management Perspective, First Edition. Gerard H. Gaynor.
© 2015 The Institute of Electrical and Electronics Engineers, Inc. Published 2015 by John Wiley & Sons, Inc.

- Improving IT Project Performance
- Advancing Project Management Practice
- Managing Project Cycle Time
- Managing with a Systems Perspective
- Key Points
- Notes

EXECUTING THE DECISION

While macro decisions are made at the highest levels in the organization, the input to those decisions comes from various levels of managers and discipline specialists at the operations level as noted in Chapter 3. The terms used for project description such as unique, new-to-the-market, revolutionary, and other such terms during the approval process quickly lose their significance when the emphasis changes to *execution*. Executing the project becomes much more difficult than providing the information required to make the macro go-ahead decision: implementation challenges even the best of project managers and their capacity to make not only the right decisions, but timely decisions. This is the time when the real and undefined complexities come into the success equation. Now, solutions to the unknown, uncontrolled, unpredictable, and unexpected problems must be resolved; and there will be many with impact on activities across all organizational units.

Assuming due diligence, the complexities in implementing the project's objectives should have been identified and understood by all participants at the time the project was approved; there will be delays and changes, but they should be managed without significant interruption. While the need for plans cannot be minimized, it is also essential that managers and the project team recognize that plans are not cast in bronze. Plans provide direction and those plans will require modification based on new information as a project progresses; this is especially true for projects scheduled for completion in 2 or more years.

The project process can be described in many different ways and in its simplest and generic form involves the following issues.

- Provide all involved team members with an understanding of the complete project: this requires a formal project launch if the project involves multiple organizational units. Too often organizations consider project launch as an unnecessary activity, and eventually pay the price.
- The objectives related to project requirements, schedule, and cost should have been identified and clarified prior to approval of the macro project, but if not, need to be developed and understood by all the participants involved

in the project; requirements, cost, and schedule must be evaluated as new information becomes available and plans put in place to accommodate the changes.

- Project plans involve more than stating the project's objectives and expectation; they include some understanding of how those objectives will be accomplished such as identifying appropriate resources of all types; developing work breakdown structures; formalizing a project communication plan; initiating a formal project reporting system; managing the delays in meeting project commitments; handling of administrative issues; and addressing the usual project management issues that determine success or failure. Each of these activities involves decisions.

- Executing the project requires *thinking before doing* and making countless decisions by many people. As mentioned, there may be thousands of decisions made on a major project spanning the continuum from those decisions made by individuals to those made after group consultation. Many decisions will be made by individuals without involvement of others, but must include consideration of other's needs and many of these decisions will be based on good practices and without any significant deliberation. The decisions requiring group participation will span a continuum from the simple to the complex. Successful project execution depends on successful management of both the individual and group decisions.

USING TOOLS AND TECHNIQUES

The arrival of the computer after World War II brought new opportunities for reaching decisions. But did it? Computers were looked on as an extension of human mental capacity with almost unlimited possibilities. Management science developed mathematical techniques to aid decision-making. The science included linear programming, operations research, queuing theory, game theory, regression analysis, followed by the Analytic Hierarchy Process (AHP) developed by Prof. Thomas L. Saaty in the 1970s, decision theory, conjoint analysis, choice modeling, multiscale decision-making, decision mapping, and experimental design. Of course there's always the option of flipping a coin. These decision-making tools provide a benefit only when needed and to the extent needed. They do not relinquish managers and engineers and other discipline specialists from *using judg*ment. This does not suggest that the aforementioned tools should be disregarded, but four major questions require a response, (1) are the decision-making tools necessary; (2) do the selected tools add information of value, and if so, how; (3) do the tools' mediation solutions meet the project's prerequisites; and (4) are the least complicated, although adequate, tools being utilized?

Peter Drucker[1] cautioned management on improving what was already known, rather than on innovation breakthroughs. He cautioned that the task determined the tools and not vice versa. He also cautioned that excessive fascination with tools and techniques might cloud the distinction between the quantitative (how to do) and the qualitative (what to do). Drucker cautioned that tools and techniques were a supplement to and not a substitute for judgments about risk and uncertainty. Drucker feared that

> "a singular stress on the tools divorced from meaningful concepts of the interaction between work and working would produce an army of technicians and specialists talking only to themselves, creating a jargon understandable only by themselves, and focusing on scientific validity over applied relevance."

Drucker said that the study of the computer in relation to decision-making was far too important to be left in the hands of management experts. Drucker's comments apply not only to executives and managers, but also to engineers and other discipline specialists. As engineers we can become engrossed in simulations and modeling, but do the results reflect the context, conditions, and take into account all the related parameters. I'm not suggesting that these tools be avoided but caution when using them we recognize their limitations. I've yet to find any tools that clearly differentiate customer's needs.

Use of techniques presents a similar issue to the use of tools that basically focus on process. The mindset persists that following the process will result in meeting the project objectives, but as noted, project performance studies do not reveal acceptable project performance. How many more project planning techniques do we need? At the dawn of management science as a means for increasing efficiency, Henry Gantt, an American mechanical engineer and consultant, proposed the Gantt chart as a technique for project planning. Very simply, the chart lists activities on the vertical axis and time on the horizontal axis. Time for each activity is then blocked out on the chart. The Gantt chart has been a very simple technique for planning and over the years has been supplemented with sophisticated techniques such as Critical Path Method (CPM), Program Evaluation and Review Technique (PERT), computerized Gantt charts that go into the minutest of details, and many other similar approaches. As computer technologies advanced, many other project management techniques evolved. Unfortunately, many planning techniques become so cumbersome that a full-time staff is required to provide useable information. Our attempts to quantify the minutest of details too often results in paralysis and unnecessary expense. I do not suggest that these techniques do not provide benefits, but must be used with a degree of discretion. Justify each bit of information and the techniques provide valuable input.

While watching the World Cup 2010, one of the narrators mentioned that, "many of these young players don't think; they just play." That's a serious allegation, but deserves some consideration. As we look at the decision-making processes of managers, project managers, engineers, and other discipline specialists are we witnessing a similar situation? Are we witnessing a situation where this group of contributors to the decision process has become disengaged in doing the "real work" required for managing the organization's resources? Are we using "tweeting" to reach decisions? Are we failing to think deeply before offering our input to the decision process?

What do I mean by *thinking*? First, in our desire to have nanosecond response to every email request, every tweet, or other request, how do people have an opportunity to think? Thinking is hard work; it requires a mindset; it requires time to sort out alternatives and come to a conclusion regardless of the seriousness or complexity of the issue. This does not mean that thinking will delay the project's completion. We resolve problems or pursue opportunities by thinking; thinking and response to the thinking are interconnected. We do not think in a vacuum; we do not just sit and think. We usually think to accomplish some result. My concern is the depth of our thinking. Here's an example. Mike presents a proposal. It does not matter where he fits on the organization chart. He's looking for a response to his proposal: discussion, acceptance, rejection, or a decision. But, responding is difficult because the proposal lacks substance and business context. If Mike's purpose is socialization of an idea, this can be a start. But if Mike seeks some form of acceptance of the proposal he needs to put some "meet on the bones." It's an idea; it's one of those 10,000 ideas that will result in perhaps one or two successful projects. This is a very common scene in both the profit and not-for-profit sectors. In the past 20 years or more, individuals and organizations seem to begin cutting metal before they have developed the pattern. Such actions remind me of the trial and error approach that may work in some exceptional situations, but not as a practice. We tend to propose solutions from some list of ready-made answers. We're prone to jumping to conclusions without exploring alternatives. Our emphasis is on a quick solution. We look at the problem from only one perspective. We allow personal biases, prejudices, and past experiences dominate the decision, although the current decision will be made in a totally different environment. My concern arises from our poor performance in meeting project requirements. As engineers we play a major role in not only meeting engineering requirements, but also business requirements. To make this transition to meeting business requirements, we need to add an additional level of thinking; a level that digs deep and considers decisions from different perspectives. One might ask, how others would think about the problem at hand. Call this creative thinking, if you wish, but it involves more than star gazing. This in-depth thinking does not take place by dedicating a specific number of hours per day for thinking.

This type of thinking requires attention 24/7 or more realistically 24/through a lifetime.

Abraham Zaleznik[2] raised this issue in "Real Work" published by the Harvard Business Review. With the emphasis on leading as contrasted to managing, Zaleznik asks, have organizations lost sight of the *real work* of managers, and other discipline specialists? Zaleznik notes that since the work of the manager is changing continually, the real work of the manager always includes one crucial component.

> "That component is thinking—the thinking that must precede action in order to inform and direct it. When leaders substitute ritual for thought, they are not performing the whole of their jobs."

Zaleznik noted that during the 1930s, academics and researchers began to consider the expectations of the individual and what is the place and role of the individual in the organization. This was the beginning of the human relations school of management that emphasized the social aspects of organizations for achieving best performance. Taking care of the social aspects was to reduce, if not eliminate, the alienation that often exists between managers and workers; this was particularly important with the increased number of knowledge workers.

This was a period when the human resource departments promoted self-esteem, participative management, and similar management approaches, but also focused less on the need for employee task performance: fulfilling the chain of events required for designing, manufacturing or supplying services, and shipping a usable product to the customer somehow lost some of its importance.

While organizations are social systems and require cooperative behaviors at various levels, all human activity brings people together, with not only different but often conflicting attitudes and personal characteristics that must somehow be blended into a workable organizational unit. Zaleznik suggests that focusing excessively on "smoothing over conflict, greasing the wheels of human interaction, and unconsciously avoiding aggression" suppresses valuable emotion that is essential for being a productive contributor.

DESCRIBING THE PROBLEM

Lawrence Gibson[3] in *Defining Market Problems*, describes a situation that illustrates how a team can engage in nonessential activities that have no relation to the problem; nonessential activities defined by the decision-makers. Such misdirected effort consumes resources directed at an inadequate statement of the problem. The situation involves a French subsidiary of General Mills, Biscuiterie Nantaise (BN). BN competed for the after-school chocolate cream-filled snack referred to as the *gouter*—a cookie. At one time BN was the most popular brand of the *gouter*. A competitor, Prince, sold a more expensive and fancier *gouter*, and became a national competitor. BN's sales began to slide, continued for a 2-year period, and then dropped significantly. BN managers, after much study and pondering over the issues, concluded that the significant drop in gouter sales was due to a lack of advertising. There was evidence that BN's advertising budget was reduced in previous years. During this period BNs French competitors were gaining market share, BNs pricing, relative to the competition, was decreasing, and major changes were made in the production processes to reduce costs. The solution recommended by BN managers: Increase the advertising budget.

Time has arrived to ask some questions. What was actually done to reduce manufacturing cost? The responses were startling. BN began recycling broken cookies into the product and began using less expensive ingredients. Cookie quality became a major issue. After considering other issues, there was general agreement that sales declined because of the degraded quality of the cookies. Quality was the issue and advertising would do nothing to change the competitive situation if BN continued its use of less expensive ingredients and recycling of broken cookies. Both activities reduced the cost, but also degraded the product quality.

Under these circumstances how would BN regain market dominance? Regaining dominance would require more than just improving the quality of its current cookies. BN made a decision to take a multi-flavor strategy; market testing various combinations of chocolate and other fillings. The market study revealed that not all children preferred the same flavors. BN positioned itself to take advantage of this information in planning its product introductions and introduced cookies with a range of flavors. BN sales decline was reversed, market share rose, and margins improved on volume gains in spite of higher production costs. There's a moral to this story: Make sure you're trying to solve the right problem. The original solution to BN's problem, invest more in advertising, failed to explore other related issues. The research required to determine the causes of a problem cannot be eliminated or short-changed in any way. Interestingly, that research only requires asking the right questions from a systems perspective; single-issue management seldom provides usable answers.

This case history raises other perhaps more important issues. What was going on in the BN organization that allowed production to make product changes without adequate knowledge of the consequences? Could the BN head of General Mills France been oblivious to these changes? Were there no procedures for making ingredient changes prior to adequate market testing? Last, but certainly not least why wasn't BN trying to improve the product? Why wasn't the multi-flavor approach considered before the crisis? Did BN become self-satisfied with its performance and not consider future business opportunities? Introducing multi-flavor *gouters* seems to be a logical product extension and one would think would have been proposed as a major competitive advantage before the quality issue arose. Who made those decisions? Just another example that shows that failure can generally be traced to questionable management decisions and lack of effort in anticipating future needs.

IMPROVING IT PROJECT PERFORMANCE

Meeting project requirements, schedule, and cost of information technology (IT) projects continue to dominate management's attention. IT pervades every organizational activity whether related to products, services, processes, communication, and including strategy and operations. Yet the performance of IT projects continues to waste not only man-hours of effort, but also drain financial resources. Deepak Sarup[4] discusses why projects fail in "To Be, or Not to Be: The Question of Runaway Projects." We know that projects will always fail; he cites a highly complex Customer Relations Management (CRM) implementation that cost more than US $100 million and took 3 years to complete. In a recent survey he found that less than a third of these projects were rated as successful by their managers; successful in terms of meeting, even partially, the business objectives.

Al Neimat Taimour[5] in "Why Projects Fail" discusses the limited and disappointing performance on IT application projects. He cites the Standish Group report on 30,000 IT applications that shows that in 2000 about 28 percent of projects were completed on time, according to budget, and fulfilled the requirements as originally specified. Twenty-four percent failed were cancelled, or never implemented. Forty-eight percent were completed and operational, but over budget, over the time estimate, and with fewer features. Although there was some improvement from 1994 to 2000 the numbers continue to show that problems continue. Current anecdotal evidence shows that as we approach the middle of the second decade of the twenty-first century, some improvement may have occurred, but far below of what should be expected.

The Standish Group cites an example of an IT failed project; the Virtual Case File project for the United States Federal Bureau of Investigation (FBI). Development took place over 5 years at a cost of $170 million dollars and never implemented. The general conclusion reached was that requirements for the FBI mission were not included in the virtual Case Design and that the failure was due more to the people than the technologies involved. The Standish Report then includes a list of primary causes for the failure of IT projects. They include

- Poor planning
- Unclear goals and objectives

- Objectives changing during the project
- Unrealistic time and resource estimates
- Lack of executive support and user involvement
- Failure to communicate and act as a team
- Inappropriate skills

The Report continues with a discussion of each of these primary causes of failure. I suggest that these primary causes of failure are no different than those related to a project of any type, whether it involved the development of a component, a subassembly, a product or service, or the design of a new manufacturing facility.

I was concerned that the Standish report did not mention *lack of attention in defining the requirements* as one of the primary causes of failure. The report does state that; "Defining clear requirements for a project can take time and lots of communication, but sometimes goals and objectives might be unclear because project sponsors lack experience to describe what they really require." Such a statement appears to contradict the fundamentals of project management since it's difficult to understand, except in the work of a purely research-oriented group, how an organization can allocate funding for a project where neither problem nor the ultimate deliverables are defined. Perhaps, more time should be dedicated to due diligence through an up-front activity at minimum cost. While preparing the requirements does take time, effort, and additional cost, an organization pays a relatively small amount for fulfilling the up-front requiems compared to what it pays when the project overruns cost and schedule and doesn't meet requirements.

The Report also notes that, detailed plans are not effective for managing IT projects. The reason is that managers do not know enough about the work to make detailed plans. We can argue just what the term *detailed plans* means, it will be described differently by different organizations, but if an adequate level of information is not available to begin a project, perhaps time must be allocated *to put that first stake in the ground*. Planning is not as much of a problem, if agreement is reached on the basic requirements. If the basics of the system cannot be identified, how could anyone think of beginning the work effort? This is not research. The programming involves using standard programming approaches to achieve some desired output. There is no doubt as to the complexity of these programs, but in most cases programmers may need to follow the same procedures used in hardware design, you don't include unproven techniques or technologies that have not been proven unless you're going to prototype and validate them.

A personal experience may help justify my concerns about going forward blindly without documented requirements and gaining agreement of the groups involved. We were in the process of putting together a proposal for a major investment for a computerized control system for a new manufacturing process. The control system was a major investment and the plan was to prepare the requirements and contract the development of the appropriate software. The hardware requirements were defined in great detail very clearly, because of the critical and complex requirements. The control systems requirements were submitted to several suppliers and after many meetings, a contract was issued to the successful supplier. After several months of work between the supplier's engineers and software developers and my counterparts, we were ready for a final review of the supplier's approach to our request.

The meeting began and after the usual introductions we began the review to make sure that our people and the supplier's software developers were in agreement on our expectations and just how they would be achieved. It did not take long for me to begin spotting body language from both sides, that there were critical differences in interpretation of the requirements. I also began to realize that while the supplier's lead people may be competent programmers, they demonstrated little if any knowledge of process control basics and knowledge of what the software programs would control. They not only lacked machine knowledge, but also an understanding of what their software would be required to control. After the morning break I suggested that instead of continuing with the meeting both groups take whatever time is required to identify, rationalize, and resolve the differences in interpretation. This was a case where the supplier's lead people had little if any knowledge of what it mcant to program a very complex measurement, instrumentation, and control system that include a mix of pneumatic controllers with many critical parameters and interactions and super-critical tolerances.

Back to the drawing board so to speak. Decision number 1, send two of my engineers to the supplier to educate the software engineers about the details of the control system and finalize the agreement on the requirements. The process requirements must be understood if the software programming is to meet the requirements. After roughly 3 months of work by both groups that included a final review, a realistic plan was put together based on a clear understanding of the requirements. In spite of the original delays, because of a misunderstanding of the requirements, the project went through its start-up on schedule. Reaching agreement on the requirements then allowed the supplier to plan the project in such a way where additional personnel were brought into the program.

Doing what I refer to as the up-front work in any project is critical to project success. Mental as well as physical rework develops headaches for every manager and every professional who becomes involved in the rework. While doing the up-front work may seem logical, too often the *fire–read–aim* approach takes precedence and violates the fundamental principles of project management. Arguments will be made that the complexity of major software militates against any possibility of clearly defining requirements, but if this should be the case, I suggest that the solution involves going back to the proverbial drawing board and find a way to fix it.

ADVANCING PROJECT MANAGEMENT PRACTICE

Doug Russell,[6] in "Effective Project Management in Semiconductor Design Organizations," provides some background based on a couple of decades in project management positions at Motorola, within the US Defense Department, for a Defense contractor working on Space Shuttle projects, Motorola's Iridium System, and the Department of Justice. It's difficult to understand the lack of improved project management performance, recognizing the continuous growth of project management tools and training and the emphasis on project management certification programs. Perhaps project management, as taught in traditional project management training programs and the subsequent dependence on tools and techniques, has lost sight that successful project management requires hands-on project managers, capable of integrating the needs of many different disciplines. And what does successful project management involve, competencies in decision-making. Russell has identified 10 Guidelines for the project manager.

Define Success—how do we measure project success? Is it possible for a project manager to optimize (1) the requirements, (2) schedule (target dates), and (3) cost of the project? Which is most important for this project? Russell suggests that all three cannot be met. If meeting the target date is the measure of performance, and in the process all requests from customers or internal sources for changes or additions are categorically denied, then meeting the target date may end with much dissatisfaction from management and the customers.

Gain Management Support—management wants results regardless of the complexity. Too often, project managers focus on the latest tools and techniques that generate data, but that seldom resolve any problems. Project managers must demonstrate leadership and that involves meeting the task requirements that require more than blindly following a process. If there is any position in an organization that requires judgment, it's that of the project manager: the project manager serves several masters, management, the project team, and the customer. A simple caveat to gain management's support; no surprises.

Know the Project Team—project managers establish the principles to be followed on a particular project, those principles will vary depending on the type of project. This is the leadership role and it involves knowing and understanding the people on the team. How do those individual competencies work to the advantage of the team? Allan Cox[7] in *The Homework Beyond Teamwork* provides a comprehensive description of the value-adding team.

"Whether established department or ad hoc, the team is a thinking organism where missions validated, problems are named, assumptions challenged, alternatives generated, consequences assessed, priorities established, admissions made, competitors evaluated, goals tested, hopes ventured, fears anticipated, successes expected, vulnerabilities expressed, contributions praised, absurdities tolerated, withdrawals noticed, victories celebrated, and defeats overcome."

This comprehensive description of the team does not recommend any team structure. My personal experience in dealing with hundreds of teams shows that team structure is of minimal importance: if the right people are available, team structure although essential is of secondary importance. While the importance of teams continues, we need to recognize the contributions of individual contributors.

Successful project managers must bring appropriate attitudes and personal characteristics to their work. These attitudes would include operating with a base of adequate knowledge and experience; understanding the technical details of the project; identifying the talent requirements; and knowing how to integrate the team's activities toward a successful completion. Will there be people problems, definitely yes, but the role of the project manager is to resolve those technical and people issues regardless of their complexity or potential controversy.

Do Not Compete with the Team—Russell is adamant about project managers competing with the team. He sees the role of the project manager as distinctly different from that of the technical people and suggests that a project manager should not try to out-engineer the engineers. However, the role of the project manager becomes more than accepting at face value every recommendation made by the team. If the project manager brings to the team knowledge and experience of the technologies and other issues, while not trying to out-engineer the engineers, the project manager does have a responsibility to use that knowledge and judgment to further the work effort. A project manager walks a fine line in such situations to avoid trying to overshadow the knowledge of team members.

Focus on the Job Essentials—project managers must focus on the real work of the project manager: basic project planning, scheduling, resource planning throughout the whole project; assessing risk at various project stages; resolving conflicts; bringing people together to resolve issues; meeting that host of issues that come under the aegis of project management responsibility; and monitoring and guiding the project to a successful conclusion. A project manager who misses target dates or fails to resolve conflicts with team members, management, customers, or suppliers may wisely choose a more appropriate profession. Conflicts within the team will occur and the project manager cannot afford to delay a decision. Decision-making is part of the manager's function.

Learn to Say "NO"—saying "NO" to a team member or a team request will result in various degrees of dissatisfaction. Russell refers this type of decision as developing a state of unhappiness. Project managers are not assigned to make team members happy; they are assigned to urge the team to provide results and at the same time obtain a level of personal satisfaction from their work effort.

There are ways to say "NO" and the method depends on the individual. Some people can take a "NO" without any consequences except with a bit of grumbling. Other more sensitive individuals may be destroyed by the same "NO." A "NO" will usually be accepted if there is justification for the "NO." However, if your team includes competent, but sensitive people, learn to deal with them, but don't indulge their sensitivities. A focused team should not require very many "NO" responses. If your team knows where you're going, sensitivities will be at a minimum. Severe cases of sensitivity require professional help.

Manage Change Control—Russell notes that engineers hate administrative work whether in paper or electronic based; they want design. While Russell relates his comments to design engineers and more specifically semiconductor design engineers, changing direction once a project has begun creates various levels of frustration. While engineers hate administrative work, they're not the only ones: they need to recognize that administrative work determines whether or not their pay check is deposited on time, their benefits package managed judiciously, an all the associated administrative work receives adequate attention. Managing change control involves more than developing a change order policy; it involves having the courage to implement the policy. But be specific so that all the stakeholders are aware of the requirements. But change control begins by the *thinking* that takes place before the change is approved and fed into the control system; who originated the change request for what purpose, with what expected results. Was this a change requested for a particular customer or a large percentage of the customer base? How does that requested change affect other related operations? Does it have an impact of manufacturing or marketing? If patents are involved has it modified in some way the original patent application? Changes will be requested. Changes will be most likely approved, but manage the changes in requirements up front by identifying the required changes in schedule and costs that may be required. However, be realistic. If the response to a change request must be a "NO," explain what must be done: the reasons and possible other approaches. Identify the benefits if any exist.

Provide Support for Offsite Teams—chances are that the project will include other internal and external support teams. It should not be difficult to integrate the efforts of several internal and external support teams. If the project requires a coordinator someone may be assigned to integrate the various operations. However, coordinators without authority provide little benefit and only lead to generating suspicion of favoritism. Most likely this appointee requires exceedingly good interpersonal skills. Very often organizations fail to develop working relations with the offsite teams. Russell notes that too often, they make one trip (if that) to an offsite team, demand a schedule, and then assume they will run themselves. That's not the way to manage offsite teams. Usually specifications are issued, bids received, evaluated, and contracts negotiated and issued. Those contracts at minimum include cost, schedule, and a description of deliverables. But too often the communication ceases with the issuing of a contract. The longer the delivery time the worse the problem. It's easy to forget about those offsite teams that are often accused of being the "problem" when the total project becomes mired in difficulties. We know that no specification totally defines the requirements. When I use the word "total" I mean "total" and that means absolutely nothing is missing. Regardless of the costs, there's only one way to determine performance and status of offsite work, personal visit to the team's site.

Ensure Adequate Reporting Project Data—what do those reams of data tell you? Project managers can spend a great deal of time creating, sifting, sorting, collating, and reporting project data. For what purpose? Most project data serves the interest of the team members. The project manager's concerns involve monitoring the work effort, developing confidence that the work effort meets the requirements, interacting with other teams as required to focus on the end result, using validated information in making critical decisions, and respecting the agreed upon timeline regardless of various types of interruptions. While projects are not all the same, Russell suggests that a project manager should spend one-third of the time interacting with others on actions and meetings; one-third working alone or on one-on-one thinking, strategizing, analyzing, and planning; and one-third working with data of all types and reporting. This apportionment of a project manager's time is only a suggestion; projects may require totally different allocations of time depending on the project manager and the complexity of the project.

Adjust the Approach—adjust the approach in dealing with your team, customers, and management, says Russell. He also suggests that the project manager develop 20 or so high level milestones, but as you reach the end of the project develop a detailed schedule for the last several weeks or months. He further suggests setting up 10 minute stand-up meetings to consider the day's accomplishments and risks. Just exactly what you do depends on the project. I'd suggest that you remain agile, flexible, sensitive, committed, proactive, and innovative. Agile to take advantage of opportunities that require quick action or reaction; flexible in dealings with your team, customers, management, and other internal and external teams; sensitive but not too sensitive to the needs of the team members and related teams; committed to meeting the requirements, cost, and schedule assuming realistic estimates were made and if the estimates were unrealistic restructure and be committed to the new schedule and costs; proactive in making personal contributions and working with the team; and last but not least, innovative in all project activities whether related to technology, marketing, manufacturing, or any discipline or organizational function.

MANAGING PROJECT CYCLE TIME

Time is of the essence is the mantra in business transactions. Fulfilling the mantra of *time is of the essence*, depends on the capability of making realistic time estimates of what it takes to complete a series of tasks regardless of their complexity and making appropriate decisions. Those decisions relate to allocating the required resources and developing an appropriate plan of action. Various approaches such as optimizing time to market, simultaneous or concurrent engineering, enterprise-wide development, concurrent process development, and other quick-fix programs, while having some impact, have failed to have a major impact on performance. Such activities only accomplish incremental improvement. While managers espouse the use of various means of concurrent work effort, insufficient emphasis is placed on managing the system. Time cannot be recovered. An alternative approach involves managing projects with a systems perspective.

Managing System Cycle Time

System Cycle Time Management (SCTM) is not something new and no research is required to demonstrate the need for managing it; it is not a new idea, concept, innovation, or management discovery. Henry Ford, Edwin H. Land, and other industrial pioneers managed cycle time: it was an implicit management behavior. Two years after Alfred P. Sloan gave Charles F. Kettering the go-ahead to develop a diesel engine, Kettering achieved a major breakthrough that revolutionized the railroad industry. We can argue that management was quite different in the days of Ford, Land, and Kettering than it is at the beginning of this twenty-first century, but the fact remains they managed cycle time from a systems perspective. The United States moon landing provides another example of managing system cycle time. President Kennedy said:

> "I believe that this nation should commit itself to achieving the goal, before this decade is out, of landing a man on the Moon and returning him safely to Earth,"

and the mission was accomplished.

SCTM involves taking a wide-angle view of a new product development program and integrating the basic functional units of research, development, manufacturing, marketing and sales, finance, and any other related functions and managing the activities and processes from concept to commercialization or implementation. So what is SCTM? SCTM involves managing three time elements: managing time, managing timing, and managing cycle duration. As an example, introducing a new product does not occur without some level of risk in the design, the marketing, and the launch: it takes a system approach and perspective that includes considering the needs of all the involved organizational units.

Managing Time

Time is a commodity that can be wasted, used effectively and efficiently, but cannot be saved. Every organization uses time with various degrees of effectiveness. Managing time goes beyond developing time-management skills. There are many prescriptions, recipes, and exhortations about making better use of the available time. But Managing Time in the context of SCTM involves thinking before doing. Our penchant for action rather than thought prior to action, often leads not only to physical rework, but also mental rework; both very costly, not only in a monetary sense, but also in a business and a personal sense. None of us appreciate rework of any kind because of a failure to give adequate thought prior to action. Hall, in *Dance of Life,*[8] makes a distinction between Monochromatic Time (M-Time) and Polychromatic Time (P-Time). M-Time emphasizes the mechanics and the processes such as scheduling, prioritizing, allocating, classifying, and adhering to procedures. All activities are linear: A comes before B and so on. P-Time stresses participation and active involvement with various degrees of flexibility. Schedules can be modified and rearranged. P-time does not count hours and minutes, efficiency and saving time; it focuses on the individual and the system to meet the objectives.

Managing time in this sense requires changing one's *mindset* toward time management. The *mindset* involves reconsidering the usual ideas of time management which focus on saving time and considering to what one does with available time and refocusing activities from a systems perspective. Just saving time by improving processes is insufficient to make any meaningful progress: saving time involves thinking holistically and integrating the functions involved in the system. As an example, product development must take into consideration at a minimum the procurement, manufacturing, marketing, and distribution requirements at the time of product development and not when product development is completed. Marketing, when proposing new-to-the-market products, must recognize the needs of product development, manufacturing, marketing, and distribution. While many organizations think they fulfill this integration, project performance statistics as noted provide a totally different picture.

Timing

Vessey[9] showed that a product that misses its launch date by 6 months loses one-third of the potential profit over the lifetime of the product. One can argue with such statistics, but whether the loss is one-third or one-fourth or one-tenth is of little importance. The simple fact is that there's a loss in profitability. What are the total costs, when management delays capital investments that require 3 or more years, and when finally they make the decision to proceed with the project, management expects the facilities to be designed, fabricated, installed in an operation in 18 months. Inflation and redesign now add additional cost. What are the costs associated when patents are not filed in a timely manner or improperly divulged prior to filing? What are the potential costs associated with, as an example, the 3-year delay of the Boeing 787 Dreamliner?

Timing of information plays a major role in business performance. Beeby[10] in "How to Crunch a Bunch of Figures" discusses the need for managers to have accurate and timely information. While this is an old case, it continues to demonstrate the over-reliance on use of data management systems in the decision-making process. Beeby describes how information from the field at Frito-Lay made its way up the organization structure. It took about 3 months for field information to make its way to the decision-makers. To provide faster feedback from field operations Frito-Lay installed a decision-support system (DSS) that gave its 200 managers detailed field inventory information from 10,000 route salespeople equipped with hand-held computers. The 3-month field inventory figures were now available within 2 weeks using the new DSS program. Beeby cites a situation where it took 2 weeks to discover a drop in market share of a particular product. The reason was traced to a situation where one major supermarket chain introduced a store brand product. Store shelf comes with a price tag. Prime space costs more. Eye level receives more attention than ground level. Visibility determines space cost. These are the observable events that make the difference; yes, the figures are important, but only part of the story. Observation and judgment do not come from the DSS.

There was an interesting response by Chambers[11] to Beeby's article in *The Wall Street Journal* titled "Don't Let Your Computers Do All your Thinking." Chambers was a visiting professor at Emory University in Atlanta and was fully aware of the benefits associated with DSS. However, he raised an important issue of being totally dependent on such technologies as DSS when other solutions might be more appropriate. Keep in mind that it took Frito-Lay's DSS system 2 weeks to recognize a drop in its sales because a supermarket chain introduced a store brand product. Chambers was concerned that the Frito-Lay field contact did not immediately inform management when the store brand product was displayed. In this case, reliance on DSS delayed an appropriate decision to deal with the situation. Chamber concluded that

> "We must be careful to let the computer replace only the information and tools it can outperform. It should never replace our own experience and judgment. The computer should be only one part of company's DSS."

Beeby also noted that the new DSS program now assists the concept of *management by walking around.* He said

> "I can, at a glance, view the performance of each of our managers and salespeople around the country. If I see something I don't like, I can fire off an electronic mail memo. Conversely, if there is good news, I'm likely to contact the manager and congratulate him."

Peters wasn't thinking of a computer tour by the CEO and other managers who were interested primarily in getting numbers from the field. *Managing by walking aroun*d involved first-hand contact with people in the pursuit of the organization's objectives: an opportunity to see and gain an understanding of how people work together and sense the spirit of the organization. Numbers alone do not tell the whole story.

You may argue that the Frito-Lay DSS situation dates back to 1990 when information system technology was in its infancy compared to today. That is certainly true, but we continue to rely on sophisticated information systems when in many cases simpler and more responsive tools are available. Perhaps, paying attention to our work environment and using our powers of observation may often provide usable information. This reminds me of the story, where an organization never questioned who was the owner of a major factory being built in there vicinity, only to find out later it was their major competitor.

Managing Cycle Duration

From a generic sense, cycle duration includes the time from "X" to "Y" to accomplish a stated task independent of scope, complexity, cost, and impact on the organization. In practice, the word *task* may refer to product, service, or process: it could refer to some segment of work related to a product, service, or process; it could refer to system of systems program such as Boeing's 787 Dreamliner; it could refer to any activity or a breakdown of an activity into many independent yet complementary tasks. The activities between points "X" and "Y" must be described to clearly identify where point "X" begins and point "Y" ends. Points "X" and "Y" depend on the task and how the points are defined. As an example, points "X" and "Y" could include the work effort from Scouting and Study, Idea Generation, Concept Development, Preliminary Design, Approval of Funding, Development, and Implementation. The cycle time, the time required to go from point "X" to "Y" will most likely include intermediate tasks as described with cycle durations of x_1/y_1, x_2/y_2 ... x_n/y_n.

Identifying points "X" and "Y" become important as organizations attempt to improve project performance. As a new product team puts together the x_1/y_1 to x_n/y_n timelines in all the related functional areas, the timelines extend beyond acceptable limits. The dictum comes down from someone at the organization's executive level that the proposed timeline is not acceptable; the process begins as the various functions begin making arbitrary changes in the timelines. Chances are very good that those timelines were very generous to begin with and included allowances for contingencies. The sum of the contingencies from activities x_1/y_1 to x_n/y_n, and then most likely an added contingency in the total sum, add up to an unacceptable total project timeline. Projecting timelines where unknown elements exist requires judgment, but that judgment can be more realistic by careful examination of the facts. Consider three examples: Introducing a New-to-the-Market product, Introducing a New Technology, and New Production Facilities.

In Introducing a New-to-the-Market Product: Consider the risks involved in developing the cycle time for the introduction of a new-to-the-market product that involves a market segment that previously has not been explored. Developing a realistic timeline may seem as an impossible task, at least at the beginning of a project. Assumptions must be made regarding the work effort to accomplish individual tasks. Facts will be limited, no history. While theoretically the sum of all the tasks determines the timeline, it's necessary to provide judgment in the design of the tasks to take advantage of parallel activities.

Entering a previously unexplored market sector provides a challenge since it requires taking a systems or a holistic approach; all functions must be involved, integrated, and a high level of agreement must be negotiated. The market issues do not function in isolation of other functions involved in the concept to commercialization cycle. Assuming a competitive marketplace, if the product is ready for shipping, but marketing and sales somehow fail to meet their timelines, additional costs are incurred not only from lack of sales, but also from what I refer to as the *frustration cost. Frustration costs* include the costs of lost time from just talking about the delays, asking for additional information, stalled sales program, and dissatisfied customers.

From a marketing perspective it's not just a matter of the customers, but identifying the customers who will buy the product or service and identifying the conditions under which they'll purchase the product. Identifying the global market; delineating its segments; meeting the different needs for the same product based on the cultural and national environments; dealing with the legal restrictions relative to safety, toxic chemicals, and general health-related issues that might require lengthy negotiation; and the financial issues, such as pricing and currency translation impact, require understanding to develop not only a marketing plan, but to determine the viability of investing in the product development. While international statistical data exist on customer segmentation and preferences, it must be applied to specific situations and often it is impossible to go from the general to the specific with a significant level of confidence. Furthermore, it's difficult to predict the economic conditions at the time the product will be introduced to the market. As an example an organization that planned on introducing a new major product in the depth of the recent recession entered at a time that could not have been predicted.

New Technology: The issues related to introducing a new technology can be identified with a high percentage of reliability. What is the state of the technology; unproven, semi-proven, or proven? If the technology is unproven in any application it may be wise to disregard it. Beginning a project with an unproven technology usually ends in a disaster unless provisions are made for a back-up technology. If the technology has been proven in practice or semi-proven experimentally, although in a totally different application, it should not be difficult to carry out the experimentation as to its applicability to the current use. This may delay the development of a full proposal, but in the end may reduce the total cycle time and the grief that's accompanied by making decisions without at least the minimum level of confidence. An advanced work schedule to prove the applicability of the new technology, at least in a prototype or simulated application, reduces the anxiety and then allows for realistic time-to-completion projections. Proving use of a new technology within a product development cycle often generates discontinuities in the project plan, because effort which was not included in the proposal immediately begins to include the possible use of the new technology. In essence, two approaches are followed: (1) do what's required to introduce the new technology and (2) provide for the backup. This approach leads other functions such as process and manufacturing to be capable of implementing either the new or the current technology.

New Production Facilities: The third example includes the actions required to develop a new production facility. While marketing basically determines the needs of the marketplace and product development has responsibility for developing the product, production depends to a great extent on the schedules and performance from the product development group. The decision-making process becomes critical in linking these three organizational units. Granted that a product specification exists, but seldom does the final product fulfill the original specification. We haven't reached the point where a specification can be developed that fully meets requirements. Fully means totally, no new additions or deletions. The real world doesn't permit such idealism. This situation requires that the production team design the process to accommodate the need of the new product. Such design activities require experienced process design people who can anticipate possible changes. The ability to anticipate depends to a great extent on the type of production facility. As an example, machine designers involved in the development of a production machine that involves the assembly of 10 or more precision parts, and possibly a subassembly, need to know the specific dimensions of the parts. Meeting the market launch under such circumstances depends on the ultimate level of cooperation and timely decision-making by product development and the production team. Meeting the final product development timeline is of little consequence without meeting the intermediate dates on the timeline and providing definitive information to the production. Kodak introduced the Disc Camera, which failed in the marketplace, required manual inspection of each assembly, because manufacturing could not meet the required part tolerances.

MANAGING WITH A SYSTEMS PERSPECTIVE

In the final analysis, projects must be managed with a systems perspective. In the situations cited, marketing, product development, and manufacturing must be integrated. Sounds obvious, but the data shows that too often each function operates with its own blinders to the detriment of the organization. SCTM requires integration of Activities, Resources, and Infrastructure (ARI) as shown in Figure 5.1 and lists the major issues that require integration.

Activities do not live in a world of their own, but must be identified and aligned within the organizational units. The three macro categories provide examples of the major concerns and must be defined by each organization because their description depends on contextual considerations. The fulfillment of the activities depends on the availability of resources and a supportive infrastructure. While people are an organization's major asset they cannot meet the organizations objectives without the other seven resources. Information technology, one of the eight resources, is vital for effective performance. All those administrative functions that are generally disregarded as inconsequential can determine success or failure. The organization's infrastructure elements affect the effective use of resources. Innovation will require a culture that provides some freedom. Meeting the organization's objectives will require an understanding of the purposes for which the organization exists and the strategies by which those objectives will be met. The organizational infrastructure elements align the activities and resources.

The ARI as noted in Figure 5.2 cannot operate in isolation of each other. Success also depends on the performance level of the Activities and the availability of the Resources and Infrastructure elements: all will be at some level below 100 percent. At the same time project success depends on their

ACTIVITIES
- Investigation, Analysis, Synthesis
- Concept Development
- Feasibility: Technology, Markets, Business
- Realization
- Commercialization or Implementation

RESOURCES
- People
- Intellectual property
- Information
- Technology
- Time
- Organizational Culture
- Financial
- Administrative Support

INFRASTRUCTIURE
- Purposes, Objectives, Strategy
- Structure
- Guiding Principles
- Policies and Practices
- Management attitudes
- Support for Innovation and Entrepreneurship

Figure 5.1. Common project activities, resources, and organizational infrastructure.

availability at acceptable levels. Figure 5.2 shows the integration of ARI. Consider the three vectors enclosing a virtual cube with equal sides (1). If 50 percent of each of the ARI requirements is met, only 25 percent of the cube would be filled. Even if 90 percent of each ARI was met only about 73 percent of the cube would be filled. While I have selected a composite figure for each ARI,

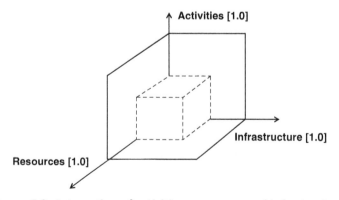

Figure 5.2. Integration of activities, resources, and infrastructure.

a more beneficial approach to consider includes identifying the critical issues in each ARI. Diligent pursuit of all Activities is essential. People, Time, and Technology may be the Resource priorities. And Objectives and Management Attitude may be the primary Infrastructure elements. I do not suggest the use of this approach in looking for exactness, but for developing awareness and a sense of the ensuing problems. Any manager scanning the elements as noted in Figure 5.2 should be capable of assessing without extensive thought, whether the group possesses the necessary competencies, and likewise, for all the other Resources. The Infrastructure elements are self-explanatory, yet very important depending on the type of project. An innovation without a Management Attitude that understands what innovation involves and an active and responsive support for innovation has little if any chance of success. These are all decision points that determine the future of the organization.

KEY POINTS

- The macro decision made by an executive group can only be fulfilled by the decisions made at the operational level: the people responsible for the implementation. This group of operational decisions spans a continuum from the very simple to the complex.
- Decision-making at the operational level requires more than tools and techniques: tools and techniques should be selected to add value and not because they're interesting and provide too much data most of which is not essential for reaching the decision. *Real Work* as described by Zaleznik and Drucker requires *thinking*. DSS have their place and should be used where applicable; misuse is a waste of time and effort.
- Describing the problem or opportunity adequately requires competencies to collect the data from many sources, synthesize the data from many different sources, analyze the data, and propose a decision. Giving short shrift or taking a laissez faire approach in describing the problem or opportunity, often leads to negative consequences.
- Successful project performance depends on timely decisions. Delayed decisions not only add cost, but demotivate staff. Focusing on doing the up-front work diligently minimizes many of the hazards.
- Project management principles call for clearly defining the objectives. Russell's 10 Guidelines provide a good starting point: define success; management support; the project team; project managers competing with the team or team members; the project manager's work; ability of the project manager to say "NO"; support for offsite teams; reporting project data; and adjusting the approach as needed.

- SCTM involves managing time, timing, and cycle duration: all the three components determine benefits to be achieved from the investment of organizational resources.

All organizational functions, and the specific disciplines within those functions, take a limited view of their respective responsibilities. Marketing focuses on marketing, R&D focuses on R&D, product development focuses on product development, and manufacturing focuses on manufacturing. Seldom do we find a focus on the total system that's required to bring a new product or service to market. Integrating activities, resources, and organizational infrastructure bring a coordinated approach for effective project management.

NOTES

1. Peter F. Drucker, *The Essential Drucker*, New York: Harper Collins, 2001, pp. 10–13.
2. Abraham Zaleznik, "Real work," *Harvard Business Review*, November–December 1997, p. 62.
3. Lawrence Gibson, "Defining marketing problems," *Marketing Research*, Spring 1998.
4. Deepak Sarup, "To be, or not to be, the question of runaway projects," *Information Systems Control Journal*, Vol. 5, 2004.
5. Al Neimat Taimour, "Why IT projects fail," Project Perfect, http://www.projectperfect.com.au/info_it_projects_fail.php
6. Doug Russell, Effective Project Management in Semiconductor Design Organizations, Freescale Semiconductor Corporation, http://www.dsp-fpga.com/article-id/?3560#
7. Allan Cox, "The homework behind teamwork," *Industry Week*, January 7, 1991.
8. E. T. Hall, *The Dance of Life: The Other Dimension of Time*, Garden City, NY: Anchor Press/Doubleday, 1983, pp. 13–54.
9. J. T. Vessey, "The new competitors: they think in terms of 'speed to market'," *The Academy of Management Executive*, 5(2), 23–33, 1991.
10. R. H. Beeby, "How to crunch a bunch of numbers," *The Wall Street Journal*, June 11, 1990.
11. R. J. Chambers, "Don't let computers do all your thinking," *The Wall Street Journal*, July 11, 1990.

6

MAKING PEOPLE DECISIONS

Many articles have been published regarding executive succession, both in the academic and business press. While executive succession remains a major issue, little attention has been dedicated to providing succession plans for engineers, scientists, and other discipline specialists, managers in the many organizational functions, project managers, and even technicians who deal with the increasing complexities associated with the introduction of new technologies into new worldwide markets. There is no doubt that succession planning at the executive level cannot be disregarded, but there are times when the availability of the technician may be far more important than that of an executive. When the information system shuts down and competent people are not available to find and fix the problem, within an acceptable time period, chaos usually prevails. We've all probably witnessed these situations. The problem arises because assumptions are made that backup competencies are available. The research regarding the poor performance record on project completions, as previously mentioned, should force management to look seriously at the causes and develop solutions; those causes and solutions are not prescriptive, they'll be made to fit the organization's operating practices and culture, each requires decisions from various levels of management.

Decisions: An Engineering and Management Perspective, First Edition. Gerard H. Gaynor.
© 2015 The Institute of Electrical and Electronics Engineers, Inc. Published 2015 by John Wiley & Sons, Inc.

Chapter 6 focuses on the people decisions related to building and maintaining the competence of the organization's talent base for the sustainability of the organization. All of the issues involve a decision about people. While some may appear to be trivial, on the surface, the consequences can damage an organization's reputation and destroy careers. It should not take years to determine that an employee has not met expectations; it does take courage to resolve situations related to inadequate performance. Chapter 6 topics include

- Energizing the Human Resource Department
- Hiring Practices
- Evaluating Employee Performance
- Assessing Employee Potential
- Promotions and Appointments
- Selecting Team Members
- Assigning Work
- Transitioning from Specialist to Manager
- Salary Schedules
- Continuing Education
- Building Succession Competence
- Key Points
- Notes

ENERGIZING THE HUMAN RESOURCE DEPARTMENT

The decisions concerning employees begins and ends in the human resource department (HR). The HR departments play a major role in organizations on any actions involving recruiting policies, salary schedules, the adjudication of any form of misbehavior, termination, labor union negotiation, or any other decision related to people. In more recent years, with the growth and expansion of organizations, HR departments have become the eyes and ears to executive management regarding the organization's human assets. As an organization grows in size and scope executives quickly become less visible. The days when CEOs knew the competencies of candidates available for greater responsibilities, from personal association and experience, appear to be limited, except for those immediate reports and their staff. Executives have lost personal contact with engineers, scientists, and other specialists in all disciplines except perhaps financial and legal. Now, HR departments often provide the executives with screened lists of candidates for new appointments. My consulting experience showed that too often HR professionals have a predesigned idea of the organization's ideal candidate. My work experience and management research also show that HR departments, too often miss the most desirable candidates, because of some particular predisposition to candidates who display certain characteristics. Being aggressive too often appears to be a questionable characteristic in twenty-first century management practice. Being aggressive should not be a deterrent. Every candidate involves some levels of strengths and weaknesses; there is no perfect candidate, at least in the long term.

Over the years, I have found many competent people in HR in all their areas of responsibility. I have also found that too many only bring the HR message and recommendations from HR management, and contribute little to the process of providing the future talent requirements of the specific organizational unit. To be effective, HR must begin operating under a new paradigm. They need to provide twenty-first century needs. Most HR groups continue to do what they have always done with perhaps little change in the process. They tend to equalize everybody toward some common denominator and allow little room for handling those who make exceptional contributions to the organization. HR units, like all other organizational units, report to a hierarchy, and some will argue they are only fulfilling the organizations policies and procedures, but more is expected, their responsibility is to take the lead. There are many opportunities for HR to demonstrate their creativity and innovation, but it must go beyond such programs as the 360 degree process.

The HR department, as a staff group, too often avoids the realities of departments responsible for moving products to the customer. When operations' people are brought into HR to alleviate this situation, they quickly fall into the staff mode; don't rock the boat. As a practicing engineer with a record of technical and executive accomplishments and as a consultant, I found HR departments generally to be stumbling blocks to creating change and are managed by enforcing policies and procedures. Fortunately, I always have found someone in HR who would support deviations from policies and procedures when necessary. It is possible to find people in HR who push the envelope and who consider their job more than following policies and procedures. The problem, HR departments generally lack an adequate number of change makers to make an impact on performance.

This new HR paradigm, that I suggest, does not involve taking drastic action; it does involve bringing in people who are willing to challenge the status quo. It involves bringing in people who can innovate in the many areas of HR responsibility. Too often innovation becomes the property of the technical and marketing organizations. Innovation usually works best when employed throughout the whole organization since innovation success crosscuts all organizational functions and outside resources. Even HR needs its complement of constructive mavericks to make progress. It needs those people who think *future* rather than *past* and attempt to introduce systemic change. It needs those people who cannot live without change. Like any technical or marketing innovation, any change must be considered based on its purpose, what it will achieve, and its chance of being implemented successfully. In HR, *that chance of being implemented successfully* requires even more consideration than when related to products, services, or processes: it affects the organization's key resource, people, and involves some of the organizations most important decisions.

HIRING PRACTICES

Hiring policies and practices originate in the HR department and on occasion with input from managers in the functional departments and subsequently approved by some executive-level committee. Bringing new people into an organization involves an investment on the part of the organization and the individual: both have a stake in each other's future. Organizations hire engineers, other discipline specialists, managers and others in two basic categories, (1) through annual college recruitment programs and (2) individuals with experience to fill particular and often very specific needs. Each requires different approaches and in both cases the process too often fails to produce the desired results.

College Recruitment Programs

The typical annual college recruiting program provides an opportunity for HR departments to visit various university campuses and screen potential candidates to meet the organization's future needs. Over time the interviews have expanded beyond people in science, engineering, and mathematics to accounting, marketing, and general business: job requirements and knowledge have expanded to the point where organizations now consider people with majors in music, history, and those related to language and the arts.

Since the HR recruiters are not knowledgeable in many of the fields for which they are recruiting, except in their own field of expertise, and often not accompanied by professionals in the fields for which they are recruiting, they focus primarily on issues related to academic performance, interests, personal characteristics and traits, hobbies and job experiences with the overall purpose to determine if the interviewee meets the organization's requirements. Does the interviewee meet the organization's values statement as interpreted by the interviewer? These are important issues to investigate and short of sending a recruiting team in each specialty, does provide a first opportunity to make a selection. The major difficulty lies in the influence of the interviewer: to what extent do the interviewers inject their personal biases of what the ideal candidate should bring to the organization. My concern comes from the fact that recruiters often miss the candidates who deal in facts, are forthright in expressing their thoughts, expect to participate in meeting the organization's goals, and lack what has been emphasized, emotional intelligence. This is not to discount the importance of some level of emotional intelligence, but in balance with all other qualifications. These people may appear to be somewhat abrasive and arrogant, but they are the organization's future.

Another critical issue arises when recruiters decide to focus on the top 5 or 10 percent of the class. Academic credentials do not translate necessarily to organizational job performance. There is no reliable evidence that correlates academic credentials with professional performance. An applicant who maintained a solid 2.5 to 3.0 grade point average, found relevant employment during the summers, and worked about 20 hours per week during the academic year may provide a far better candidate than the applicant who managed a 4.0 as a full-time student. I found that these applicants brought far better personal and behavioral skills to the work environment. I would not disregard anyone with a grade point average of 3.5 to 4.0 for 124 to 148 credit hours, but performance is not about grade point average: it's about using that knowledge by working with others which requires general people skills. Technical competence by itself is insufficient in today's global environment, except in relatively few positions.

As an example, I doubt if Bill gates of Microsoft fame would have been an acceptable candidate to the average recruiter. Bill Gates and others who never completed their academic credentials were far more successful in their careers and made significant contributions in introducing new technologies and products that served society than many with advanced degrees. The examples go beyond the few known exceptions like Gates. If you're searching for someone who can design complex intricate mechanisms, such as we see in our daily lives, if we stop to take notice of them, a degree in mechanical or mechanisms engineering may not be necessary. The majority of these designers completed a couple of years in college, became bored because they prefer to focus on design: they have a penchant for "doing." They want to focus on showing what they can design: like the artist or the composer, they have an innate desire to bring their ideas to some form of reality. I would not ask these designers to calculate the stresses expected in the Boeing 787 Dreamliner at 40,000 feet. College recruiting often misses the creative, the innovative, and the people who will build the future of the organization. These are the nonconformists, the somewhat eccentric, and the constructive mavericks who become the organizations innovators and entrepreneurs. These are the tinkerers who, because of some sixth sense, bring forth those new technologies and products. They not only generate ideas, they pursue them to a conclusion.

If an organization requires relatively few new recruits annually, building relationships with professors in the academic community provides an opportunity to short circuit much of the campus recruiting. Such arrangements often recognize individuals in their third year for summer internships, where organizations have an opportunity to determine what the potential applicant may offer the organization. It's preferable if more than one university is involved, since professors have their biases, like the rest of society and it's necessary and more beneficial to introduce atypical and unfamiliar elements.

Hiring the Experienced Specialist

Hiring people with experience poses totally different problems. Selection of the appropriate applicant requires due diligence that goes beyond the usual give and take during an interview. Applications for specific disciplines come with different levels of experience. Hiring a person with 20 years of experience generally requires more diligence than hiring a person with 5 years of experience, so judgment dictates the extent of the effort. Either situation depends on the level of specialization or breadth of the job requirements. The requirements for a web designer to do routine web design would be quite different from the candidate who explores areas in superconductivity. The requirements for an applicant to design automation systems of various types would be quite different from those of an applicant expected to develop new automation concepts: concepts that would take automation to the next level. The requirements for an applicant to develop new manufacturing processes would be quite different from those of an applicant in materials research. These distinctions may appear to be self-evident, yet they are too often disregarded. In hiring a person with experience, the organization is making an investment and the long-range needs must be considered. The experienced applicant's risks also deserve equal consideration. Selection of experienced applicants cannot be done in a perfunctory manner.

What do managers need to know in selecting experienced engineers and other discipline specialists? Job requirements' statements seldom establish realistic requirements: too often they fall someplace along the job requirements continuum from "the insignificant" to "impossible to meet" and lack specificity. It's not enough to find an engineer, scientist, marketer, or any professional with a degree in a particular discipline with x-years of experience. The requirements must be sufficiently specific to meet the needs of the position and that position depends on current and projected workload; the disciplinary and other competencies must be defined. The selection requires identification of the required disciplinary and cross-disciplinary competencies. While checklists are often denounced, they do serve a purpose for identifying the critical issues.

Managers often fail to prepare for an interview and fail to grasp the nuances in making a new appointment. The interview process requires time and often the time for an interview is limited by the HR department. As an example, the HR department, if it goes to the expense of bringing a candidate into the work location, will choose to offer the applicant an opportunity to interview several different groups. That usually means a limit of 2 hours per reviewer. It is impossible, except in rare occasions, to interview an experienced applicant in 2 hours and determine whether or not that person meets the requirements. Yes, educational credentials can be reviewed, job history and accomplishments can be discussed, but more is required. How do you find out what the applicant brings to the table?

Bringing a new experienced employee into the organization involves an investment. As a Director of Engineering, I insisted when interviewing an upper-level experienced candidate, for an opportunity to spend a full day. I wanted every offer to be a successful offer that provided an opportunity for growth, both for the organization and the individual. The process began with finding out as much as possible about the applicant, prior to offering the invitation to visit the organization. The interview process usually began with breakfast, followed by a couple of hours of detailed discussion. The applicant would visit several managers, senior engineers with whom he'd be involved, and perhaps a lunch with a select group of senior engineers. At some time during the day the applicant would meet with the engineers who became engaged in the discipline discussions, to determine the depth of understanding in the field: a casual discussion to determine the contributions the applicant made in prior positions. If possible, I met with the applicant and a selected manager or two and a discipline specialist for a casual dinner, where my colleagues and I had an opportunity to get feedback from the applicant and send him on his way home. The next morning, a selected group came together to review the previous day's conversations: question did the applicant meet, not meet, or meet our expectations with reservations. All the participants did their homework, so reaching a conclusion was relatively simple.

Over many years of experience, I watched managers hem and haw in reaching a decision about a candidate. I concluded from questioning them after holding an interview, they included too much unimportant chit chat; never dealt with what would make the applicant a desirable employee; did not learn much about the applicant's specific competencies, interests, and work preferences; forgot to focus on issues such as communication and leadership, and basically reviewed the application with the applicant. My usual approach included disregarding the application form after I read it.

Learning to interview is a teachable skill, so after reviewing managers' interview reports, I established a short program on the basics of interviewing. I found that managers spent very little time preparing for the interview, failed to be forthright with the candidate, and failed to ask the types of questions that would identify the applicant's capabilities as well as shortcomings. A candidate who meets every requirement seldom exists. Supervisors and managers also spent too much time attempting to confirm all the details on the candidate's resume. You may ask, why go through such a lengthy process in a global economy where long-term employments appears to be a custom of the past? Bringing professionals on board involves an investment or cost depending on how you view the process, and I doubt that we have a desire to repeat the employment practices of the dotcom era.

Most requests for experienced people involve preparing the job requirements in some sort of formal format. This document usually spells out the job description, education and an experience requirement, personal characteristics required for the position, and asks a candidate to provide a short paragraph about personal job objectives. The difficulty arises when managers, in the process of hiring a new senior engineer are asked after the interview, if the person interviewed met the requirements. I often received responses to my questions, such as: "What did you think of the candidate you interviewed today?" or "Did the candidate meet the requirements, and will you make an offer?" with various levels of disappointment. I'd receive responses such as "I think the applicant meets all our requirements and everything we expect, but I'd like to interview some others. I might find someone better." I usually ended the conversation with the following response: "Look, the applicant either met or did not meet the requirements. If the applicant met the requirements, make an offer. If you choose not to make an offer of employment, rewrite the job requirements and we'll discuss them." Looking for an unknown undefined quality seldom yields results.

EVALUATING EMPLOYEE PERFORMANCE

About every 5 years, HR justifies to top management the need to change the performance review process. Over the past 50 years the process has gone from the manager completing a two-sided page to the current in vogue 360 degree process which consumes multiple pages, and in some situations completed on a 6- and occasionally a 3-month schedule. A process that was at one time very simple has grown into a monster that provides little information to guide future organizational directions.

Why does performance evaluation of employee performance present such difficulties for the reviewer and the reviewed? Reviewers delay and the reviewed fret over not knowing the outcome. Performance evaluation of competent employees requires little effort, confronting the nonperformers creates unbelievable amounts of stress for the reviewer and the reviewed. It's not easy to tell someone that their performance somehow misses the mark, but why does this take place during the annual or semiannual review process. This action by the manager should take place when the lack of performance occurs or some other misguided action is recognized, and the individual is informed immediately and provided guidance to avoid repeating the same act. Poor employee performance begins when managers fail to recognize it when it occurs, and confront the individual or group involved.

Over the years many elementary schools adopted the practice where everybody is a winner; everybody receives a trophy, just for attending. Also, various school sports parents and coaches stopped counting the number of runs in a baseball game after one team exceeds a certain number of runs, so as not to affect the self-esteem of the less successful team. Such actions usually made to protect the self-esteem of the individuals. There's nothing wrong with protecting self-esteem, but self-esteem is not given by somebody, it's earned. Such practices have found their way into organizations dominated by adults. That performance evaluation distribution curve has shifted dramatically to the right. It appears that most employees are rated as meeting or exceeding requirements or the equivalent on some other scale. How can that be when overall performance regardless of the metric used is something less than expected? Such results expose the deficiencies in evaluating personnel. In the process, performance scores have been inflated to the point where in some organizations over 40 percent of the employees are graded as exceeding performance. As previously noted in Chapter 1, James M. Kilts[1] in *Doing What Matters*, reports that when he became an outsider CEO of Gillette, Gillette's vice president of HR informed him that 65 percent of the managers had received performance ratings of *exceed expectations or outstanding*. At the same time, Gillette's earnings were flat for the prior 4 years. This is not an uncommon situation.

From my early days as a neophyte engineer, I had an opportunity to participate in several task forces asked to evaluate performance evaluation practices and provide more appropriate methods for making evaluation process more realistic and workable. Unfortunately, these task forces that included members from HR, plus a selection of people from operations in different disciplines, seldom were willing to provide something that would simplify the process and at the same time focus of the few issues that needed improvement. Review processes became more complicated, the documents requesting more information, and basically attempting to remove judgment from the reviewer. Those areas identified for improvement mean nothing unless both manager and employee show diligence in pursuing the recommendations. Those recommendations require an investment of time, energy, and often financial resources. There is a simple answer to the employee evaluation process: a single blank page with the date, name of the employee, and name of the reviewer. The usual criticism of this approach, from the HR staff, was that most supervisors and managers were not capable of writing an appraisal in such an open system. My usual retort was, then why are they supervisors and managers? Why not focus on the root of the problem. Evaluating performance is a serious issue, yet often, few HR staff members, beginning with the vice president of HR, have the courage to take steps to halt the process of performance inflation. They should take the lead.

I learned my approach to appraising performance within 6 months of my first job as a newly minted engineer. I asked my manager about the organization's review process and his response was interesting. He said, "Gus, just remember that every time we meet, you're being appraised." This manager was one who *walked around* long before managing by *walking around* became the flavor of the day. At appraisal time he opened a folder with all kinds of individual notes. Our discussion focused on the future not the past. For all practical purposes, and especially since he was always visible, I always knew where I stood. I didn't have to wait until review time to know how I would be rated. These notes reflected what he had talked to me just about every time we met. If something needed correction, it was done immediately.

I followed that same process once I was appointed to my first supervisory position. As I reached the stage where I had supervisors and managers reporting to me, I instituted the same procedures that resulted with varying degrees of success. Changing behavior takes time, and sometimes a great amount of time. Performance reviews present so much frustration for the appraiser because appraisers fail to have adequate information required to make a judicious appraisal. Depending on memory for evaluating past events, shortchanges the employee being appraised. Supervisors and managers often fail to confront employees at the time a problem arises; such as a failed design, some type of unacceptable performance, difficulties with colleagues, missed communications, and so on. Those personnel reviews to be valuable must be based on performance over the period involved, and not on the last good or poor performance event. The point I wish to make is that supervisors or managers responsible for the activities of a group of engineers or in any other discipline cannot evaluate performance equitably without knowledge accumulated over the time period. Employees should know where they stand at any time. The evaluation process should not reveal any surprises.

Evaluating an employee's performance is just about the most important function of anyone with a supervisory or management position. These evaluations determine not only the future of the organization in maintaining a cadre of competent employees, but also in fulfilling the employee's career aspirations. Allowing an employee to underperform without corrective action of some kind only creates future problems for the employee and the organization. Overrating an employee's performance also has its downside, both for the organization and the employee. Eventually some manager will arrive on the scene and be expected to make the necessary difficult hard and often unpleasant decisions. In the meantime a career may be destroyed, because of the inability of a manager, and in many cases a series of managers who lack the courage to evaluate an employee and take timely corrective action at the appropriate time.

ASSESSING EMPLOYEE POTENTIAL

Evaluating employee performance and assessing employee potential require two different mindsets: evaluating performance tells the past history with input for the near future and within the same immediate environment. Assessing employee potential looks at the potential in the current organizational unit (OU), other OUs within the corporate organization, and perhaps with the need to even suggest departure of an employee, not for poor performance, but as recognition that the employee's career expectations cannot be fulfilled. Too often managers become protective of their people, because the loss of a key person may create operational problems: such actions prevent an organization from developing the cadre of specialists and managers who eventually become the new organization. Assessing an employee's future potential in the organization should begin with data available from the performance reviews, but that is only the beginning.

The mindset for assessing employee potential requires an understanding of the organization's future personnel needs. Managers are primarily interested in meeting today's objectives: their future is measured by what goes out the door and not their ability to plan future personnel needs. While executive management may bemoan the lack of interest in providing for the future, they seldom take constructive action to actively promote it. It's too late to begin searching for specific competencies when they're needed. Such needs require prior planning and execution. What are those new technology needs? What changes will take place in the marketplace to require new competencies? Where are those new managers? Unfortunately and too often, organizational leadership fails to provide for the future in some systematic manner. It's really not that difficult to project future needs, if managers understand the organization's strategic directions. However, too much information is hidden in those strategic plans sitting on the shelf without defined operational plans: strategic directions become a reality only when linked to an operational implementation plan that is staffed and understood by those responsible.

Question to Ask

After 5 years of working on challenging projects, educational credentials provide little if any direction as to the future potential of an employee. In appraising future potential, managers need to consider work experiences and characteristics and attitudes. The process begins with asking the simple what and how. Some questions must be answered.

- What has the employee accomplished and how was it accomplished?
- What were the individual's contributions to the group?
- What was the group's contribution to organizational results?
- What did the employee propose that failed? What was learned? How did the employee handle the failure?

- What did the employee propose that was successful and what was the impact on the organization?
- What are the individuals thinking processes? Do those thinking processes provide depth?
- Does the employee play it safe or take calculated risks?
- Did the employee take on projects that others chose to avoid? Were any of those projects beyond the person's knowledge and experience base and produced exceptional results?
- Where has the employee demonstrated leadership, personal initiative, and ability to develop working coalitions?
- How has the organization assisted in fulfilling the full potential of its employees?

These are just a sampling of questions that must be asked whether considering future engineering potential or management areas. As noted in Chapter 1, studies by Heike Bruch and Sumantra Ghoshal, 10 percent of managers move the company. I suggest that about the same percentage of engineers move the organization forward. The 10 percent that move the company need the other 90 percent for support: obviously some percentage among this 90 percent may even influence organizational performance negatively. Managers and executives, at all levels, have opportunities to test the spirit, determination, and courage of an employee interested in taking on senior-level responsibilities cither in the engineering or management ranks. This is not a difficult task, just provide significant stretch targets that require more than the employee has to offer.

PROMOTIONS AND APPOINTMENTS

Policies regarding promotions span a continuum from very broad to very narrow and include many issues. Here are several approaches we need to consider: should promotions be made, (1) if the appropriate level of work is not available; (2) should promotions be based on longevity; (3) should promotions be based solely on performance; (4) should promotions be based on multiple factors such as longevity, need, and performance.

Some organizations espouse a policy of promoting an individual when a specific event occurs, based on some predetermined longevity period in a position, whether that promotion is necessary or not. Here is an example, assume that on a scale of seven levels of seniority, we're promoting an engineer from Group 5 to Group 6. Each of these groups has specific performance requirements as to the type and level of work, amount of individual initiative required, nonsupervised activity expectations, and requirements for innovation depending on the organization. But there is no Group 6 work required and none appears to be required in the immediate future. So, now there's a Group 6 engineer doing Group 5 work or lower. I believe extreme caution must be exercised under such conditions to avoid future obsolescence; such promotions should include a plan to limit the time under which the employee may be required to work below grade level, otherwise the organization begins a downward spiral toward mediocrity. Working below level for a year or more, too often results in setting lower expectations in performance for the future.

Basing promotions on years of service for engineers raises the perennial issue, 5 years of experience or 1 year of experience five times. If promotions are based on years of acceptable performance, independent of the need to promote, then managers must somehow find work at that upper level. In the example cited, the manager would have to find a way to provide Group 6 work, and since Group 6 involves emphasis on personal initiative, and nonsupervised performance, and innovation, that should not be difficult, assuming this engineer met the requirements. Promoting engineers or others when the work does not exist at the promoted level, at best demonstrates poor judgment. There must be a better solution and a better solution involves a critical appraisal of the current and future workload. Organizations might take heed and appraise not only their hiring practices, but also their educational and training programs. As a manager who preferred to promote based on performance, plus all those necessary behavioral characteristics and attitudes, I also included the future potential of the engineer. I recognize that there are many opportunities for partiality and even injustice. Performance can be inflated and exaggerated and can also be minimized and underestimated depending on the manager's experience and background. So, there's a need for a caveat, "don't appraise what you don't know." If measures of performance are based on meeting objectives, the need to know the specifics loses its significance.

Elevating to the next grade obviously has several conditions that include more than exceptional performance in a discipline. An engineer, within his or her first year apprenticeship, could make a significant technological advancement that supersedes those of longer term colleagues. But, does that engineer meet all the other requirements related to the expected knowledge, skills, and attitudes. If not, the manager has a new challenge: level with the individual and provide the necessary guidance. Developing talent is the manager's responsibility. There are times when this same engineer does have all the knowledge, skills, and attitudes and does perform above and beyond colleagues and thus should not be held back. These people are the ones in the top 5 percent, not top 5 percent academically, but the top 5 percent in making things happen. They have what I call the put-it-all-together competence. You do not have to tell them what to do.

Consider the following quotes from the 24 September 2007 issue of Business Week about Gen Y. "Gen Y needs a bucket of praise." "There is a strong, strong millennial dislike of ambiguity and risk, leading them to seek a lot more direction and clarity from their employers, in terms of what the task is, what the expectations are, and job progression." With such attitudes, regardless of their technical competence, Gen Yer's will not make the top 5 percent, unless an organization decides to change or even lower its standards. Being an engineer involves more than being proficient in the technical areas, the profession requires good interpersonal skills, communication competency, and a business mindset.

SELECTING TEAM MEMBERS

Building teams is presented as though it was a late twentieth century phenomenon. Using teams requires managing relationships among people who come from different disciplines and different levels of accomplishments within those disciplines. The team members will span the continuum from the proactive to the inactive; from those who think out of the box to those who don't even know they're in a box, and from those who limit their interest to their discipline, to those who consider their discipline, in relation to the business. But what is involved in building a value-adding team. Alan Cox[2] in *The Homework Beyond Teamwork* offers a comprehensive description. NOTE: I repeated Cox's statement here so as to maintain continuity and not expect the reader to return to Chapter 5 to search for the reference.

> "Whether established department or ad hoc, the team is a thinking organism, where problems are named, assumptions challenged, alternatives generated, consequences assessed, priorities set, admissions made, competitors evaluated, missions validated, goals tested, hopes ventured, fears anticipated, successes expected, vulnerabilities expressed, contributions praised, absurdities tolerated, withdrawals noticed, victories celebrated, and defeats overcome."

This description of a team does not specify any particular structure. My years of experience have taught me that structure really doesn't matter if the team includes the right combination of people, with the appropriate competencies. If the team does not include the right people, no amount of tweaking with the structure will make a difference. But developing competent teams involves (1) setting the direction and style and (2) selecting the right people.

Setting the Direction and Style

Managers determine the direction and the basic plan toward meeting the team's objectives. As a young manager I quickly learned that when dealing with people issues, *the shortest distance between two points is not a straight line*; I mean this from a behavioral perspective. Finding an appropriate way to deal effectively with people's differences and idiosyncrasies often poses major challenges and involves

- Building the team: Using teams is not a management panacea. It's too late to begin building team competence and capabilities when the need arises. It is absolutely necessary to be sensitive and guard against William H. White's admonition that group activity (teams) has a downward leveling effect on the individual, forces conformity, denies expression of individualism, nullifies creative activity, and in general hampers and limits human activity.

- Learning from research: John C. Redding[3] asked the question, which of two methods is more effective in resolving an issue using a team to address the issue, (1) Team A, follows an established and structured process or (2) Team B, uses an unstructured approach that allowed for a free flow of ideas. The results showed the teams structured like Team A, were less likely to develop innovative solutions, if left to their own devices. Unstructured Team B type discussions were twice as likely to develop innovative solutions.

- Asking the tough questions and getting the answers: There are many reasons why teams fail to deliver positive results. If all the problems associated with a team effort were communicated to management, innovation would be buried with all other activities that involve some sort of change. The question, how much bad news should be communicated to executive management since it will determine success or failure? This is a judgment call and the risks need to be evaluated carefully. These decisions involve asking the hard questions which often fail to surface. Those PowerPoint presentations seldom tell the complete story. The messenger of bad news may even be isolated by the team members for raising a controversial point for discussion.

- Defining the role of each individual: Defining a team participant's role requires knowledge of the individual and a clear understanding of his/her expectations. Not all positions require brilliance: brilliant people often fail to demonstrate their brilliance because of an improper assignment. But brilliance may not be a prerequisite for all team participants: the team requires a combination of competencies to fulfill the requirements. You may say that this is obvious, so why repeat it here. I repeat it because team composition too often leads to failure. In the final analysis any team effort must conclude with a recommendation that takes into account the integrated thinking of the team. Work should provide opportunities for growth, notwithstanding the need to also complete the mundane: those activities performed by using rules of thumb or that have been pursued so many times that they seldom require significant amounts of thought.

- Using teams: As noted, teams provide a useful avenue for resolving all types of issues, problems, and dilemmas. Peter Senge[4] author of *The Fifth Discipline* asks the question, "How can a team of committed managers with individual IQs above 120 have a collective IQ of 63?" Chris Argyris[5] writes in the *The Fifth Discipline*, "The team may function quite well on routine issues. But when they confront complex issues that may be embarrassing or threatening, the teamness goes to pot." Argyris notes that "the consequences of such actions results in *skilled incompetence*—teams full of people who are incredibly proficient in keeping themselves from learning." While Senge was referring his remarks to upper management, the same dictum pertains to all organizational levels and disciplines. Collective inquiry forces us to find new ways to resolve issues: it forces new thinking to determine whether or not our biases and the baggage that each of us brings to the table prevents us from providing value-added contributions in a dynamic and interconnected global economy. Argyris refers to this condition of not facing up to reality as *skilled incompetence*. Argyris also notes that there's a significant difference between advocating views and inquiring into complex issues.

- Pursuing excellence: Pursuing excellence requires hard work, dedication, and a passion to accomplish some purpose. Of course the word *excellence* spans a continuum of descriptions. What may be *excellence* for one person may be *mediocrity* to another. Nonetheless market forces ascribe some level of attention regarding quality of products and services. Excellence is not perfection although too often it's interpreted as such. Even the best quality standard allows one deviation in a million. Pursuing excellence is a mindset that requires discipline: it must be designed into the system. Discipline in this sense means developing a mindset about excellence and mastering the body of knowledge that allows for effective application. There is no cookie-cutter approach to promoting excellence: it's a mindset and practice to guide performance.

- Making diversity work: Why should managers concern themselves about diversity issues? The simple answer, federal and state laws generally prohibit discrimination. David A. Thomas and Robin J. Ely[6] have suggested that diversity initiatives are guided by (1) equal opportunity, fair treatment, recruitment, and compliance with federal and state laws and regulations and (2) it just makes good business sense; it's the right thing to do and serves the enlightened self-interest of the organization and the community. Diversity is not about numbers or imposed quotas: it's about finding the talent wherever it exists and allowing that talent to actively participate in determining the organization's future. We live in a global economy and all the talent no longer resides at the motherhouse. Global goals cannot be achieved by limiting sources of talent. But there's another type of diversity that seldom receives consideration; diversity in thinking which may have far greater significance. In our digital age, I find considerably less interest in thinking deeply about a decision or topic of importance; *average* seems to be good enough rather than the pursuit of excellence, excellence, not perfection.

- Motivating the team: If you need to spend any time motivating the team you probably have the wrong team leadership or team members who do not meet team requirements. There are basically two types of motivation and lie on a continuum from intrinsic at one end and extrinsic at the other end. Few people are intrinsically motivated at all times and under all circumstances: most people need some form of extrinsic motivational help. Intrinsically motivated people receive satisfaction from their accomplishments, executed through their own capabilities and self-discovery. Extrinsically motivated people need the fringe benefits, the status, and look for the rewards for meeting their objectives. In the final analysis, work assignments determine to a great extent where a person operates on the intrinsic/extrinsic continuum. Someone, with a desire for recognition and working on a project of low importance in the organization's project hierarchy, may find it very difficult to be motivated. If someone is assigned what may be classified as "junk projects" that have no visibility whatsoever, don't expect the person to be motivated unless you find that person who lacks the competence to participate in major projects.

Researchers like Abraham Maslow, Frederick Herzberg, and Douglas McGregor have set forth some guiding principles regarding motivation. Maslow[7] suggests a hierarchy of needs that span the low to high level needs: they begin with meeting the lower level physiological, safety, and social needs, followed by the higher level needs of self-esteem and self-actualization. Our current culture, unfortunately, focuses too much attention on meeting the self-esteem needs without the effort put forth for gaining self-esteem. No one can give another human being self-esteem; self-esteem is earned through accomplishing something of value, first to yourself and then to others.

Herzberg's[8] research focused on the differences between motivation and hygiene factors. He described *hygiene factors* to include approaches to supervision, policies and procedures, interpersonal relations, working conditions, and salary and benefits. He found that attitudes toward a specific work effort, a form of mindset, were *hygiene factors* and not motivation. Herzberg's motivators included a personal achievement, recognition from peers and management, the work-effort itself, responsibility, satisfaction, and opportunities for advancement.

McGregor's[9] research produced the concept of the *Theory X* and *Theory Y* manager. Theory X managers operate under the principle that the average human being dislikes work and will avoid it where possible and must be coerced and controlled to meet personal requirements: basically a control and command mindset. Theory Y managers operate under the principle providing freedom to exercise initiative and ingenuity; a focus on achievement; and full utilization of talent. While many managers fall into the extreme ends of this Theory X and Theory Y continuum, competent managers manage someplace on that continuum between the extremes depending on the circumstances. Managers must provide for meeting individual differences within reason and thus will use different means for managing the activities of those unique people charged with meeting the objectives of their organizational unit.

SELECTING THE RIGHT PEOPLE

Selecting the right engineers requires operating at the micro level rather than the macro. The macro level considers basic classification by discipline and grade; the micro level also considers discipline and grade, but focuses on specifics. It's not sufficient to make decisions based on an engineer or a marketer or a production process engineer by just considering their technical qualifications. The needs must be described in specific terms. Selection of candidates for specific positions requires operating at the micro level. The micro-level analysis focuses on just what the person under consideration has accomplished and how: it looks for the specific talents that have been demonstrated in work-life situations. The selection of people with the required competencies determines the success of any organized effort; people assignments eventually define the organization. Those competencies involve not only discipline knowledge, but also a delineation of the specific skills, attitudes, personal characteristics, and experiences. Generally, it's too late to start on the learning curve when work must begin. Learning on the job can be a costly experience for the organization. Selection of people with available competencies requires serious rather than cursory reflection: it requires consideration of a person's total history of accomplishments and failures and how the failures were managed. But often it's difficult to adequately describe competencies because standards are not available: it requires judgment.

Identifying competencies presents various levels of complexity. Here's an example: A young manager prepared a survey asking her engineers to identify their work-related competencies and those outside of the work environment. She thought such information might be helpful in identifying key talent that might need development for the future. She was also searching for engineers who possessed good writing skills. Surprise! The more talented engineers identified the fewest competencies. The majority responded that they were proficient in writing. A review of some of their past attempts at writing reports showed clearly their lack of writing skills. A wide gap exists between personal evaluation and management evaluation. Other studies also identify the discrepancies between how professionals, in all disciplines, view their competencies compared to how their management views their competencies.

The analysis of critical engineering needs and in related disciplines for a particular macro project is seldom codified prior to making the decision to proceed. This process does not involve specifying a total complement of individuals involved in the project, but identifying the gaps that exist and determining the means for acquiring the necessary talent and filling the gaps. Lack of some unique competencies both within and outside the organization can be one of those knockouts previously described. To begin any approved effort with less than adequate talent is bound to result in something less than expected. This seems such an obvious conclusion, but too often goes unheeded. We are all aware of what occurs when people are assigned to positions without the required competencies to fulfill the requirements of the position. At the very least, the lack of specific competencies that could eventually scuttle the project must be identified. Lack of the required people competencies is just one, but a major potential project "knockout." This analysis of potential knockouts should be assessed prior to approving a project: first, find a solution to the knockouts.

ASSIGNING WORK

Linking competencies to workload involves (1) managers who make the assignments, (2) people assigned to fulfill the workload requirements, and (3) the organization. Too often this activity becomes a juggling act by moving people from one project to another and in the process creating various levels of dissatisfaction. The major difficulties arise when managers make major assignments without considering an individual's competencies: it's insufficient to make assignments based on second-hand knowledge. If people are assigned below their level for any length of time that level of performance may become the new standard. If people are assigned too far above their level of competence, frustration sets in and the project may suffer those unintended consequences. Good career planning requires setting stretch targets. At one time, I suspected some senior people were working far below their competency levels and raised the issue with a colleague director. The director's response justified the action; his response was that those were the only types of projects available in his department. Under further investigation, I found that another part of the organization lacked senior level people, but had an excess of junior level people. We managed the exchange from one department to another with of course some grumbling.

We live in a society where the word apprenticeship has been forgotten and that attitude begins at an early age. There's the story of a young boy Tim, whose participation in the class play began by holding a sword and standing in the corner. By the time Tim was ready to enter junior high he had the lead in the class play. Upon entering junior high, Tim once again began by holding the sword in the corner and when he was ready to enter high school he had the lead in the class play. And the story goes on and on where every new entry placed Tim at the bottom of the ladder: starting from the new bottom, but with greater expectations. Today, if Tim had the lead in the kindergarten class play he'd want the lead in class play as he progressed to the next educational level. *I did it once, so I learned everything I need to know*: such an approach provides little when it comes to looking for breadth of experiences.

TRANSITIONING FROM SPECIALIST TO MANAGER

Organizations continue to struggle in developing managers who become responsible for managing the activities of the people who report to them. Unfortunately, what it takes to transition an engineer and other discipline specialists to management positions involves more effort than is usually anticipated. When a vacancy arises, a few candidates are considered, one is selected, Friday afternoon arrives, the announcement is made, some praise and grumbling occurs, and the new manager begins Monday at 8:00 A.M. This may be overstated, but not by much. As a technology executive, I often faced the situation when a manager's position required replacement, someone would ask me: "I'd like to put my name on the list." My usual response included a question: "What have you done to prepare yourself for the position." The response, a blank stare! What was I expecting? Why would I even think of considering someone who has not demonstrated any interest in managing as a candidate? Organizations have many opportunities to develop competent managers by beginning with small assignments as project managers and tracking performance. Even at this level, some basic knowledge must be acquired and the principles mastered. Becoming a manager is not a destination, it's a journey that never ends as one advances in the profession.

The discipline of managing is probably one of the most difficult of all disciplines: it deals with human behavior that does not operate by the defined principles of physics or the periodic table of the elements. There are no algorithms to govern human behavior. Managers need to understand their role. As a young engineer, the CEO of the organization informed us that he spent over a quarter of his time on people problems. That was difficult to believe, but here is a very simple example.

Managing is an ancient practice. Modern management is a mid-twentieth century invention. The expansion of information systems, and their capability to analyze and easily manipulate data, model performance, and simulate operations, has provided new tools for managers. However, those tools are too often replacing judgment. The academic community, through its research, has provided industry with many new insights and theories regarding the art and practice of managing. Managing is not science; it's an art and a practice. Those insights and theories may not follow the laws of nature, but they need to be explored for the gems of wisdom they often unveil. Peter Drucker,[10] in *The Essential Drucker*, warns against considering managing as "a bag of techniques and tricks." Managing involves more than using these techniques and tricks: it's the body of knowledge that supports the act of managing.

Managing also involves looking beyond meeting the objectives of the group. Those objectives are linked to objectives of other organizational units. We are all familiar with situations where every group has accomplished what was expected except when those subassemblies were being integrated nothing worked as was expected. Managing the pieces is insufficient: it's necessary to integrate all those requirements throughout the complete process and manage the whole. Managers manage the use of organizational resources and the managing goes beyond managing the people's activities and money, it includes managing the intellectual property, technology, time, distribution channels, customers, suppliers, production capability, operating facilities, and all external resources.

A quote from Henry Mintzberg[11] provides a word of caution to engineers and other discipline specialists and their managers.

"No job is more vital to our society than that of the manager. It is the manager who determines whether our social institutions serve us well or whether they squander our talents and resources."

Those are potent words and every engineer and manager should be vigilant to avoid squandering organizational and other related *talents and resources.*

SALARY SCHEDULES

Some of the most important decisions a manager may make relate to compensating an employee for exceptional performance: the amount of compensation affects the future not only of the organization, but also the employee. Current salary schedules generally link compensation to employee performance assessment. However, employee performance has been distorted in recent years with a tendency to exaggerate the accomplishments. Employee evaluation results, as noted previously continue to show a continuing increase in the number of people rated as *exceeding requirements* or in some other equivalent metric. These misguided efforts, to lower standards of performance, have yielded an essentially automatic progression system with little room for adequately compensating exceptional performance. While such an approach relieves the manager of using judgment in compensating for exceptional performance, it negatively affects future organizational performance.

While compensation may not be the driving force for becoming committed in pursuing a project, it must be there if the effort is to continue. Managers have a tendency to avoid judging performance realistically, so it's easier to give everyone the same nominal increase, but that's not the way to build capability in an organizational unit. Some years ago, many organizations basically discontinued merit increases; a 1 or 2 percent merit increase on top of the cost-of-living increase hardly qualifies as a merit increase. When an organization proposes an across the board increase and disallows any substantial merit increases, the organization is bound to lose some of its most promising talent. Also, employees contribute at different performance levels and with different levels of initiative and energy; compensation should be based on their contribution to the organization's success. Implementing merit-based approach forces managers to exercise individual judgment.

CONTINUING EDUCATION

Lifelong learning begins on the day after graduation. You may argue that it begins earlier, but that first degree or first professional level position begins a transition to building a career. There is no shortage of courses whether through university extension programs in many forms or from commercial producers. Too many professional specialists like marketers and engineers fail to take advantage of educational opportunities, not only in their specific discipline, but also in other related disciplines. It may even be advantageous if these two groups learned something about each other. There are also courses often referred to as professional development that include topics such as communication, interpersonal relations, leadership, and project management.

Some people have a built-in penchant for learning and take every opportunity afforded, others have little interest. Whether the half-life of an engineer's knowledge is 5 or 10 years makes little difference. The fact remains that technologies change and the value of an engineer is limited by his or her ability to keep up technologically with the times. But continuing education in any field needs more than learning, it also involves applying that learning; in essence application of what was learned. Learning also can be experiential. An engineer working on leading-edge technologies probably need not fear obsolescence, but the engineer who in mid-career finds that 10 years on the job assignments has not provided any growth opportunities ought to be concerned about the future career opportunities.

Much of today's university curricula focus more on specialization than on breadth. The electrical engineering curricula in particular have become very specialized. So the question I ask, are universities graduating electrical engineers or well-educated electrical and electronic technologists? As a graduate in EE from the University of Michigan in 1950, I took courses in strength of materials, statics, dynamics, fluid mechanics, AC and DC machinery, electromagnetics, heat transfer, chemistry, physics, math though differential equations, descriptive geometry, and yes, a full year of drafting where final drawings were made on linen with India ink. I'm not suggesting that students spend a full semester developing the intersections of cones and cylinders and so on. However, knowing how to develop those intersections might be of value. I'm not suggesting that we revive drafting, as it was called, but knowledge of how to sketch on the back of a napkin or envelope would be helpful. Many of these courses are missing in the EE curricula and if included are often more likely to be a survey course rather than fully accredited course. We were taught to be engineers and able to solve problems in just about any engineering field. We were taught fundamentals and how to apply them. We didn't have to have knowledge to solve every problem, we needed to know the fundamentals and know what kind of expertise we needed and where to find it.

Unlearning

While continuous learning is necessary, organizational unlearning may be a necessary requirement. Any effort that attempts to tear down the organizational silos, usually fails. Any effort to eliminate e-mails between people sitting in adjacent cubicles usually fails. Any effort to change those actions, methods, or processes that have been internalized throughout the organization, over many years, usually fails. Those HR policies regarding appraisal need to be discarded because they fail to develop the back-up people to sustain the organization: somehow recommendations to change to more meaningful instruments are not implemented. Those long-established work processes that provided a benefit at one time, no longer meet the requirements. Each of these served a purpose at one time, the question is do they continue to add value. As an example, there was time when organizational functions could live in their somewhat isolated world. Engineering focused on engineering. Marketing focused on marketing. Some executive would probably reconcile the differences. But engineering and marketing are no longer independent functions. The product that customers now expect requires integrating engineering and marketing activities. Engineers cannot dictate market requirements and marketers cannot dictate technical solutions, but the customer's needs now take precedence. If both go in their own direction, the organization fails. Now it's important for the organizational silos to consider the needs of each other's silos and take a systems approach. What do I mean by a systems approach? Take community responsibility for the outcome of the activities of the many silos; that can only be accomplished by understanding the needs of the total process from concept to delivery to the marketplace.

BUILDING A SUCCESSION COMPETENCE

Succession planning begins at the bottom of the organization rather than at the top: by bottom, I mean hiring the professionals responsible for moving ideas from the laboratory to the customer and then over a period of years bringing them into top level positions in all the organizational disciplines. This may be considered to be an idealized perspective, but it does make sense to avoid continually bringing in new people without any knowledge of how the organization functions. Prior to the early 1980s there was social contract between employers and employees. Executives, managers, engineers, and other discipline specialists enjoyed lifetime employment. But when major downsizing began and globalization reaches far beyond the organization's headquarters, lifetime employment began to erode significantly. According to some observers loyalty was relegated to the trash can. I repeat a quote here from Amanda Bennett,[12] a writer for *The Wall street Journal*, from Chapter 1; she presented a description of the 1980s middle manager in the article "Broken Bonds" and she noted that middle managers thought they had an unwritten and unspoken contract with their employers. It said

> "Take care of business and we'll take care of you. You don't have to be
> a star; just be faithful, obedient, and only modestly competent, and this
> will be your home for as long as want to stay."

While Bennett's statement may appear to be an exaggeration, we need to keep in mind that during this period many organizations were being accused of being too paternalistic: they began providing almost cradle to the grave security which under any circumstance is not sustainable. The comfort zone was expanded and under such conditions attitudes toward maintaining organizational discipline declined with intended consequences: less discipline in meeting organizational objectives.

Leavitt[13] in *Corporate Pathfinders* divided the managerial process into path finding, problem solving, and implementation. He was careful to point out that the lines between these three activities are blurred, but there is little reason to believe that when dealing with people and organizational issues that there would be clear lines of demarcation. Management is not mathematics, it's fuzzy. But, where do corporate pathfinders come from? These pathfinders, problem solvers, and implementers can be grown within an organization as long as the creative and innovative spirit lives within all organizational units. If, the organizational status quo prevails, the comfort zone expands; management must begin a rebuilding process.

KEY POINTS

- **Energizing the Human Resource Department:** Bring innovation into the HR department.
- **Hiring Practices:** Provide for the organizations engineers, other discipline specialists, and managers according to requirements and not according to some predetermined HR perspective.
- **Evaluating Employee Performance:** Do it the right way even if it hurts. Managers are expected to resolve employee non-performance in a timely manner.
- **Assessing Employee Potential:** Every employee should be able to reach their level of competence.
- **Promotions and Appointments:** Think before promoting. Automatic progression systems limit the opportunities to garner the right talent.
- **Selecting Team Members:** You build a winning team with members who meet the required competencies; either be confident you can build the competencies or have the courage to make the difficult decision.
- **Assigning Work:** Provide growth opportunities in assigning work to make sure that 10 years experience yields 10 years of experience and not one year of experience 10 times. Managers share a joint responsibility with employees for their growth. A tremendous responsibility!
- **Transitioning from Specialist to Manager:** Managing involves taking risks. It takes courage. It involves making major decisions with minimal information. And, managers must recognize that they do not manage people, they manage their activities. Knowledge workers cannot be managed.

- **Salary Schedules:** Make room for substantial merit increases. Dont try to bring everyone down to the lowest common denominator.
- **Continuing Education:** Needs support from the organization and the employees. The competition requires that employees adopt a lifelong learning approach. Invest in learning; you own it when you acquire it.
- **Building Succession Competence:** An expectation, not a choice. As the global economy expands, executives needs to come to terms with succession competence across all organizational unite. Focusing on CEO

NOTES

1. James M. Kits, *Doing What Matters*, New York: Crown Publishing Group. 2007, pp. 5–14.
2. Alan Cox, "The homework beyond teamwork," *Industry Week*, January 7, 1991.
3. John C. Redding, *The Radical Team Handbook*, San Francisco, CA: Jossey-Bass, 2000, pp. 5–12.
4. Peter Senge, *The Fifth Discipline*, New York: Doubleday Currency, 1990, pp. 3–25.
5. Peter Senge, *The Fifth Discipline*, New York: Doubleday Currency, 1990, p. 25.
6. David A. S. Thomas and Robin J. Ely, "Making differences matter: a new paradigm for managing diversity," *Harvard Business Review*, September–October, 1996, pp. 3–25.
7. Abraham H. Maslow, *Motivation and Personality*, New York, Harper & Row, 1970.
8. Frederick Herzberg, "One more time: how do you motivate employees?" *Harvard Business Review*, 1986, January 2003, Reprint No. 388X.
9. Douglas McGregor, *The Human Side of Enterprise*, New York: McGraw-Hill, 1960, pp. 3–57.
10. Peter F. Drucker, *The Essential Drucker*, New York: HarperCollins, 2001, pp. 10–13.
11. Henry Mintzberg, "The manager's job: folklore and fact," *Harvard Business Review*, Reprint 90210, p. 12.
12. A. Bennett, "Broken bonds, special early retirement supplement," *The Wall Street Journal*, December 8, 1989, p. R23.
13. H. J. Leavitt, *Corporate Pathfinders*, Homewood, IL: Dow Jones Irwin, 1986, p. 4.

7

DEVELOPING DECISION-MAKING COMPETENCIES

How do people learn to make decisions; what are their sources for learning? Industrial and political history provides many examples of a spectrum of decision-makers at many different levels and under different circumstances. While I have noted that most discussions take place about decision-makers at the highest organizational levels, those decisions seldom have any effect on fulfilling the requirements. Fulfillment of those macro decisions becomes more dependent on decision-making competence of engineers and other discipline specialists and their managers. These are decisions that generally cannot be made by acting out some predetermined business model. There's not much point in arguing which decision level is more or less important, because decisions made by the very highest to the very lowest levels have generated their share of failed results. So, how do the people that span this decision-making continuum learn to make decisions? Like any topic, making decisions will involve more than taking Decision-Making 101. Even deciding to do graduate level work and receiving a PhD in decision-making will not necessarily enhance one's competence in making decisions. We learn like we learn to master any other skill, through experience. Start with the small somewhat inconsequential decisions,

Decisions: An Engineering and Management Perspective, First Edition. Gerard H. Gaynor.
© 2015 The Institute of Electrical and Electronics Engineers, Inc. Published 2015 by John Wiley & Sons, Inc.

learn from the bad decisions, and practice and practice, and learn that decision-making requires practice like any other skill. Learning to make decisions, like any other kind of learning requires dedication to the process and using ones innate sense of the environment in which the decision is made. Many of these decisions, after consideration of the facts, will be influenced by intuition and personal preferences.

Chapter 7 focuses on approaches for developing decision-making capabilities of managers, engineers, and other discipline specialists. I leave the education of executives in decision-making to the academic community and the consultants: they have much work to do. Chapter 7 topics include

- Decision Dilemmas
- Learning to Make Decisions
- Educating for Decision-Making
- Dealing with Ambiguity
- Executing the Deliverables
- Key Points
- Notes

DECISION DILEMMAS

The process of learning how to make effective decisions begins by gaining an understanding of an individual's propensity for making decisions. People eventually make decisions, even though they may struggle in reaching that decision: it's a matter of how long it takes to reach a decision and the confidence level that the appropriate decision resulted from the required level of analysis; whether the decision was appropriate to the situation will be determined at some time in the future. Some people just cannot bring themselves to make timely decisions without a great deal of anxiety. It is not my intent to engage in any psychological analysis as to why some people have difficulties making decisions, but to propose some approaches for improving the process. Making a decision involves accepting responsibility for the decision. It may involve accepting failure and learning from the experience. Accomplishment requires experimentation and experimentation involves living with mistakes and learning from the mistakes that at times can be devastating. Management needs a high level of tolerance of people who make well-intentioned mistakes.

Jim Collins[1] in *Good to Great* explored and analyzed the processes behind key decisions in business history. The general conclusions indicate that the emphasis is not on the "what" but on "whom."

"Lasting excellence in corporations seems to stem less from decisions about strategy than from decisions about people, and seeking consensus is not the way to make the tough calls."

Decisions has considered the histories of the auto industry with bail out of General Motors; the succession of investors in Chrysler that eventually led to a joint investment by the US Government and Fiat of Italy; delays in the Boeing 787 Dreamliner; demise of the icon Eastman Kodak; and others. Did all of these organizations lack a cadre of people, from the executive to the operational level to respond to all the environmental clues? Were they so engrossed with strategic planning or other single-issue management initiatives that they disregarded the fact that strategies are useless unless accompanied by implementation plans? Implementation determines level of success. Were executives and managers so insensitive to the fact that people who may be characteristically independent thinkers and somewhat irreverent were their ticket to success? Did the engineers and the various discipline specialists fail to take the initiative and force the appropriate decisions to the upper management and executive levels? Was taking individual initiative encouraged or suppressed?

So, how do we learn to make decisions? Let's put decision-making in perspective. Collins[2] notes;

"No decision, no matter how big, is any more than a small fraction of the total outcome. Yes, some decisions are much bigger than others, and some are forks in the road. But as far as what determines outcomes, the big decisions are not like 60 of 100 points. They're more like six of 100 points. And there's a whole bunch of others that are like 0.6, or 0.006."

So the success of a decision depends on the cumulative effect of all those micro decisions.

Decision-making, like any activity, begins with making small decisions and learning from them, and especially to begin building a base for making more important and difficult decisions in the future. We can't expect to make multi-million dollar decisions without having made those that only involve thousands of dollars. We can't make a good decision to introduce a new technology unless we understand the technology and its limitations and consequences: it's not just an issue of understanding the technology but its applicability to meeting customer needs. We can't make a good decision to enter a new global market, if we have no experience in recognizing the different cultural needs and the priorities of those cultures. We can't make the decision on building a new manufacturing facility without having made decisions regarding production processes, materials and inventory control, or wrestled with supply chain system requirements. We can't make a decision on hiring a person without having participated in evaluating requirements with senior level professionals and learned how to ask the right questions? We can't make a good decision to purchase an automobile if we haven't made a decision on buying a bicycle, or other sports-related equipment. But, how do we learn to make progressively more important organizational decisions, not only related to finance, technology, marketing, manufacturing, procurement, human resources, distribution, customer service as individual functions, but also when multiple functions are involved? We need to learn the full meaning and the consequences of the term "due diligence."

We come to an organization's decision-making table with various decision-making skills and competencies. Those skills and competencies will range on a continuum from those who lack even the minimum requirements to make timely decisions to those who can make timely decisions with a minimum of information and with great ease. At one end of the continuum, we have those who struggle and delay decisions, and at the opposite end of the continuum, people who are comfortable in making timely decisions and then accepting and living with the consequences. Some will be slow decision-makers, who unnecessarily ponder over the minutest of details to those who, because of experience, make a decision, recognizing that risks are involved and no decision will ever represent the optimal. Arguments will continue about the benefits from quick decision-making but research shows that quick decision-makers make better decisions.

As noted in Chapter 1, Eisenhardt in "Making Fast Strategic Decisions in High-Velocity Environments,"[3] explored some of the factors affecting the speed in decision-making and concluded that fast decision-makers

- use more information than slow decision-makers;
- develop more alternatives;
- recognize that conflict is essential and critical to decision-making;
- integrate strategic and operational plans;
- avoid centralized decision-making which slows the process;
- rapid decision-making is positively related to patterns of emotional, political, and cognitive processes.

Each of these may appear to be almost self-evident. People process information at different rates and much is based on prior knowledge and breadth of experience. At the same time many people, executives, managers, discipline specialists are just not attuned to making decisions. Some people fear failure and often their managements respond inhumanely. Learning to make decisions, like developing any other competence, requires practice. I will continue to repeat that every organization must make provisions for *well-intentioned* failure; this is the real world, and the intent is to make sure that those *well-intentioned* failures are ones the organization can afford.

From this point, gaining decision-making experience depends on whether we take advantage of those often obscure opportunities or hesitate and flee from any opportunity that requires making a choice. In my years of experience, I've seen senior executives delay making a decision on crucial investments with statements such as; it's an excellent program, but now is not the right time to go ahead with it; there's no way we can get approval because the CEO or some top executive would be against it; even though it's a good project, it poses too many risks by introducing new technologies and venturing into new markets; or I'm not willing to take the risk, because I know it won't get approved. I've seen engineering and marketing managers spend weeks deliberating before making a decision, hoping that the answer was available by finding the right crystal ball. There are no crystal balls. I am continually amazed and quite distressed how often engineers and other discipline specialists have difficulty in coming together and making a choice. There's always more that must be known. There are always other directions required for further exploration. Unfortunately most were immersed in computing data to the nth degree of accuracy and couldn't recognize that their decisions only required a range of plus or minus 10 to 15 percent. This difficulty, in reaching a decision, is not just limited to engineers and other discipline specialists; it crosscuts every professional discipline, management levels, and often the executive suites. I've seen people in finance hesitate to make a recommendation, even though the ROI and all the other elements of the analysis were positive. I've witnessed human resource people failing to propose realistic merit-based compensation programs, from fear of possible conflicts with upper level executives, so necessary for organizational sustainability. By the time some people make a decision to engage in any new activity, the competition has captured the marketplace.

Developing a solution to a problem is quite different from making a decision. Decisions involve choosing alternatives and in most organizations, large or small, many different needs require consideration. While decisions usually involve resolving a problem, those problems often present opportunities. At face value, every problem presents opportunities. A malfunction in production equipment, viewed as a deviation from some predetermined standard, presents a problem that must be resolved as quickly as possible. But, it also presents an opportunity. If the problem is resolved temporarily, will it occur again? If so, there's an opportunity to review the situation and take steps to prevent the situation from occurring again. That's the opportunity and it may take many different forms: it may require major redesign; it may require total replacement; it may even require reevaluation of the product line as to its future viability. While the initial issue involved a problem, another look at the problem could suggest future opportunities. A negative response from a customer regarding a product can be viewed as a problem or opportunity. Be thankful for the negative response which allows fixing the problem or disregard it and suffer the consequences. Perhaps others have the same problem. Perhaps a study of the problem with the customer will provide an opportunity to enhance the product's performance. Problems also come about as new information becomes available regarding markets and market segmentation; introducing new technologies; possibilities for global expansion; or outsourcing of non-proprietary activities. What is an organization's response to changes in the economy, changes in national and industry cultures, and changes in natural phenomena that provide for new exploration?

LEARNING TO MAKE DECISIONS

As a manager, how do you begin providing decision-making experiences for those under your supervision? Most likely, by being a role model in how you make decisions or at least how others perceive that you make decisions. Every manager has opportunities for providing learning experiences in making timely decisions. But, too often the manager makes a decision where someone more closely engaged with the task should make the decision. The process requires (1) presenting the issues clearly, (2) creating a situation that fosters debate, (3) intentionally creating some dissonance, if necessary, (4) reaching a timely decision, and (5) managing by consensus. By using a multistep process to resolve a certain class of issues, neophytes can begin learning how to make decisions. No decision can wait until all the facts are gathered and analyzed. It's often difficult to separate fact from fiction. There are ambiguities and uncertainties that need to be considered. But ambiguity is the "X" in many decisions. There is no perfect decision; there is only a best-choice decision that appears to meet the requirements as established by the organization's objectives, operating policies, and procedures. Consider the following five-step process which is not a panacea but a generic approach to the decision-making process.

Present Issues Clearly

Wouldn't this be an expectation? Should it be so difficult? No, but it is. Framing a problem in any discipline or function involves more than noticing a problem and fixing it. One fix after another and after another eventually creates a situation where the original fix is no longer required, but part of it remains in the system and consumes time and energy every day. The easiest way to spot such issues in manufacturing involves doing a thorough process review. Case in point: A group was asked to review an organization's process that included strict manufacturing and safety standards because the devices involved insertion in human beings. The process flow sheets were requested and included several sheets of paper with much of the information comprehensible only to those who knew he process. When the group met to lay out the process, the flip charts began to cover the walls of the conference room. After a full-day of back and forth questioning, the current process flow was clearly delineated. The next day, the discussion focused on how all of these steps got into the process and how they continue to serve a purpose. At the conclusion of the review almost 60 percent of the steps were eliminated. These redundancies not only included production time, but also downtime in process for manual testing. The process review included the reasons for making those many changes that were instituted over a period of 8 years. Over the years, one fix after another was made, without consideration of the previous fixes.

Creating Debate

Referring to the same situation in No. 1, we found a great deal of disagreement among the organization's participants about why each fix was implemented and if it needed to remain. There were tense moments as we tried to elicit responses that would give us confidence that we had the correct information. In such situations, there are people who basically object to outsiders evaluating any of their activities and others who look upon it as a new workload, so it's absolutely necessary to gain sufficient insight from different people. This lack of agreement does not come from any cover up or untruthfulness, but from the philosophical orientation of each person involved. One person may follow a strict practice of eliminating all redundancies and nonessential requirements; while another may take the stand that the particular action doesn't create any problems, so why change it. Someone in upper-level management must say, do it! The fact remains that all organizations find themselves in such situations especially on new product start-ups that the scale-up process will require modifications to the manufacturing process. When you begin to ask, why are we doing this, or why is this step required, or what happens if we eliminate it, you begin to take a serious look at the process. This is where decision-making education and training begins.

Intentionally Creating Dissonance

What do I mean? In any group of people, we always find those who have something they want to say, but for many different reasons will not voice their thoughts or opinions. We also find those who want to dominate and push their particular agenda. We also have managers who fail to reveal the true state of a project; those who are on schedule for 12 months, and in the 13th month need 6 more months to complete the work. Then there are those groups where there is too much agreement and no one raises the burning issues: those issues, known to be potential problems sometime in the future, but not disclosed. These situations are only resolved by the group leader who intentionally creates dissonance by asking the hard and potentially embarrassing questions or having others ask them, to get at the root of the problem. While creating dissonance should not be a matter of standard policy, it serves a need and must be used judiciously and diplomatically. Smart managers read the environment and head off situations that require such actions. Force the issue privately before the meeting and not during the meeting. There's nothing wrong with people agreeing to disagree.

Reaching a Timely Decision

There comes a time, when a decision must be made to accommodate all requirements: technology, markets, manufacturing, the business or any organizational unit within the business. Single-issue management doesn't work. This responsibility could fall to an executive, manager, engineer or other discipline specialist, usually the highest level person. But when we consider the research of Bruch and Ghoshal[4] that showed 30 percent of managers are procrastinators, 20 percent are disengaged, 40 percent are distracted, and only 10 percent are purposeful and focused, our confidence in reaching the appropriate decision decreases significantly. One can argue whether these same percentages apply to engineers and other discipline specialists. While I have only anecdotal evidence that engineers and discipline specialists would fit into the same categories and percentages as managers, it all depends on how we define each of the categories. What constitutes a timely decision depends on the circumstance at the time the decision is made. What may be timely for one person may not be timely for another. Such statistics leave us with little confidence in reaching a timely decision. If you're involved with the 90 percent that lack purpose and focus, reaching the appropriate decision of any kind may be problematic.

Decisions by Consensus

Decision-makers too often attempt to reach a decision by consensus. Such actions diminish the authority and responsibility of the decision-maker and allow the decision-maker to justify failure if it should occur. Much has been written about the pros and cons of consensus decision-making. I suggest there's a significant difference between *reaching a consensus* and *consensus decision-making*. Reaching a consensus depends on seeking all the inputs possible, considering alternatives, deciding on the pros and cons of different scenarios, and then making the decision. The decision then will most likely be made by one individual. Not everyone is expected to have their individual desires satisfied. In consensus decision-making, a group is brought together for discussion of a specific issue, and various solutions are suggested. The ultimate decision must satisfy the group to the greatest extent possible but definitely not all the participants. Too much of consensus decision-making includes extensive hours being allocated for discussing minutiae. Some people have a tendency to fight for the ultimate point to the extent that the collegiality required for consensus decision-making is destroyed.

Any decision-maker, at any level in the organization, has the ultimate responsibility for making a timely and responsive decision. In today's business environment, they receive credit for success and blame for failure, right or wrong that's the situation. While decision-makers do not have the privilege of making arbitrary decisions, they do have a responsibility to gather the information and make the decision. If a group can reach consensus on an approach to resolving an issue, that may be commendable, but not essential. The same applies to engineers and other discipline specialists who may be involved with junior members in reaching a decision.

EDUCATING FOR DECISION-MAKING

Managers play a major role in educating their people about the competencies that are seldom taught in an academic curriculum: they basically accomplish this task through coaching. Some of this coaching may be personal, some may be in groups, but it's a role that cannot be disregarded. Sophisticated tools and techniques might be taught in academia, but not the practice of decision-making that engineers and other discipline specialist require to meet their goals. Most of the time professional specialists provide their specific discipline knowledge, but unless that discipline knowledge is integrated into a team effort, little will be accomplished. It's up to the manager to take all the disparate personal attitudes and characteristics and the skills and experience of many people and mold them into a functionally superior team. That's not an easy task. Each day provides opportunities for managers to develop competencies in decision-making. Looking at the results of Bruch and Ghoshal's research, previously noted, does not provide a great deal of confidence. Perhaps organizational executives need to develop a program to educate the managers. Be that as it may, the education for effective decision-making is a defined responsibility of managers at all levels. While some people may not have any difficulty making decisions, the vast majority feel uncomfortable, especially if the decision involves large sums of money or people.

Presenting the Issue

Much can be learned by asking the right questions and receiving meaningful responses to those questions. The process begins by presenting a current issue and working through the process. The issue must be real and one of immediate interest to the organization and not some hypothetical issue that has no relation to the organization. Consider the following two cases.

Case 1: Realigning an engineering group: A personal experience. I was assigned to head an engineering group that required some realignment. For several years the group failed to meet the organization's expectations. The group included seven supervisors with various levels of capability, but not aligned to build a successful organization. I quickly realized that the supervisors lacked any formal education in what the job of supervision involves. I discussed my situation with a university professor in management and we put together a proposal which I submitted to my management for funding. The proposal was rejected because of the economic situation at the time. I knew that if I did nothing, I'd face the same problems as my predecessor. I put together a self-taught program. My solution: Select seven books related to fundamentals of supervision and assign one book to each supervisor. Each supervisor will read the assigned book and give a book review to the group, followed by a discussion of how the *material relates to the organization's issues.* The assignments were viewed as a stupid idea, a great deal of grumbling about reading a book and giving a review. Realistically, this was quite a challenge to the supervisors. It's easy to talk mathematically, but to explore behavioral issues was quite a different matter. Nevertheless, since I was the department manager, they had no choice but to comply. The meeting for the first book review was scheduled to take place 30 days after the books arrived and would take place weekly on Monday morning for 2 hours or for whatever time required.

The books were assigned and general guidelines adopted; each supervisor would read the book, give the book review, moderate the discussion, and pre-pare a short report on the session. The results of the first meeting brought out many of the issues; no lack of technical competence, but a total lack of under-standing of what it takes to move an idea to a conclusion, when more than one group of people is involved. I chose to sit back, listen, and observe the interac-tions of the participants. While the first book review left something to be desired, the discussions that followed began the learning process. *Real work* issues came forward that demonstrated the problems within the department. After 7 weeks of intensive Monday morning discussions the mindset of the group began to change. An inexpensive supervisory development program, focused on the department's real issues, eventually became exceedingly realistic and was a first attempt at developing competent managers. In later years, these supervisors, who over the years faced many challenging assignments and ascended in the organization's management, concluded that this simple program was the best management development they ever experienced. The training was based on resolving real issues, and at the same time provided the fundamentals required for effective supervision.

Case 2: Meeting design requirements: Consider the decision where the machine design group is asked to propose the design for a new automated process and the associated equipment to assemble eight components, each weighing less than 3 ounces, at a theoretical rate of 60 per minute. The details regarding part size, while important are irrelevant at this time. Four of the eight parts would be considered high precision; the other four parts must meet generally accepted production tolerances. The assembly process also included showing product characteristics and labeling of batch and dates, and other imprinted information related to future processing by the customer. Current assembly speeds were limited to 10 per minute and assembly must be accomplished in closely controlled environmental conditions.

The request to study the possibilities of designing the above described machine was presented to the machine design group by a newly appointed business unit manager. Within 2 weeks the response came back, impossible. There is no way that the described task could be accomplished with a single machine. Engineering concluded that 20 assemblies per minute would be the upper limit. The business unit manager called for a meeting of the automation group to discuss their decision regarding the technical limitations of fulfilling this request.

After a short introduction of the issues, the engineers began to make their case regarding the impossibility of increasing productions rates beyond 20 assemblies per minute. The engineers raised the issues related to design, machine dynamics, tolerances, static, environmental conditions, machine integration, and flexibility for different configurations. The manager suggested that they consider each of these issues independently. The following conversations followed.

Engineers	The engineers gave a clear description of the machine concept and much discussion followed. There was a discussion of why certain types of controls were given preference, direct drive automation, types of materials, assembly complexity, potential maintenance problems, and all the other factors that would be included in such a discussion. The automation group focused on the dynamics of the mechanical systems that would be the primary difficulty.
Manager	The manager asked about the differences of this concept from what's used in the present 10 assemblies per minute machines. The concept presented by the engineers was based on the current design and the redesign of certain machine parts, making provisions for speeding up the present machine concept, and making relatively minor modifications. The manager raised concerns about *the machine dynamics*.
Engineers	Machine dynamics will not permit assembling at 60 per minute on a single machine. There are just too many interacting machine components to provide reliable equipment.

Manager   The manager followed with series of questions. What do you
                 mean by dynamics and where? What led you to conclude
                 that 20 assemblies per minute was the practical limit? Do
                 you have any data from past tests that you ran on the current
                 machines that led you to the conclusion? You mentioned
                 tolerances of component parts as an issue in the assembly
                 process, can you identify the specific parts? Our current
                 machines operate at 10 per minute; did you ever try to gain
                 any additional output from them, say, 12 or 13 per minute?
                 Are the parts fed at random or do they come to the machine
                 ready to pick and place?

Engineers   They're fed through our usual pick and place mechanisms.
                 Some parts need to be held to tolerances of + or −0.0001
                 inch and the rest are the usual + or −0.001 inch. The 0.0001
                 parts are the problem because they must be located accu-
                 rately or otherwise the assembly will not meet requirements.
                 We also have one of the parts made from a composite
                 that also has critical tolerances, and must be fitted during
                 assembly.

Manager   What can you do to eliminate the fitting operation? Is this the
                 primary operation that limits the speed of assembly? Do we
                 have evidence that the high tolerances are essential? Is there
                 any way of redesigning around the high tolerances, even
                 though additional costs may be involved in the assembly
                 operation? While tolerances do play a major role in the
                 assembly process, what can be done to modify the design to
                 work within the + or −0.001 inch tolerance range? Should
                 we completely reevaluate the design? You mentioned the
                 issue of static, what are the issues?

Engineers   Generation of static is a common problem not only in this
                 case, but in most of the work in this plant. Static discharges
                 increase significantly as speed increases and the use of static
                 discharging devices does not reduce static to the minimum
                 required levels.

Manager   Do you have any recent test data to show what the static limits
                 might be? If not, what do you have to do to determine the
                 limits? Have you recently tested the new types of polymer
                 compositions for static generated and at what speeds? What
                 are the possibilities of substituting other materials or other
                 compositions of similar materials? Can the static problem
                 be minimized, if you change the environmental conditions,

	such as changing the dew point? You also mentioned that machine fabricators would not undertake the building of a 60 per minute per machine.
Engineers	Integrating all the machine functions into an operable and efficient machine will involve some designs that have not been undertaken by others in the machine-tool industry.
Manager	If the machine design and build firms we work with can't do what we'd expect, maybe we need to engage some new suppliers? We've worked with the same suppliers for many years; you might consider investigating new suppliers. Are any of the current parts or subassemblies capable at operating continually at the required machine rate? Which subassemblies are an absolute "no" and which are possible. Let's identify them. Are the data available to show limitations? Why the reticence to explore totally new approaches? If we don't, our competitors will.
Engineers	It's impossible to meet the manufacturing schedule for other products and projects if a new design is contemplated and introduced.
Manager	What brings you to this conclusion? Do we lack adequate staff and if so in what areas? Maybe there are certain programs that could be delayed. Are the concerns related to potential start-up problems? What does it take to define the specific issues that prevent us from meeting production schedules? What do we have to do to resolve the issues and still go forward with a new design? Can you be more specific about all of these issues? It's difficult to make a decision without any facts.

The engineers continued to took a stand that assembling at 60 units per minute was impossible: if not a stand against the concept, at least not willing to accept the responsibility. These questions asked by the manager may seem to be frivolous recognizing that the engineers are well qualified in these areas. But engineers, like all other people, have blind spots and often take the path of least resistance. Do we really want to come up with a totally new design and fight the scale-up problems of the equipment one more time? Everyone clearly understands the problems associated with bringing any new process online, independent of its complexities. The simplest of new processes includes headaches, not foreseen in the design.

The manager came to a conclusion: forget about the current design and begin thinking about a totally new concept. Start with a blank sheet of paper and look for new approaches that allow operating at high speed and at the same time resolve all the issues raised during the interchange.

The engineers immediately brought up the issue of insufficient staff; inability to meet projected schedules; delay of other projects unless additional people were assigned or hired; test runs to debug the new machine would be costly; adding new materials would require qualification and certification; and the list continued. To be sure, the engineers' comments would be supported by manufacturing because manufacturing clearly understands the cost associated with introducing new equipment. Relatively few executives and not too many managers are aware of what it takes to scale up a new process. The manager interrupted; he told the engineers, start over, and tell me what we need to do to develop a machine that produces assemblies at 60 per minute. Just tell me what you need and let's stop discussing the issue; it's time to get to work. Within 6 months and many interim discussions with the manager, the engineers returned with a proposal for a machine that would produce 60 assemblies per minute.

What does this case tell us about making decisions? It's very easy to make decisions on Case 2, looking at it from a macro perspective without considering all the details involved in the design, construction of the machine, its scale up, and meeting production requirements. It's very easy to look to the past, and continue with a design that's been proven over years of experience. And there's good reason to ask, why change the design, if what's available works? There are two perspectives, an engineering perspective and a business perspective, Why object to three 20 assemblies per minute machines versus one machine at 60 assemblies per minute? Basically, three machines require three crews instead of one, scale up of three machines instead of one, plus all the services that go with the additional space requirements. Further, competition has been steadily improving their output per machine.

After that macro decision is made though, the countless number of decisions involve understanding the requirements and the technologies involved; doing the design to meet the requirements; choosing from suggested alternative designs; selecting materials based on limitation of specific operational parameters; designing the assembly processes; and considering the other requirements to integrate the new machine into a workable production system. It requires thinking which is complex and time consuming: solutions do not come from 2-hour brainstorming sessions. The design involves more than the machine: it requires the definition and design and development of all the ancillary functions that allow the new machine to function and meet requirements and integration into the business system. These functions include parts processing and testing, prototyping designs of any mechanical or control actions, and making revisions as new data is presented.

DEALING WITH AMBIGUITY

Teaching and learning are different sides of the same coin; professors' lecture and students are expected to absorb. But such teaching does not develop skills in any discipline, especially decision-making. Coleen Burke[4], a businesswoman related her story as she tried to become a teacher.

Coleen and Richard, an artist, were neighbors and shared a property boundary with a cluster of tulips on Richard's side but with the flowers overflowing on Coleen's property. One day she was describing to Richard, how she attempted to convince her students to go beyond the outline of a situation, and deal with the subtleties and ambiguities, Richard asked her to describe the tulips.

Colleen said the tulips were white, paused and looked a bit harder and continued to ponder the bed of flowers. Were they really white, maybe they weren't white, maybe they were a blue-gray, or a bleached coral, and perhaps a complete range of colors. In the shape, she saw overlapping petals that created shadows, non-forms, and finally considered the subtleties of the individual petals, the stamen, and the interwoven cluster. Colleen thought about her students; was it this difficult for them to comprehend what she was attempting to teach. How does this experience reflect on the subtleties involved in teaching organizational behavior? Did Colleen's original lack of excitement about the tulips, reflect the attitude of her students as she attempted to convince them about the benefits of putting human behavior into a mathematical box? Were the students threatened by ambiguity, the unknown, and the need to understand the complexities of dealing with human behavior? Reflecting on the experience, Colleen concluded that she will never again see a white tulip as a white tulip, and hopes her students will never again see a simple group as a simple group. She will not ask her students to see everything in such detail, but will introduce them to the complexity of a situation and focus on the specifics as well. This is not the end of this story.

Colleen asked herself, how teachers communicate the skills of seeing, analyzing, measuring, interpreting, and presenting; all the basics involved in reaching a decision. Colleen enrolled into an elementary painting class to see if she could learn anything that would apply to her teaching activities. Being an adult, she arrogantly skipped over the prerequisite basic courses in three dimensional designs. Colleen's first assignment was to paint a still life of crumpled tinfoil. She attacked the canvas with resolve and after many attempts could not interpret or present what she was looking at. She tried a mixture of colors, but the canvas never saw the crumpled tinfoil. The various geometric surfaces did not come to light. Colleen, once again, asked herself, is this how my students feel when I ask them to deal with ambiguity.

After three hours Colleen went to teach her class of 25 freshmen who had just read a handout on structural analysis of industries. The students looked as though they were given a piece of crumpled tinfoil. She concluded that to understand teaching, one must experience being a student of the foreign. Colleen contemplated the need for students to develop a sense of humor and perspective, she asked herself, can her students be comfortable with the shades of gray; can she teach them their mix of colors; can she guide them to develop a sense perspective as a skill and not by accident.

The environment in the art studio was quite different from the classroom in which Colleen tried to challenge her students. No standing teacher and sitting students. Students wander around, exchange insights, go back to their canvas, make mistakes, much trial and error, and eventually interpret, present, and learn within themselves. Grading of the interpretations is a social event. After each assignment of the same subject, students sit on the floor and critique each other's work. With the instructor they first look at the successes in each canvas in a constructive exchange. The teacher seldom teaches, but when called to my canvas, he explained what I was doing wrong and urged me to "lay on the color" which Colleen does not understand. Eventually Colleen understands. As time goes on, Colleen becomes bolder and more subtle in her rendition. In Colleen's business class, such actions would be considered dumb, scary, and risky. She now asks herself, what assignments she can give her business students to see the grays between the black and white analyses and learn through experiencing.

As Colleen reflected on how the painting course reinforced the student's responsibility for learning, she realized the amount of student interaction, spontaneous communication, constructive criticism, and experimentation that took place in contrast to her business classes. The art studio was filled with learning; mistakes were made accepted and encouraged, critiques were welcomed. How would she bring this perspective to her business students?

Why this story! We do not learn to make decisions by listening to a teacher lecturing on the subject. We learn to make decisions by asking questions of ourselves as well as of others. As with Colleen's students, decisions involve dealing with ambiguity, dealing with the unknown, the unpredictable—that's when we enter the danger zone. It's our responsibility to learn how to make decisions, to understand the basics, to interact with colleagues, to communicate, accept constructive critiques, experiment, learn, make mistakes, learn more, make more well-intentioned mistakes, search for the facts, integrate information from many sources, ask and respond to questions, and learn to make decisions with a minimum of information, since all the required information will never be available.

The following personal vignette provides an example of a learning experience. As a young boy at the age of 16, I took a part time job painting storm sash for 15 cents per hour. Storm sash, once a major industry before the appearance of thermo pane windows, are basically windows placed over an existing window, as a barrier to the effects of cold winter weather. The glass was built into a wooden frame and was usually inserted for the winter and removed in the spring. Some windows were single pane and others divided into multiple sections of glass. The glass was secured to the frame with triangular metal clips, and the contact area between the glass and the frame filled with putty. I was confident that I could do the work, and told the owner of my expertise. Since I had painted storm sash at home, I was obviously qualified for greater opportunities in the world of painting storm sash.

I worked for 4 hours the first day and felt proud of my accomplishments. When I returned the second day, the owner confronted me and asked where I learned to paint. I explained in detail. He was not happy with my painting ability. He showed me the windows that I had painted, and asked me how long I thought it would take to remove all the paint that I managed to put on the glass, and what the paint on the glass would do to the bond between the putty and glass. He then suggested I begin removing the paint from the glass, and informed me that I would not be paid for the time it took for removing the paint. I spent 4 hours the previous day painting the sash, and then 3 hours removing paint from the glass. I then told the owner that I completed the clean-up. He asked me if I wanted to continue to work, and if I did, he'd teach me how to paint storm sash.

The owner brought out a new window, the paint, and the brush and the learning experience began. He showed me how to hold a brush properly, how to dip the brush in the paint, and how to remove the excess paint to make sure there was sufficient paint on the brush, but not any excess. He then began painting the areas where the glass joins the putty. I stood there and could not believe what he did; not a drop of paint on the glass. He then asked me if I was ready to learn, which I was. He didn't ask me to paint. He took my right hand in his and together we began the process. We went through the process several times, and he then suggested, I try it without any assistance. He left me on my own to practice and in about 15 minutes, I was on my way to becoming a real pro. The owner came over to inspect what I had done and was very pleased with my work. He told me he'd pay me for the time it took to remove the paint from the previous day's effort and I continued to paint for 15 cents per hour. As different paint formulations were introduced, I was taught what kinds of brushes were required on what types of wood and some of the nuances that required consideration.

Why this story! This was a learning experience for me. The owner took the time to go through the steps and provide the training I needed to meet his expectations. The same type of learning applies to decision-making. While the decision-making process is mental, there are steps that must be learned to become effective in making decisions. This is not to suggest that decision-making occurs by the numbers and if you follow the process you'll necessarily reach the correct decision; it is this kind of taking by the hand and walking a person through the process that enables a person to begin making decisions with some level of confidence. That process needs to start at an early age. It's never too late to begin the process, but preferably long before the day your name is called to receive your degree. At the same time we must be cognizant of the fact that some people may not reach conclusions to their satisfaction to make a timely decision. The question not only involves making a decision, but making a decision in a timely manner.

EXECUTING THE DELIVERABLES

Projects fail to meet performance requirements because of (1) incompetent management, (2) inadequate level of the required competencies, (3) lack of alignment on objectives, and (4) inattention to details. While the big picture decision leaves all with a sense of euphoria, the next morning brings the project realities to life. Often, discipline specialists from all functions, who really put the proposal details into a saleable package, now begin to reassess and redesign. Such actions start the project down the wrong path and a competent project manager would immediately put a stop to the changes. If the changes were necessary, the people or the group that approved the project must be informed. Obviously this depends on the scope of changes, but such actions tend to expand as a project progresses. Executives and upper level managers do not like surprises. It's better to face such situations when they occur. The problem begins when the changes are not reflected in the cost or schedule. I'm not speaking of minor changes, but changes that affect other organizational functions or add cost and time to delivery. There was a commitment made for certain deliverables and those commitments need to be acknowledged and met. This section deals with executing the deliverables and raises the issues related to Support for Business Strategies, Project Objectives, Project Scope, Project Importance, Project Manager, Project Staffing, Project Cost, Research, Technology, Marketing and Sales, and People Decisions. The questions require making a timely decision: learning to make decisions begins by responding to questions and then implementing the responses asked in the questioning process.

Support of Business Strategies: There is no doubt that an organization's strategic directions supplemented with supporting operational plans allow it to meet its performance objectives. But strategic directions, like the accompanied operational plans, must relate to the real world. Facts and only facts from all the organization's functions! But are the financials real or made to fit some predetermined algorithm? Are there two sets of financials, one internal and the other for Wall Street?

Questions: Do objectives support the organization's business strategies and those of the business units? Assuming that the organization's strategies have been updated, do they also include the strategic directions related to research, product development, and manufacturing? If any of these strategic directions were changed in some respect, would the project objectives continue to be viable? Would costs need to be reevaluated? Where does the organization fit in relation to its competitors, not only in marketing, but in research, product development, and manufacturing, distribution systems, revenue, profits, and ROI?

Project Objectives: Developing objectives for any activity provides a means for directing resources in an effective and efficient manner, and then measuring performance against projections. But those objectives need to be considered within the capability of the organization's resources and infrastructure.

Questions: Are project objectives stated in clear and unmistakable language? Are all those sub-objectives clearly stated? Are they translated into language everyone understands? Do all the participants involved in fulfilling the objective fully understand the what, the why, the how, who, when, and where? Responses to these questions must be answered at the time objectives are defined.

Project Scope: Projects seldom include one discipline or organizational function. A change in any one aspect of a project inevitably requires changes in other parts of the project. Projects can originate in any organizational function; research, product development, marketing, and manufacturing, but live in the organization's project management world.

Questions: Is this a technology project, market project, or a business project? If a technology project, can the potential new products or services be projected? If a market project, can sales projections be made within acceptable levels of accuracy? Customers are important, but customers' users must be identified since they are far more important. If a project affects customer's employees' in the future, has input been considered from the employee's perspective? If this is a business project, what is the driving force?

Project Importance: Achieving business objectives requires setting priorities. Not all ideas can be considered. Financial resources are limited. People resources are limited. Timing and introduction to the marketplace determines not only amount of generated revenue but more importantly net income.

Questions: The major question, does the project meet the fields of interest of the organization and if not should it be considered? Why is this project important? Is it necessary? What does it do for the organization? What are the expected unique results? Is it a me-too project: a competitive catch-up project; does it leapfrog current generation of competitive products? Would it be more appropriate to include this project with others for a longer-range project with greater benefits? If the project failed what could be salvaged that was of real value? What are the consequences if the project is not approved?

Project Manager: The choice of a project manager (PM) depends on the scope of the project. A PM who may have the capability to build a new manufacturing facility may not have the ability to manage the plant checkout. A PM with experience in managing microchip projects may not have the competence to manage the design and construction of an automated assembly line. So PMs must be selected based on the needs of the project. An excellent track record with experience in a totally unrelated field may not be of value.

Questions: Is there a project manager with the credentials plus the experience and a track record in successful project management? Have the requirements been identified for the various functions such as research, product development, marketing, and manufacturing? What unique expertise does this project manager need: requirements would be quite different if this was a project that crossed international boundaries? Could the assigned project manager resolve conflicts that occur among functional interfaces? Does the project manager bring a balanced perspective to the project; ability to understand the language of other disciplines? If you think this is not a problem, think again and recall your own past experiences. Is the project manager business oriented? Can the selected manager function in an interdisciplinary and multifunctional environment? Can the selected project manager instill the essential discipline in meeting commitments and at the same time develop an environment that stimulates innovation, dedication to the project, and strive for excellence? If the credentials, experience, and track record of the assigned project manager do not meet requirements, how does management compensate for the deficiencies?

Project Staffing: Project staffing requires critical thought before making assignments. Lack of appropriate project staff often plays a role in the high percentage of projects that fail to meet requirements, schedule, and cost projections. Developing the team cannot begin at the start of a project. There is no doubt that people react and relate differently with colleagues, peers, and their managers, and especially in situations where time for completion requires paramount attention. A qualified project manager knows how to bring people together and if someone creates too many difficulties the project manager has no alternative but to take appropriate action.

Questions: Are staff needs fully defined? Will project require new skills in research, product development, marketing, and manufacturing and other functions? Is staff available either internally or from outside the organization? Are specific knowledge and experience levels of expertise defined? Are they available? Have the required competencies been demonstrated through past performance? Do the recommended project participants have a track record of project performance? Are the various functional groups capable of interfacing effectively?

Project Cost: Project cost under any circumstances will always be an issue. The financial barrel does have a bottom. But those costs must be realistic. We all know about the horrendous cost overruns on not only government projects but those in academia and industry. The major problem about costing arises from organizations setting financial targets, and those of us who have been project leaders know how to respond to such dictums: if management demands a specific ROI they'll always get it, they know what we're doing, and they go along with us. Such approaches to estimating cost seem ludicrous and upper management should understand the folly of establishing such criteria. But, that's the way it is.

Questions: What are the new capital requirements? Are all those overhead items included? Are all costs related to necessary research in all disciplines and functions included? Are the marketing and sales organizations in place? Does the product need a new or modified distribution system, from order entry to customer delivery and customer service? If not, what are the alternatives? What are the potential product liabilities? What are the costs associated with meeting governmental policies, laws, and taxes at the federal, state, and local levels? Does the project meet the organization's financial targets and are those targets realistic? What are the total costs? Who developed the costs? Engineers please note, the only cost estimates the major organizations depend on are those that come from the finance department, so work with them to gain a full understanding of the cost.

Research: Investing in research, in its many different forms, determines the future of most organizations; it keeps the organization on the leading edge in its industry or relegates it to a has-been organization, or may even lead to its demise. But research operations must be managed effectively and efficiently: that means not only doing the research, but documenting it in readable terms so the benefits can be recognized. The level of project success would increase if all organizational functions operated using the project management approach.

Questions: Why does a research department exist? What are its limitations? How much freedom are researchers given to explore new opportunities? What has been the past payoff from investments in research? Could cost of research be reduced by joining forces with other organizations? Likewise, could time to completion be reduced? The same question can be asked of related activities from engineering, manufacturing process engineering, marketing, etc.? Were the pros and cons of using other organizations analyzed realistically or was it just easier to justify doing everything in-house? Has the research department built relationships with appropriate academic communities?

Technology: Technology usually drives growth. However, adopting the latest technologies, those leading-edge technologies, may not be the most effective. It may be better to adopt technologies that are adequate: the ones that only meet the requirements.

Questions: So does the proposed activity leverage the organizational technology bank? Are the technologies understood by those who will use them? Can the benefits of these technologies be clearly delineated? What is the "value added" by using the technology bank? Is it time to review the technology bank for its relation to competitors? Are any of the technologies proprietary? Are they covered by patents? What technologies could competitors develop to achieve the same or better result? Are the technologies applicable globally? What are the specific technologies to be used? Are the known and unknown aspects of the technologies clearly stated: are those unknown aspects identified? What problems exist without a solution?

Marketing and Sales: Research and product development activities provide no useful organizational benefit unless their results meet the expectations of marketplace needs or wants. So marketing and sales become responsible for making the results of research and product development a success and provide a benefit to the organization.

Questions: Who are the people making the marketing decisions? Are they well-educated neophytes or experienced marketers with an experiential understanding of the market sectors involved? Are they focused on marketing statistics or innovation and bringing new products and services to the marketplace? Does the sales force possess the necessary competence and experience to promote the new product? Are customer service specialists in place to respond intelligently to customers' problems? Will special accommodations be made to meet global requirements? Who are the customers? How many new customers are required to meet sales projections?

People Decisions: Overall performance in either individual or group activity depends more on the people involved than any other factor. Funding, while important, will not provide the expected result without the required people competencies. The attributes including knowledge, experience, skills, attitudes, and characteristics that each person brings to the table determine the success of any venture. While no one person may possess all the desirable attributes, the collective attributes of the group must reach some minimum acceptable standards. What questions can be asked to determine if a person possesses the required attributes? First, consider the specific position requirements. Not every position requires the same complement of attributes. The attributes required for managing a major project such as the construction of a major airport are quite different from those required for developing a new-age aircraft, or developing the next computer chip. In reviewing attributes, I suggest that academic credentials after 5 years of experience tell very little about a persons' competency. Consider the following questions related to knowledge, experience, skills, attitudes, and characteristics that each person brings to the table: they determine your potential for success of any venture.

Knowledge Questions

What are specific complementary needs of the project? Does the project require a specialist in some narrow field of technology, marketing, or finance; someone with cross-disciplinary knowledge; a specialist who also brings some business sense to the issues; a tinkerer, but one who tinkers with discipline; a person able to become knowledgeable on the issues facing the organization in the future; someone who requires structured and formal education or one who follows the self-learner approach? Does the effort need someone with a PhD, an MBA with experience, a college graduate educated in the practice of the discipline, or a Bill Gates who dropped out of college to build one of the major US corporations?

Experience Questions

Does the function involve a specialist or someone with breadth of experience? Some people can function exceedingly well in their own discipline, and also have some sense of the requirements of other disciplines? Should engineers understand something about how their product designs are accepted in the marketplace? Should marketers be comfortable in discussing the technologies involved in the products they promote? Where did the experience come from? How was it acquired? What were the consequences of gaining the particular experience? What was the value-added component? How did the experience affect the results? Was the experience gained during working in the primary discipline; from interacting with related disciplines; from participating in business activities; from observing the consequences of interdisciplinary activity; from an avocation that somehow provided insight?

Skills Questions

We all work within a system that professes a mission with certain visions, and values. Availability of the required skill sets determines the results. What are the expectations? Leadership, considered an essential for managers, is equally a requirement for the engineers and other discipline specialists. Has the person under consideration demonstrated leadership in his primary discipline and in related disciplines? Is there evidence that shows the person communicates effectively? Can you gain a glimpse of how this person thinks, through a narrow lens or wide-angle lens? Is the person a problem solver, problem finder, or problem solver and finder? Does the person know how to work in a project and team environment? Can the person influence others? How will this person react when put in a position to make choices?

Attitude Questions

You have probably heard on many occasions that it's all about attitude. Maybe not always, but often attitude does make the difference between success and failure. What kind of mindset does the person bring to the organization, positive, negative, or thoughtful? Does the person display a level of arrogance that could destroy the cohesiveness of a group? Will the person avoid conflict or face up to the differences and resolve them? Does the person display any passion about a particular issue? How would the person respond to criticism? You determine this by searching for clues during discussions. Is this person willing to join the organization to be a leader or sit on the sidelines?

Characteristics Questions

Personal characteristics include integrity, dedication, honesty, energy and drive, thoughtfulness, respect for others, curious, tenacious, persistent, agile, focused, flexible, reliable, and proactive. Has the person demonstrated high ethical and moral principles? Does the person's past history show dedication to any project in the past? Honesty cannot be compromised, so have you decided that your discussion has been based on truthful comments? Has the person provided thoughtful responses or canned answers throughout the discussion; shown respect for colleagues and peers? Curiosity drives innovation; does this person bring a mindset that focuses on future events? Tenacity and persistency are two overlapping characteristics: holding on to an idea and pursuing it and continuing as long as there's a light at the end of the tunnel. How do you judge such characteristics as agility, focus, flexibility, reliability, and being proactive? Ask the right questions. For agility, develop a scenario and ask the person to respond. That scenario might simply provide a situation that requires a person with agility to meet the requirements. Agility becomes important because too often managers hear grumbling like, why is she changing priorities. Priorities often need to be changed and thus accommodated. You determine focus during a discussion by determining how often the person deviates from the subject at hand. You develop an understanding of a person's flexibility by asking questions related to future opportunities and asking for a response. As an example, would you consider Foreign Service for three years? Would you relocate within your country's national boundaries? Reliability is a characteristic that drives results, it's absolutely essential. It means doing what you said you'd do regardless of any inconvenience. It means meeting requirements, schedules, and costs. But how do you determine reliability? Delve into the past history regarding performance. The level to which a person may be proactive can be revealed through a review of the person's employment record. What's in that record that shows that the person took personal initiative without being asked?

KEY POINTS

- Learning to make decisions doesn't occur by the numbers or through some algorithm: start early in life; understand the available facts; make the decision, if you made the right decision, fine, if not learn from the mistakes; try again, fail, learn and restart the process. Just make sure the mistakes aren't too big.

- Project success depends on the cumulative impact of all the decisions beginning with the macro decision that authorized the project. Each contributes or detracts from meeting requirements.
- Take advantage of every opportunity that presents itself to make an important decision. Bring all your experience and knowledge into the decision process. Every decision involves some level of intuition: all the facts will never be available and will change throughout the life of a project.
- Educating to make decisions begins and takes place in the normal activities associated with the organization. Executives work with managers, managers by working with their engineers and discipline specialists while performing daily activities.
- Managers teach and learn while clearly defining issues to be resolved, creating debate on issues, intentionally creating dissonance if the group doesn't face up to the issues, and taking the various comments into consideration and making the decision. Consensus management only works with disciplined groups who speak with knowledge.
- Take advantage of the teaching moments when major issues are under consideration: asking the questions shows those involved the process by which a decision can be reached.
- Success of any activity depends on the knowledge base, the lifelong experiences, the particular skills, both the good and the not so good attitudes, and the sometimes offensive personal characteristics to the workplace. Don't look for the ideal, it doesn't exist.

NOTES

1. Jim Collins, Collins on tough calls, *Fortune*, June 7, 2007.
2. Ibid. Collins on tough calls.
3. Kathleen M. Eisenhardt, "Making fast strategic decision in high-velocity environments," *Academy of Management Journal*, 32(3): 743–776, 1989.
4. C. Roland Christensen, David A. Garvin, and Ann Sweet, *Education for Judgment: The Artistry of Discussion Leadership*, (Harvard Business School Press, 1991), pp. 37-48.

8

IBM ROCHESTER, MINNESOTA: THE SILVERLAKE PROJECT

The history of IBM Rochester (IBMR) began in 1956, when IBM President Thomas Watson Jr. arrived in Rochester, Minnesota, to announce the company's intention to build a manufacturing plant. At the time, Rochester, MN, a city of about 70,000 people, was dominated by the Mayo Clinic. The IBMR site included 401 acres of prairie grass, a few structures, a windmill, and a barn: it would eventually became home to 8,000 engineers; programmers; marketers; managers; manufacturing facilities; and all the support units required by any industrial enterprise.

The Silverlake Project[1] (code name) story tells us how a group of engineers, programmers, and planners, totaling about 2,500, transformed themselves from a technologically driven laboratory, into a customer-focused and market-driven organization. This transformation of IBMR shows the role of decision-making, at many levels in the IBM organization, in meeting organizational expectations, creating a major change in organizational culture, and taking full advantage of the competencies of the available talent. The transformation began when Tom Furey came to Rochester as manager of the IBMR Development Lab. This is a story of decision-making, which integrates the activities of the technology

Decisions: An Engineering and Management Perspective, First Edition. Gerard H. Gaynor.
© 2015 The Institute of Electrical and Electronics Engineers, Inc. Published 2015 by John Wiley & Sons, Inc.

and marketing functions, on their journey from success, to overpowering by competitors, to building one of IBM's most successful businesses. Chapter 8 topics include

- Birth of IBMR Minnesota
- Project Fort Knox
- IBMR Faces Market Challenges
- New Directions for IBM Rochester
- Furey Asks the Hard Questions
- Ambitious Goals
- Market Launch
- Lessons Learned
- Key Points
- Notes

BIRTH OF IBMR MINNESOTA

IBMR entered computer manufacturing in 1966, when a group of engineers designed a card reader that included a processor. IBMR began making readers for punched cards that today are only a memory. The Rochester operation grew as engineers and software developers created a steady stream of well-received computers for small- and medium-sized businesses. These developments gave IBMR a base of electronics expertise, so when IBM decided to make a computer for small- to medium-sized businesses, IBMR was tapped to be the source. Subsequently, IBMR gave birth to the System/3 in 1969 for a computer that met the requirements for small businesses. Successor machines included: the System/32 in 1975, System/34 in 1977, System/38 in 1979, and System/36 in 1983. System/38 embodied major advances, which made programmers 7 to 10 times more productive. However, many of its capabilities were not appreciated by the marketplace. According to the authors, System/38 was too elegant; it was not compatible with the System/3 and the System/34 software. However, System/38 did become the choice of sophisticated users and the engineers and programmers who created it.

IBMR was successful: it delivered on time. Morale was high and overtime exceeded as much as 20 percent. IBMR reached a point where it became one of the largest computer companies, only exceeded in size, by IBM its parent. Rochester was so far from White Plains, NY, the IBM Headquarters, that seldom, if ever, did executives take the opportunity to visit an organizational unit that met its sales and profit targets year after year. IBM Headquarters left them alone.

As the authors note, they lived in "relative obscurity; they left us alone and we kept to ourselves."[2]

Competition

As often happens, all good things come to an end. Current products were losing competitive position, and no breakthrough replacements were on the drawing boards. IBMR came under siege from many competitors: Hewlett-Packard, Wang Laboratories, Data General, Tandem, NCR, and Digital Equipment Corporation (DEC).[3] While DEC focused on scientific, engineering, and other technical applications, that success led them to enter the commercial markets. DEC had a definite advantage because of its compatible structure to work and share data with mainframes, mid-range computers, and personal computers.

PROJECT FORT KNOX

In its attempt to recapture the mid-size market, IBM Headquarters, in 1982, approved project Fort Knox (project code name), and IBMR's Development Lab became home for the project. The purpose of Fort Knox was to develop a single successor to IBM's diverse range of mid-range computers with an emphasis on meeting system compatibility requirements. This was a top-down decision coming from IBM Headquarters. While simple in concept, it turned out to be a nightmare. As the authors note, "Fort Knox would have been tantamount to combining the features of a sports car, a station wagon, a compact, a luxury car, and a pickup truck into a single all-appealing vehicle."[4] IBM decided to drive Fort Knox from headquarters.

At one time the Fort Knox project included almost 4,000 people at Rochester and three other IBM Development Labs. Each site became attached to its designs and machines. Fort Knox reached the state, where jokes were common, "We really believe in multi-site development. We wish all our competitors would use it."[5]

The failure of Fort Knox left the IBMR staff with a feeling that they had "something to prove." There were many reasons for the failure of Fort Knox and they all relate to decision-making: justification for the project was questionable; too much top-level decision-making; combining the requirements of too many machines into one; using multiple sites with control from headquarters, yet with no control; lack of adequate leadership; delays and rework; ineffective coordination between engineers and programmers working in different locations; and relieving those who criticized the project of their responsibilities and sending them to technological Siberia. Fort Knox never received buy-in from the cooperating organizational units. IBM Headquarters decided that System/36 would be the machine that challenges the competition in office automation; declared System/38 as nonstrategic, leaving 20,000 customers without any future upgrades.

IBMR FACES MARKET CHALLENGES

It's 1985 and IBMR was in trouble. Times were changing. The economy changed, new professional skills entered the picture, and knowledge workers would not perform very well under a *command and control* system of management. According to the authors, managers were expected to be technically knowledgeable and capable of "authoritatively addressing" all technical questions. Relying on technical experts was seen as a sign of weakness. IBM failed to mutate the command and control philosophy to an operation where managers made the business-related decisions, and the experts made the technical decisions.

Even more disturbing was the fact that in spite of meeting their sales and profits numbers the Development Lab was ranked in the lower third of the 15 IBM development sites when measured on "technical vitality." IBMR applied for fewer patents, had only one Senior Technical Staff Member, and no IBM Fellows. The Development Lab and manufacturing were organized as two independent entities, both part of a business, but not the IBMR business and this would create problems as Silverlake grows in importance.

There really didn't appear to be any great excitement over what engineers and programmers were doing. Jobs were at stake. But, as usual someone in the depths of the organization comes up with the big idea. Hansen, an experienced engineer and software programmer and not exactly an "organization man" type, made a pitch to launch a new machine. Hansen was given approval to develop a skunk works, with four other people that included a hardware product designer, a product planner with the competence to convert customer needs into product features, a reticent technological thinker, and a former innovative IBM salesman. This was the beginning of what will eventually be code named the Silverlake Project. The Silverlake Project was now official. It would cost about one billion and be developed within 3 years. IBM Headquarters gave its approval, but this effort, unlike the Fort Knox project, comes from the guts of the organization and not the top.

NEW DIRECTIONS FOR IBM ROCHESTER

Steve Schwartz from IBM Headquarters, to whom IBMR reported and was known for his wide-ranging business perspective, assigned Tom Furey to Rochester, as director of the Development Lab and to provide the leadership necessary to bring the Silverlake project to a successful conclusion. Furey's arrival didn't bring out the flags and the marching bands. Staff wondered what this hand-picked headquarters manager could do for IBMR. What assistance would he provide for realizing the Silverlake goal? Furey now became responsible for the output of 2,500 engineers and programmers involved in designing computer systems.

Tom Furey was handpicked by IBM Headquarters. He was a twenty-four year IBM veteran, age 45, joined IBM as a systems engineer, and advanced through many technical and managerial positions. Furey was pegged as a "manager who could think strategically and had the breadth, depth, and the knack to run IBMR's Development Lab as though it were a *real business*."[6] Once Schwartz appointed Furey, he got out of his way, and let him manage the situation as he saw fit. As far as IBMR staff was concerned, Fury would be over his head. While he had a well-rounded career, he never was a lab director and certainly never managed one as large as the Rochester Lab. Furey did not exactly receive a vote of confidence. He didn't endear himself to the staff, when one of his first actions was to redecorate his office and expand the conference room.

FUREY ASKS THE HARD QUESTIONS

Furey asked two questions of the IBMR management team: (1) Who are our customers, and (2) what do they want? Those questions related to the number of customers, location of customers, computer models owned and used by customers, age of computers, and so on. But, Furey received blank stares. Staff felt it was their business to design, build, and program computers. It was beyond their scope of thinking to look at the business issues that determined IBMR's business viability. So, Furey decided that the customer-base information was so important that he formed a cross-functional task force, involving people from manufacturing, development, and marketing to develop the answers. Furey appointed a Bill Harrod, a former manufacturing manager, to look at the aforementioned business-related issues.

A preliminary report by the task force showed that IBMR had 200,000 customers worldwide, 60 percent outside the United States of America. Furey began seeing a vision for IBMR and realized that with the right computers and attitude, IBMR could become the *undisputed leader in the global mid-range computer market*. Furey began to think that Silverlake was not just another computer, but a breakthrough product. He perceived the possibilities of Silverlake before all the information was available. Furey began to refine his vision for IBMR.

As additional information became available Furey's vision of Silverlake solidified with two objectives (1) IBMR will be the industry leader in the mid-range computer market, and (2) IBMR will be an exemplar of a market-driven enterprise. Both objectives focused on anticipating and being responsive to customer needs and fulfilling them better than any competitor—in essence, taking the market lead. To accomplish these goals, Furey concluded that "managing by information, facts, computer modeling, planning, doing market research, and forecasting must be disciplines on a par with engineering and programming."[7] Also, IBMR would need to be more responsive, empower its people, nurture their skills and talents, introduce new products to market more quickly, and develop outside partnerships. A decision to empower, to nurture, and to introduce new products more quickly, sets the stage to call a meeting and explain the future *direction of the organization.*

Communicating the Plan

Furey decided it was time to call a meeting of the whole organization, and lay out the plan to the group, not too willing, to listen and accept the changes required to not only build a viable organization, but also to save their jobs. Tom Furey proposed his vision of the future and applause was not to be heard; the room was silent; there were no cheers, just quiet polite Midwestern resignation. The plan for IBMR to become the worldwide leader in the mid-range computer market did not stir their imaginations. They didn't buy it; they labeled Furey as having delusions of grandeur, and playing the role of a cheerleader. Widespread skepticism abounded about the possibilities of success: Silverlake would be a repeat of Fort Knox. Furey's continual requests for answers to questions, that previously never had been asked, resulted in open rebellion from some. The consensus, Furey will be gone in two years, and things will get back to normal. The decision by staff, disregard what Furey was proposing.

Furey decides it's time to act. He begins hosting a series of "roundtables" at lunch time, calling in various groups and listens rather than lectures. Furey expected piercing questions, and established himself as a non-vindictive manager. Those questions had to be asked and answered. When employees found that they could open up without risking any type of repudiation, the roundtables flourished. They had an opportunity to vent their concerns. Furey began to communicate his vision by answering their many questions.

Organizational Structure

Furey needed to modify the organizational structure. The Development Lab included 1,800 engineers and programmers assigned to System/36 and 600 working on System/38. These two groups were not exactly brothers-in-arms. Furey tapped people with longtime Rochester experience, recruited some outsiders, including some with whom he had worked in the past, and some Rochester outcasts, who opposed the Fort Knox project. Once he selected the team, he gave them freedom to manage their activities. Staff began to learn something about the Furey psyche. He refused to make decisions for others. He repeated that he'd rather be wrong than indecisive. He established clear objectives, and set the benchmarks for organizational behavior. There was plenty of leeway to exercise judgment.

Agreeing on Specifications

Furey recognized that developing product specifications requires a great deal of discipline; he's also aware that marketing and the technical communities want to add the bells and whistles, which seldom are required. IBMR had to make choices from a 2,000-item laundry list of specifications. At the same time, they were simultaneously required to consider the eventual price tag that the market would accept. Two pieces of information were required.

1. Who are the customers?
2. What do they want?

The available information from Bill Harrod's study of that identified the IBMR's customer base and customer's needs was too broad to be of any value. While lists of requirements existed, insufficient information was available to serve as a means for executing business decisions. It appears that marketing assumed that customer needs remain static and what was acceptable yesterday would be acceptable today and in the future. IBM did know that the market for Silverlake, a mid-range computer, would be over $200 billion over the strategic period for machines priced from $15,000 to $1 million. The market for mid-range machines was not only big, but diverse.

Market Focus

The principles of market segmentation by geography, size, industry, various demographics, and need are well known. The principles related to market focus and differentiation and positioning are also well known. While this sounds to be very straightforward, it took IBMR 18 months and 25 people to embody these concepts in its strategy. Since IBMR was product driven, customers were the ones who mailed the check. The contract was with the enterprise. As an example, their customer the U.S. Department of Agriculture had 2,400 locations, each of which was a customer. And amongst this group of 2,400 locations, the needs may have differed considerably, because the area served by the particular location had different needs. After considerable study and analysis, the team was able to identify what a customer in a particular segment of the customer base needed and wanted.

The study also showed that the hardware was only part of the decision; software and service were pivotal factors, in the buy decision. The conclusion, customers do not buy machines, they buy solutions. Rochester's analysis showed that demand for mid-range computers, like Silverlake, depended on customers (about 15,000 in the United States) with 5,000 or more employees at a single location. This group accounted for a miniscule percentage of the total demand for mid-range computers. This was where IBMR focused its attention. The *small-to medium-sized enterprises and organizations* constituted the largest share; organizations with fewer than 5,000 employees.

A meeting was finally called to hash out Silverlake's position in the market. The planning people presented the competitive analysis; the list of special characteristics, the benchmarks, and the usual analyses in terms that users would not understand. Someone reminded the group that they better think about Silverlake from the perspective of the user. The benefits of Silverlake were then expressed as

- Simplicity: requires minimum expertise to use it; provides thousands of menus and help screens. Internal software is available in native languages.
- Solutions: many application programs are available; compatible with System/36 and System/38; improved networking capability.
- Productivity: Silverlake comes with programming languages, tools, and utilities that allow owners to create software faster and with fewer programmers.
- Design: includes "artificial intelligence" capability and an integrated relational database.
- Growth; offering the market six computers ranging from $15,000 to $1 million, and some advanced capabilities for system growth.
- Support: Silverlake includes an "internal classroom."

One More Model

The original Silverlake was to consist of four models as noted previously. As the project got underway, the Rochester Management Board decided that a small version of the System/36 must be part of Silverlake. Furey gave the responsibility to a hardware engineer, who had just returned from Japan. Furey told this engineer, "We want a low end model; go do it." Go do it when nothing like this was conceived in the scope of Silverlake, and you have 24 months to do it. This group came up with some ideas and ways to adapt parts and components from Silverlake's bigger models for use in the low end model. The critical problem, in offering small computers, was finding the right mix of features and functions. Two of the people in this group, one from engineering and one from planning, took it upon themselves to study the issues and develop the appropriate price–performance balance. This group had the small model, ready to meet the Silverlake project requirements, when Furey realized, it became necessary to simultaneously reinvigorate the thinking and innovation, and build a solid reputation of being technically vital to IBM's success.

Allocating Resources

Difficulties in allocating resources were not unlike those of all major projects: satisfying virtually unlimited need, with limited resources. According to the authors, the heated debates among engineering, programming, and marketing generated more heat than light. Not unusual. As usual, most claims for funding can be legitimate, but everyone's wish list cannot be satisfied. Each of the three groups, engineering, programming, and marketing had no understanding of how their decisions affected the whole. There was no methodology for negotiating trade-offs in a holistic fashion. The background material was compiled in what was called the "System Plan." It included over 2,000 engineering specifications where each line item included a dollar estimate. The bickering had to stop; Furey and his managers struggled to find a way to allocate the available resources. They made a decision, set the priorities.

A decision was made to use the Analytical Hierarchy Process (AHP)[8] to bring a degree of quantification to the process. "Expert Choice" was selected as the decision-making tool to bring some order to the process. For Silverlake, the process included considering the business goals and objectives, prioritizing markets and technologies, prioritizing technologies within market sectors, and establishing financial targets. The first factors included market attractiveness, in terms of growth, sales potential and competitive intensity. The second included the ability to offer customers a complete solution. A weight was assigned to each and every market, in comparison to each and every market. The same approach was used in prioritizing the technologies. The next step was to understand the interdependencies among markets and technologies, relative to investment criteria. AHP had its limitations, but the exercise showed which technologies and markets were the most important. The remaining decisions became a matter of judgment.

AMBITIOUS GOALS

The Silverlake Project set some very ambitious goals, and was three or four times more complex than any previous major Rochester project. The group finally realized that their commitment to complete the project in approximately 2 years would require introducing some new thinking and some new processes.

Two years was a tight schedule for bringing not only a product, but a product line into the marketplace. The hardware included more than 50,000 different parts. The software instructions consisted of over 7 million lines of code. That meant the project would require over 3,000 person years of programming. Silverlake had to work in no less than 27 languages. The system required 33,000 pages of operating instructions, and training of 32,000 sales and service people. To meet these requirements Furey needs to change the IBMR culture, and introduce a Council of Customers and a Migration Invitational that challenges IBM's Secrecy Policies.

IBMR Culture

The management philosophy, where managers were expected to be technically knowledgeable and capable of answering all questions, led IBMR managers to become micromanagers. So, managers found themselves putting in countless hours of overtime. Furey became aware of some of these issues as he often heard from the technical community that

> "We're capable of taking the ball on this matter or that one and running with it. We're grown up, mature, educated adults, and we've spent years developing our competence. We think we can be trusted to do these things on our own—who knows half as much as we do—without having a Manager get in the way."[9]

These complaints from technical staff reinforced Furey's frustrations with IBMR, because when he wanted technical information, he went directly to the sources—the technical experts.

Furey appoints Bauer, head of the human resource department the task of finding a way to limit the extraordinarily long hour's managers and others are providing, in order to meet the agreed-upon deadline. Bauer conducted interviews across all organizational lines. The results provided a new direction regarding the responsibilities of IBMR employees.

- Managers must lead more and manage less; managers set broad goals and support the discipline professionals.
- Manage the process as much as the people; managers make sure people understand the goals to be achieved; yet not abdicating complete control.
- Managers must push authority and accountability down into the ranks.

Bauer then formed a cross-functional work team representing all the functions within the Lab. The team defined the job requirements for each laboratory position. In many cases this list included more than 50 criteria that were classified as quality, productivity, planning, technical competence, leadership, relationships, and communications. A senior engineer, in product development in order to earn an excellent rating, "had to deliver high-risk work with high quality, carry an unusually heavy work load, maintain the highest performance during a crisis, generate one patent per year, publish something in a professional journal, and influence group morale positively."[10] Bauer's team was attempting to balance a bureaucratic restrictive approach and empowerment. The document also showed what responsibilities managers could shift to others. This effort identified what the potential workload could include for every employee.

Bauer's conclusion was that IBMR may be suffering from a scarceness of managers. He began a monthly series of luncheon briefings called Management Preparation Seminars. At each session, front-line managers appeared before the group to speak about what management entailed, discussed the rewards and frustrations of managing, and highlighted the role managers play in dealing with people. This exercise turned out to be a self-screening process as many people involved in engineering and programming can manage the technical issues, but fail to find ways of resolving the people issues. This decision begins to build the required management staff for the future.

Council of Customers

This decision broke down IBM's self-reliance and secrecy in the creation of any new machine, and recognized that no organization has sufficient money and manpower to compete worldwide, in many different markets, solely with its own resources. Outsiders now will be welcome, but with prudent precautions. With this change in organizational attitude toward using non-IBM resources, the door opened to bring in the necessary talent to meet the Silverlake specifications, and help keep the project on schedule. With this background Furey establishes the Council of Customers.

The first Council of Customers included two representatives from the invited organizations. On the first day, council members were briefed on the Silverlake design, the software, migration from System/36 and System/38 to Silverlake, and tentative pricing. During the question and answer period it became obvious that there were communication problems. IBMR people spoke the language of engineers, peppered with specifications and the internal workings of the machine. Customers wanted to speak in the day-to-day language, and wanted to know what the machine would do: how will the new machine help them. The Council reported that IBMR was on the right track. They went beyond what was requested and suggested that IBM needed to simplify doing business with them. The first council was deemed an unqualified success. Councils were then organized in Rochester about every quarter, and also in Europe and Japan. The decision to establish the Customer Council allowed the Silverlake team to gain an understanding of their needs.

Migration Invitational

In addition to the Council of Customers, Furey began what it called a "Migration Invitational." Customers and business partners would be invited to Rochester at IBM's expense, to spend anywhere from 2 days to 3 weeks on a prototype machine, converting their software to operate on Silverlake. To support these activities, Furey established a Software Partners Laboratory at IBMR. Customers and Business Partners, who participated in the Migration Invitational, used this facility. Participation was not limited to current customers. By the time Silverlake was ready to hit the market, 175 customers and business partners participated. The program resulted in the conversion of 2,500 applications, encompassing more than 200,000 programs and 70 million lines of code, for use with Silverlake. This experience taught IBM, that no enterprise can any longer depend solely on its own talent, and thus it's imperative to develop partnerships with other sources of talent.

MARKET LAUNCH

Time came to consider the market launch. Normally IBM did not consider preparing for a market launch, until development was three-quarters of the way to project completion. Usually IBM Corporate Sales was brought in to manage the launch. The launch of Silverlake was to be like no other IBM launch. John Akers, IBM Chairman, said Silverlake was so important to IBM's future, that he personally appointed a key executive in charge of the Silverlake launch. John Akers also became involved personally. A Cross-functional Executive Committee was appointed and began the planning of the launch.

The executive, appointed by Akers to launch Silverlake, was known for his organizational acumen, decisiveness, and his ability to get things done. He immediately began putting the right people in the right place and formed a cross-functional team called the Executive Steering Committee. This committee included representatives from all the functions involved in Silverlake, including Furey and from each of IBM's five geographical business areas. The committee relied on the IBMR segmentation and positioning studies. Part of the launch included the activities of the Red Team, made up of 20 battle-hardened sales veterans. For 3 months they placed Silverlake under a microscope and focused on finding all the weaknesses of the system. They eventually arrived with a list of items that competitors would consider as weaknesses. The Red Team concluded that "nothing would damage Silverlake's credibility more than if it failed to deliver on our promises." Manufacturing ramped up production and through an early ship program placed 4,755 machines with customers and the Business Partners. These machines were placed with the understanding that the machines would be used as test machines, but some customers were so enthusiastic, that they immediately switched over to the test machines. While Silverlake was the code name for this major effort, it was time to decide the commercial name that would be used by the sales department; IBM opted for the "AS/400," AS for *advanced solutions* and 400 connoting the middle ground of computers.

The launch of the AS/400 worldwide was a spectacular event starting in Japan, Australia; on to the European capitals of Rome, Bonn, Paris, London, and others; and New York City.[10] In New York City, IBM assembled more than 2,000 members of the press and guests, and arranged for telecasting the event to 100,000 customers and prospects gathered throughout various IBM operations. The launch was a great success, and IBM received all types of accolades for a product launch that exceeded all expectations. Within 4 months, IBM sold more than 25,000 units and the AS/400 became IBM's most successful product introduction in its 75-year history. Within 18 months IBM sold 100,000 units worldwide. IBMR went from being a "nice little business" to being a "nice big business" and the installed base of all IBMR systems grew to 450,000. By the end of 1990, IBMR became a $14 billion business. As a business by itself, it would place number 28 in the 1991 list of Fortune's 500 companies. IBMR was now a customer-centered and market-oriented operation.

LESSONS LEARNED

Why select the Silverlake Project as Case Study on Decision-Making? The history of IBMR demonstrates the rise of an organization; its decline from a lack of business focus; the lack of understanding between engineering and marketing; increased competition in its field of interest; a culture that failed to integrate the organizational functions; many decisions, from the highest executive levels to those at the technology and marketing work benches; and a turnaround to a successful organization.

The Silverlake Project was completed in the unheard timeframe of 28 months. IBMR accomplished what many IBM Headquarters' executives doubted, even though they put Tom Furey, their hand-picked manager, to revitalize IBMR. They completed Silverlake, by turning the IBMR culture upside down and by changing attitudes; integrating efforts of engineers, programmers, managers, and a supportive team from manufacturing and marketing giving people the tools, techniques, skills; and providing opportunities for individual leadership. Managers were educated to be both managers and leaders. According to the authors, IBMR[11] learned the following about managing major projects when they faced the live or die situation.

1. Appoint a leader with a vision
2. Institutionalize the vision with the right people and mission
3. Empower the people
4. Use cross-functional teams
5. Segment the market
6. Research and model the markets
7. Set priorities and allocate resources
8. Use parallel processing
9. Form partnerships with outsiders
10. Shape and exceed customer requirements

These 10 findings could be a model for any organization, but were known long before IBMR came into existence; they are basic management principles. Here's a closer look at the IBMR lessons learned, grounded in three periods; pre–Fort Knox Project, Fort Knox Project, and during the Silverlake Project.

Pre–Fort Knox Project

The Pre–Fort Knox project period illustrates how IBMR failed to read its market environment regarding product offerings. IBMR established itself in the mid-range computer market, but failed to read the entrance of the competition. IBMR developed a series of computers that lacked compatibility features. This is difficult to understand, as compatibility was and continues to be an essential feature of any information system. Evidently, the engineers and programmers built the organization, by being oblivious to the needs of the marketplace. This is well demonstrated when Tom Furey asks for information about the IBMR customer base and receives blank stares. IBMR was financially very successful during this period and IBM Headquarters evidently concerned itself only with the financial performance. As the authors noted, IBM Headquarters disregarded IBMR, and left them live alone and IBMR liked it that way. Why is this scenario relevant?

The IBMR situation repeats itself and continues as executives lose sight of their priorities and the operating groups take the path of least resistance to satisfy management's dictums. In previous chapters, examples, such as Eastman Kodak, Hewlett Packard, the US auto industry, and others demonstrated how successful organizations lose their grounding principles of operation and tend to decline.

Fort Knox Project Period

The Fort Knox period not only received attention from IBM's top management, but was managed from the top. How an organization like IBM could attempt such an action raises significant questions about IBM's management expertise from top to bottom. However, some non-managers, engineers, and programmers realized from the start that dividing the project effort among four different Development Labs in four different locations would end in chaos. Unfortunately, management failed to listen. Managing Fort Knox from the top ended in disastrous results: 4 years of work and a loss of millions of dollars. Just what was recoverable is unknown. IBMR management finally resurrected Drucker's admonition about managing the activities of knowledge workers. Someone does generate the *big idea* that gives birth to the Silverlake Project.

The Silverlake Project Period

After the death of Fort Knox, an experienced developer with extensive experience as an engineer and programmer presents a proposal to launch a new machine and receives approval for assignment of a hardware designer, a product planner, a technological thinker, and a former salesman. IBM Headquarters approves the Silverlake Project and selects Tom Furey, a veteran IBMer with major accomplishments, as director of the IBMR Development Lab. Tom Furey launches a turnaround.

- Redecorates the office and conference room. Not a good start with the Development Lab staff.

    Such an act is not a big issue, presents negative optics, but often is essential. As I attend presentations, I am surprised how little attention is paid to providing facilities that allow for good communication.

- Manages by facts, figures, computer modeling, market research, and forecasting disciplines and these must be part of the engineering and programming groups: continues to ask for data to make decisions. Furey's management style that requires information before making decisions appears to be a problem for engineers and programmers in the Development Lab.

    Good decisions depend on facts, but we need to accept the fact that all facts will not be known at the time a project is approved. In addition, on projects scheduled over several years the original facts may no longer apply and new facts may be presented.

- Presents his vision for the Development Lab: be the undisputed leader in the global mid-range computer market and proceeds with Silverlake.

    Defining the purpose of an organization provides a general guide as to what the organization wishes to accomplish. Describing a "vision" looks toward the future as what the organization plans on being and achieving. Tom Furey defined that vision and subsequent actions allowed the fulfillment of that vision.

- Faces people problems among engineers, programmers, and managers.

     While people are an organizations' most important assets, their inter-actions with colleagues and others take up a considerable amount of managers' time. Employees bring all their preconceived ideas, practices, experiences, and prejudices to the workplace, even though some may no longer be relevant to the current situation. Tom Furey, with the help of key people, managed to synchronize these disparate into building a major IBM business.

- Refuses to make decisions where others have responsibility.

     If only all managers and senior-level discipline specialists could adopt such a point of view! Making decisions involves taking risks and accom-plishing even the most insignificant results requires accepting the risks involved. The sooner managers allow those under their responsibility to make the appropriate level decisions, the sooner they'll find time to per-form their manager/leader function.

- Lays out the Silverlake plan to the organization emphasizing the need for the Development Lab to be market driven in all functions. Staff response, Silverlake will be a repeat of Fort Knox.

     Introducing change creates a level of discomfort even for those who accept change as inevitable; the unintended consequences always surface in some form or another. Most technically oriented people do not think of themselves, in relation to the business; they think technology only. Tom Furey demonstrated the value of integrating technology with marketing; recognize different customer needs and deliver quality products that the user wants.

- Starts a series of meetings to allow people to vent their concerns. Brings in the people, who were exiled to *technological Siberia*, when they voiced their concerns about the Fort Knox project.

     It was unfortunate that IBM Headquarters executives did not listen to those dissident voices, who doubted the possibility of a successful Fort Knox Project. Tom Furey, by listening rather than talking, engaged the Development Lab in a conversation about their environment. This is not a new concept, but a concept too often forgotten by managers. Engagement does not occur by directive; it requires an opportunity to vent, to rethink, and then get to work.

- Selects a group to develop an organizational structure that will meet the needs of the Development Lab and Silverlake.

     Tom Furey could have put together the organizational chart without the help of the Development Lab staff, but by selecting a team to do it, he received buy-in. Managers might take note, that when it comes to people, "the distance between two points may not be straight line." There's a lesson throughout this case study; involving people, although more cumbersome, yields longer lasting results.

- Establishes clear objectives and benchmarks for organizational behavior. Expects team members, at all levels, to exercise judgment.

  There was a time when Management by Objectives (MBO) dominated the management process. Set the objective, organize the team and assign a team leader, and reap the benefits. Unfortunately, MBO did not consider the human element; meeting objectives requires more than following a process; it requires judgment. Tom Furey's actions showed how setting objectives and benchmarks guide the work effort to a successful conclusion.

- Challenges the information required and the means for prioritizing the 2,000-item laundry list on the Silverlake specification.

  If you ever worked on any project, you will be aware of the laundry list of requirements identified by customers, executives, managers, and the technical and marketing communities of the organization. That list may not have been as lengthy as the Silverlake Project list, but you recognize the importance of rationalizing the list regardless of the number of items. Requirements must be prioritized; there are always insufficient resources to meet everybody's expectations. While the Silverlake team used the priorities, individual judgments guided the process. Our emphasis on algorithms, modeling, and simulation too often disregard the the impact of human behavior on performance.

- Asks for information on the customer base for the mid-range computer market that could reach $200 billion at maturity for computers would sell for $15 thousand to $1 million.

  An organization like IBM, not knowing the segmentation of its mid-range customer base, demonstrates how successful organizations go through a cycle of ups and downs. IBM had its share. When Tom Furey asked about the customer base on his arrival in Rochester, he received blank stares. The fact that the results of Silverlake could approach $200 billion in sales, required a detailed market segmentation study and an analysis of customers' individual needs; customers' requirements spanned this range of computers that would cost anywhere between $15 thousand to $1 million.

- Introduces concurrent engineering principles, but expands it to concurrent management of all organizational functions.

  The principles of Concurrent Engineering often referred to as Simultaneous Engineering generally focused on research, development, design, and some aspects of manufacturing; how could IBMR be so oblivious to

*the values associated with practicing the principles. Tom Furey, by intro-
ducing concurrent management, integrated the organization. In essence,
a system that forces all organizational functions to meet the cycle time
requirements; marketing doesn't wait to begin its work until the product
is developed, marketing needs are anticipated and flow concurrently with
the product development. Likewise, new marketing needs are integrated
into the development process.*

- Breaks with IBM policies and practices and organizes a Customer Council
  and Migration Invitational.

    *Breaking organizational policies or traditions requires accepting cer-
    tain levels of personal risk with the attendant consequences, but leaders
    risk their reputations as part of the leadership function, It's a given. Tom
    Furey, because of his longevity and reputation within IBM, knew the lim-
    its and most likely consulted with Steve Schwartz who assigned him to
    the Development Lab. Both the Customer Council and Migration Invita-
    tional were innovations for the Development Lab, but not uncommon in
    other organizations, although implemented in different ways. In essence,
    develop products and services that customers need, but also bring certain
    customers into the process to ratify the assumptions.*

- Changes management philosophy: (1) no more command and control, and
  (2) leave business decisions to the managers and the technical decisions
  to the experts.

    *The business community, did not associate managing by command
    and control with IBM, although IBM's operating guidelines and principles
    were well engrained in its employees; there was a type of IBM discipline
    regarding dress, customer contact, and living within the IBM community.
    However, it was difficult to understand how the Development Lab could
    practice command and control management where staff included predom-
    inantly knowledge workers; how could these knowledge workers subject
    themselves to such a management philosophy. Tom Furey introduced the
    second change, a policy where business decisions became the responsibil-
    ity of the managers and technical decisions to the experts. Making business
    decisions and technical decisions require different skills and occasionally
    someone comes on the scene and brings both competencies to the table.
    However, rigidity in implementing such a policy also presents negative
    consequences, since it accepts the assumptions that experts always pro-
    vide advice that yields successful outcomes. At the same time, business
    and technical decisions are co-dependent; they do not operate in isola-
    tion. Establishing the Customer Council and Migration Invitational were
    business decisions, but those decisions required input from the experts in
    the technical community, and an evaluation of credibility by the technical
    community.*

- A study found the Development Lab suffered from an absence of competent managers. Tom Furey establishes workshops for managers and the engineers and programmers on management fundamentals, innovation, strategy, operations, and marketing.

  What Tom Furey found at the Development Lab raises serious issues in the larger global technical community; managing involves dealing with human behavior and not focusing as Drucker noted, "management is not a bag of tricks and techniques." Managing has little to do with all the project and program management technologies that often only delay decisions, because of their dependence on preprogrammed analyses, those algorithms that fail to account for the non-quantifiable human behavioral aspects of the situation; numbers alone do not guarantee success, managing effectively requires certain competencies that must be developed into capabilities, since managing effectively requires competence in many different yet related competencies.

- Hires a full-time communications professional who published a Development Lab newsletter and continued the roundtable discussions, and the all-manager and all-employee meetings.

  Lack of meaningful communication creates organizational disasters as has been shown in preceding chapters; witness the demise of Eastman Kodak, HP's difficulties, the US auto industry, and more recently with the grounding of Boeing's 787 Dreamliner. Yes, those written or email communiques are essential, but Tom Furey continued with the roundtable discussions and the all-manager and all-employee meetings. I suggest that discontinuing the roundtable and all-manager and all-employee meetings that Silverlake may have floundered and instead of beating their schedule launch date would have faced considerable delays. Remember that list of 2,000 requirements; these lists are not rationalized by multiple email interactions or off-the-cuff tweets, they require negotiation and especially in a timely manner.

- IBM advances product launch through its President John Akers parallel with development of the AS/400 Series of computers.

  As you read the section on the Product Launch, you probably concluded that IBM met all the launch requirements and demonstrated what can be done in an environment that values its staff, provides a vision and relentlessly pursues it, and integrates all the organizational functions into a cohesive whole. Introducing a new product into the global marketplace on the same day and in this case a series of new products that fulfill a wide range of needs requires realistic planning and concern for details. While the transition of the Development Lab, from a lack luster operation of technical professionals, to one that proved its competence in developing the AS/400 Series of mid-range computers, demonstrated what can be accomplished by the managerial guidance of Tom Furey, the successful Product Market Launch should have provided motivation for the technical team. What greater satisfaction can the technical community expect but to see its work effort accepted by the users?

KEY POINTS

- Decision-making requires the organization, regardless of size or scope, to provide an identified strategic direction, organizational structure and discipline, competent management, the required talent in all disciplines, and the mix of competencies to execute.

- Good decisions depend not only on the facts but a verification of those facts modified with personal experience and judgment.

- Attempting to lead knowledge workers with a command-and-control mindset eventually leads to an organization incapable of adapting to changing requirements.

- When executive management prefers reading reports to visiting and seeing and hearing it loses the personal contact with key people; performance will gradually decline.

- Let the managers make the business related decisions and the experts make the technical/professional decisions, but both understand the inter-relationships.

- When an organization finds itself in a declining mode, identify and understand the scope of the problems; appoint a manager with a combination of the professional and managerial competencies; one capable of bringing together the disparate functions into an operating team, inspire others, develop direction, and meet the expected goals.

- Some level of leadership is required in all organizations. So, appoint a leader who can codify the vision, inspire others to accept and understand and pursue the vision, and work collegially with all involved in the process of fulfilling the vision.

- Communicating the vision, if it departs from the ordinary, involves more than a casual announcement; it requires discussion, analysis, constant reinforcement, and refinement as additional facts are uncovered.

- Transitioning an organization from mediocrity to excellence involves a disciplined process; it does not occur in zero time. It requires a day by day struggle to bring the disparate functions to focus on the needs of system.

- The technical community cannot be solely responsible for developing product specification. Consideration must be given to what the market-place will accept; who are the customers and what do they want.

- The hardware an organization provides its customers is only part of the package and the decision; customers do not buy machines, they buy solutions.
- Engineering specifications for complex projects often include thousands of requirements that must be negotiated. By applying a cost to each requirement, the allocation of funds allows for disciplined evaluation of each requirement.
- Setting ambitious goals generally leads to discontent at some level, but achieving ambitious goals requires the resources, a mindset that guides the process, and an operational discipline. It requires a culture that not only provides freedom with discipline, but also encourages freedom of thought; it values the unconventional thinkers and doers.
- The successful market launch, of a major improvement or a new-to-the-market product or service, depends on providing the required level of effort in developing a plan that integrates the launch resources with customer's/user's needs.

NOTES

1. Roy A. Bauer, Emilio Collar, and Victor Tang with Jerry Wind, and Patrick R. Houston, *The Silverlake Project*, Oxford University Press, 1992.
2. Ibid., pp. 1–5.
3. Ibid., pp. 19–20.
4. Ibid., p. 21.
5. Ibid., p. 22.
6. Ibid., p. 28.
7. Ibid., p. 32.
8. Ibid., pp. 86–87.
9. Ibid., pp. 146–147.
10. Ibid., pp. 157–178.
11. Ibid., pp. 9–13.

9

BOEING AND THE 787 DREAMLINER

Boeing's development of the 787 Dreamliner provides an excellent case study in decision-making that spans the continuum from the executive suite to the operational levels within Boeing, its outsourced partners, and to the factory floor. Boeing embarked on the design of a totally new aircraft based on (1) extensive use of reinforced composites as a substitute for aluminum; (2) not only extensive outsourcing to suppliers, but also outsourcing to investment partners; (3) dependence on an extensive use of modeling and simulation of design, manufacturing, and assembly operations; and (4) reliance on high levels of precision in managing a major global supply chain.

My sources of information for this chapter include Boeing[1] documents and information from major publications collected for many years. The question, how could a successful and innovative organization like Boeing embark on a program like the 787 Dreamliner and be forced to delay deliveries by more than 3 years? Who are the people making the million plus decisions? There is no doubt that attempting to introduce new technologies, designs, production and assembly processes, a global supply chain, probably more than 3,000 suppliers and thousands of engineers and technicians, presented many challenges. My comments should not be considered as criticism of Boeing's executives, its

Decisions: An Engineering and Management Perspective, First Edition. Gerard H. Gaynor.
© 2015 The Institute of Electrical and Electronics Engineers, Inc. Published 2015 by John Wiley & Sons, Inc.

managers, its engineers and other discipline professionals, or others responsible for implementation. There's no single reason why the delivery schedule of the first Dreamliner was extended on seven separate occasions. A history of the 787 Dreamliner, from concept to commercial flight, would provide many management lessons. Chapter 9 topics include

- Dreamliner Scope and Expectations
- Boeing—The Enterprise
- The 787 Dreamliner Challenges
- Commentary
- Key Points
- Notes

DREAMLINER SCOPE AND EXPECTATIONS

The Dreamliner represents a major investment by Boeing in introducing not only new technologies and management processes, but also developing more efficient aircraft. The following scope and expectations put the Dreamliner advancements in perspective.

- Market size: 3,300 units over 20 years
- Seat range: 200–300
- Seats by model: 210–250
- Range:7,650–8,200 nautical miles
- Wing span: 197 ft. (60 m)
- Length: 186 ft. (57 m)
- Total cargo: 4,400 cu. ft.
- Flight speed: Mach 0.85
- Material breakout: Composites, 50%; titanium, 15%; steel, 10%; and others, 5%
- Parts reduction: Aluminum sheets, 1,500; fasteners, 40,000–50,000
- Holes drilled: Fewer than 10,000; Boeing 747: 1 million holes
- Fuel efficiency: 20% greater; emissions: 20% less than similar size aircraft
- Maintenance savings: 30%
- Amount of copper wire eliminated: 60 miles
- Computer design time: 800,000 hours on Cray computers
- Hours of wind tunnel tests: 15,000 hours
- Final assembly: one aircraft every 3 days

BOEING—THE ENTERPRISE

A view of the Boeing website provides the following information. Boeing, now headquartered in Chicago, employs approximately 160,000 people worldwide. The employee base includes over 120,000 with college degrees from approximately 2,700 colleges and universities: about 32,000 with advanced degrees. The company is organized in two business units: Boeing Commercial Airplanes; and Boeing Defense, Space & Security (BDSS). These two groups are supported by Boeing Capital Corporation, a global provider of financing solutions; the Shared Services Group, which provides a broad range of services to Boeing worldwide; and Boeing Engineering, Operations & Technology (EO&T), which helps develop, acquire, apply, and protect innovative technologies and processes.

Over the years, Boeing Commercial Airplanes Division (BCAD) has demonstrated a long tradition of aerospace leadership and innovation in the commercial, defense, space, and security sectors of the economy. Combined with its purchase of McDonnell Douglas in 1997, the combined organization shares a 70-year history of leadership in commercial aircraft. Boeing has been the premiere developer and manufacture of jet aircraft for over 40 years. We all know them by such designations as the 707, 737, 747, 767, 777, and now the 787 Dreamliner.

The Shared Services Group (SSG) provides the infrastructure services required to run their global operations. The group includes facilities services; employee benefits and services, staffing, recruitment, wellness programs, security; fire protection; site operations; disaster preparedness; construction; reclamation; conservation programs; virtual workplace; creative services; transportation; business continuity, and the purchase of all nonproduction goods and services; and other related services.

EO&T drives for technical and functional excellence across the enterprise. EO&T provides services in information technology, research and development, test and evaluation, integration of functions, supplier management, and the general functions assigned to engineering geared to providing competitively progressive and highly disciplined and efficient engineering operations. The organization pays particular attention to ensuring the success of development programs, and strives to attract, develop, and retain a world-class technical and functional work force.

BDSS provides end-to-end services for large-scale systems related to air-, land-, sea-, and space-based platforms for global military, government, and commercial customers. In addition, it provides design, production, modification, and other support services for various product lines. The group also provides system integration services for NASA's space shuttle and International Space Station programs, the Missile Defense Agency's Ground-based Midcourse Defense program, and the Army's Brigade Combat Team Modernization program.

Boeing Operating Principles

William M. Allen,[2] Boeing President from 1945 to 1972 established the following basic principles of operation to guide the company's operations.

- Avoid hasty decisions or actions when angry or under emotional stress.
- Base decisions on merit alone. Apply rules uniformly.
- Keep the promises you make. Avoid making any you can't keep.
- Acknowledge your own mistakes and refrain from buck passing.
- Avoid decisions or actions before all facts are in and carefully considered.
- Avoid delaying decisions and actions after all the facts are carefully weighed.
- Explain reasons to back your decisions and actions.
- Be reasonable in your requests and expectations of others.
- Be diligent and efficient. Do your job as well as you expect of others.
- Be friendly, patient, encouraging. Give compliments whenever deserved.
- Get acquainted with your men. Get their point of view.
- Invite and welcome suggestions. Be courteous and interested.
- Where differences of opinion exist be calm, pleasant, open minded.
- If in doubt, ask a neutral person to appraise your judgment.
- Constantly strive for fairest possible distribution of jobs, wages, and promotions.
- Apply the Golden Rule. Ask yourself; "will this be fair?"

Management Problems Surface

But all was not right at Boeing in 2003. Michael M. Sears,[3] the chief financial officer was removed from his position on November 24 because of alleged ethical misconduct. Phil Condit,[4] Chairman and CEO , resigned on December 1 as a result of ethics violations in its Defense Division. Harry Stonecipher, who sold McDonnell Douglas to Boeing and subsequently served as CEO and Director on Boeing's Board, returned as CEO and promises to restore the company's reputation. In March of 2005, Stonecipher[5] was forced to leave Boeing after emails revealed inappropriate activities.

The merger of Boeing and McDonnell Douglas in 1996 into the current Boeing involved the integration of two totally different cultures. Boeing used collaborative problem solving; McDonnell Douglas used aggressive cost control. Boeing people were referred to as the *boy scouts*; McDonnell Douglas people, *the mercenaries*. Stonecipher's appointment as Boeing CEO, upon his second attempt as CEO, generated a significant amount of employee discontent; he did not endear himself to the Boeing people when he declared

> "When people say I changed the culture of Boeing; that was the intent, so that it is managed like a business rather than an engineering firm. It is a great engineering firm, but people invest in a company because they want to make money."

James McNerney,[6] a Boeing Board member, became Chairman and CEO of Boeing effective June 30, 2005, replacing Harry Stonecipher; he is the first outsider to be brought in to run Boeing. When asked the question during an interview, "what do you observe about those who grow and those who don't?"

> "At the personal level: openness to change, courage to change, hard work, and team work. But they get trapped in a bureaucratic environment where their jobs become narrower and narrower and they're not connected to the organization's Mission—they're cogs in some manager's machine."

McNerney evidently sensed some of the problems at Boeing when he made these comments: openness and courage to change, hard work, and team work.

At Boeing, McNerney inherited problems which he may not have foreseen; however, he served on the Boeing Board of Directors prior to his appointment, so must have been aware of the problems. Reshaping an organization provides significant challenges to any executive and Boeing's size and extensive global involvement adds an order of magnitude to implementing the required changes. To this end McNerney[7] focused on his plans "to expand the $60 billion company while restoring the shine of one of the world's most recognizable brands." Two key executives, Alan Mulally and Jim Albaugh, respectively heads of BCA and BDSS, and rivals to the appointment of McNerney, were expected to remain at Boeing. On September 2, 2005, 18,300 Boeing machinists walked off the job. Management thought it had a strategy that would prevent a strike, but in a vote a two-thirds majority sanctioned the strike. *Business Week*[8] reported Boeing's Strike: Go Figure with a subtitle: The shutdown is costing much more than it would to meet the machinists' demands. What McNerney[9] brought to Boeing can best be summarized in his statement

> "I think we've opened up the culture a bit internally. We're not afraid to talk about things. I think what happens in successful institutions, is you begin to believe everything you say to yourself. It morphs into a form of arrogance. And so you've got to discuss that."

THE 787 DREAMLINER CHALLENGES

The development and commercialization of the Boeing 787 Dreamliner provides an excellent example of the impact of decisions at all levels on decision-making. At the writing of this chapter the Dreamliner is about 3 years behind schedule and all organizational units have shared the frustrations of bringing a new airplane with unproven new technologies in practice to the marketplace.

Dreamliner Virtual Rollout December 2006

Boeing[10] rolls out the virtual Dreamliner to several thousand employees. In a news conference following the rollout, Mike Blair, Vice President and General Manager of the 787 Program said

> "The engineering data behind these simulations gives us confidence in our assembly processes and our ability to meet our commitments to our customers. We found errors in simulation that would have been costly to find in production and have been able to design corrections quickly to keep the program on track."

A Succession of Problems

There is no doubt that the 787 presented many engineering, technology, manufacturing, assembly, integration, and fitness-to-fly challenges. The 787 was the first attempt since the birth of Boeing's 747 series of aircraft to depart from traditional materials of construction; global outsourcing of design and construction of major sections of the aircraft to partners rather than contractors, and an advanced delivery schedule compared to the development of any previous Boeing aircraft. The Dreamliner project included 43 top-tier supplier-partners plus several thousand subcontractors connected virtually at 135 data sites around the world. More specifically

- Forward Fuselage—Wichita, Kansas
- Forward Fuselage—Nagoya, Japan
- Center Fuselage—Grottaglie, Italy
- Aft Fuselage—Charleston, South Carolina
- Cargo Access Doors—Sweden
- Passenger Entry Doors—Latecoere of France
- Horizontal Stabilizer—Foggia, Italy
- Tail Fin—Fredrickson, Washington

- Wing—Nagoya, Japan
- Fixed Movable Leading Edge—Tulsa, Oklahoma
- Fixed Trailing Edge—Nagoya, Japan
- Movable Trailing Edge—Australia
- Wing Tips—Korea
- Engine Nacelles—Chula Vista, California
- Wing/Body Fairing and Landing Gear Doors—Winnipeg, Canada
- Main Landing Gear Wheel Well—Nagoya, Japan
- Center Wing Box—Nagoya. Japan
- Landing Gear—Gloucester, UK
- Engines—GE-Evendale, Ohio; Rolls Royce-Derby, UK

Resolving the potential design, manufacturing, assembly, communication, coordination, cultural, and internal political issues would have required significant emphasis on due diligence. These issues are not resolved through spreadsheets, models, or simulations, or project management tools; they're resolved through interaction of human beings, who bring all their knowledge, experience, and prejudices accumulated over a career. Managing this array of partner/contractors in the supply chain appears somewhat incomprehensible and will create major program delays.

In December 2007, *The Wall Street Journal*[11] (*WSJ*) reported that the supplier problems ranged from overcoming language barriers to snafus that erupted when some contractors outsourced chunks of the work. One Italian company spent months to gain approval to build a fuselage factory on the site of an ancient olive garden.

On October 26, 2006 the *Financial Times*[12] (FT) reports that Boeing's new 787, scheduled to come into service in mid-2008, was suffering from supplier and weight problems, but CEO Jim McNerney stated that "this plane will be delivered on time and it will be done within contractual commitments." McNerney also mentioned an increase in research spending and aggressive contingency planning to fix the problems.

On June 19, 2007, *WSJ*[13] reports a nuts-and-bolts problem facing the 787 Dreamliner. While the major concerns of the engineers focused on being able to make the huge sections of the wings and fuselage from carbon-fiber composites, the program slowdown occurred because of a lack of nuts and bolts. Mike Bair, Boeing's Vice President responsible for the Dreamliner referred to this situation as a "near-term nuisance." The unveiling of the Dreamliner is now scheduled for July 8, 2007. Scott Carson, Boeing Commercial Airplanes President and CEO, described the fastener shortage as one of the biggest short-term problems in the industry. He said, "Fasteners are just aggravating as hell."

The *WSJ*[14] reports that some Boeing suppliers are saying that all must go right if Boeing is to meet the May 2008 delivery target. Boeing's top leaders suggest that they can overcome the 4-month delay caused by lack of the required hardware. Boeing's suppliers are not so sure. A Boeing supplier listening to Boeing executives discuss the delays with Wall Street analysts and reporters, remarked "Are they kidding." Interviews with suppliers showed that Boeing was at least 8 months late in delivering specifications to the companies responsible for manufacturing.

Boeing[15] announces further delays. Some criticism begins to surface from customers and analysts about CEO Jim McNerney and senior Boeing executives for being overly optimistic in their projections and not revealing the full scope of the problems. Repeated changes in delivery schedule, from an organization with Boeing's reputation, begin to raise serious credibility questions.

Boeing[16] acknowledges a new problem with the 787. Engineers conclude that the *wing box*, a massive structure to which the wings are attached and also serves as a large fuel tank, must be redesigned. A Boeing spokesman states that this is just the normal situation associated with the design of a new aircraft. At this time the schedule of the first test flight is delayed to the fourth quarter of 2008.

By this time Jim McNerney[17] recruits some executives from the defense unit to help straighten out the program to analyze the situation, implement the fixes, and provide customers with delivery schedules that will be met.

Boeing[18] continues to schedule the Dreamliner fly date in the fourth quarter of 2008. The first delivery is now pushed back about 14 months. Pat Shanahan, General Manager of the 787 program, revealed delays in the final testing of the hydraulic system. The fuselage for the fourth test plane will arrive 3 weeks late because the wrong fasteners were used, supply chain difficulties continue, and every effort is being made to provide a continual stream of certification reports to the Federal Aviation Administration (FAA).

Boeing[19] now faces a 57-day strike that focuses on job security. Almost 27,000 machinists walked off the job after contract negotiations failed between Boeing and the International Association of Machinists and Aerospace Workers. The 787 Dreamliner becomes the hotspot of negotiations: outsourcing of the Dreamliner; problems with outsourced suppliers; and increased reliance on subcontractors since the mid-1990s. Boeing[20] suppliers face the possibility of slowing or stopping production and furloughing workers.

The Boeing[21] strike continues into its third week without any resolution. The picket lines continue at Boeing.[22] The discussions continue. Scott Carson notes that, "The issues at the root of this strike are so critical to our ability to run the company and be competitive that there are lines we cannot cross." On October 28, 2008, after a strike that continued for 53 days with intensive negotiations and mediation, Boeing and the Machinists Union reached a tentative 4-year agreement.

Boeing[23] faces new delays bringing the Dreamliner into the test phase. Thousands of fasteners were installed improperly and must be replaced. Engineers identified the problem due to "Specifications that weren't specific enough." Boeing management made no predictions regarding possible additional delays on the project which seems to be plagued by one problem after another.

Boeing[24] announces management changes aimed at improving oversight of supply chain and quality, both largely responsible for the project delays. Maiden flight is moved to second quarter of 2009 with the first delivery to sometime in the first quarter of 2010. The previous schedule called for the first flight to take place in December 2008 and the first delivery of the Dreamliner in the third quarter of 2009. Boeing undergoes additional executive changes to resolve 787 technical and supplier problems.

Problems continue at Boeing[25] after the machinists strike, the economic turndown, and now a release of approximately 10,000 workers, with about 4,500 in the commercial airplanes unit. Mr. McNerney is optimistic about the future, but also recognized that 2009 would be a business challenge. The company hopes to make the first test flight in the second quarter of 2009.

At the Paris Air Show a Boeing[26] executive, just 1 week after Boeing asserted that the Dreamliner was on schedule for its first test flight before July 1, announces the schedule is tight but doable. Pressure for delivery comes from the 787 buyers. One aviation consultant noted, Boeing has this habit of saying "Everything is fine, everything is fine, and everything is fine: until it isn't."

Boeing[27] considers becoming more involved in manufacturing by buying a facility from Vought, one of the subcontractors, that makes sections of the 787 fuselage.

The Dreamliner presented not only technical challenges, but also integration of the partners and subcontractors. Boeing[28] overhauls its production methods and tightens control on manufacturing processes. Boeing now finds that many suppliers were not capable of managing their subcontractors. Boeing didn't have enough engineers to assist the contactor's subcontractors. CEO Jim McNerney said: "The initial plan outran our ability to execute. I think we got the balance wrong at the beginning of this program."

In March 2008 Boeing[29] identified a problem with the wing box which delayed the test flight. Engineers now discover another issue with the composite materials in the plane's wings. Inspections showed that the metal bolts, called freeze plugs, slightly damaged the surrounding material causing some delamination or cracking. Company officials announced that delamination of the composite material would not delay the test flight. The *WSJ* article reviewed a work order written by one of the engineers: "Noted conditions are structurally and functionally acceptable to engineering for Ground Testing Only" and adds "No Flight Test Allowed." Boeing continued to project the test flight by December 22, 2009.

The moment of truth arrives on December 15, 2009 when the 787 Dreamliner is scheduled to take to the air from Paine Field in Everett, Washington on its flight test. The crowds of 16,000 plus onlookers witnessed a bit of history as the 787, made essentially of reinforced composites, gracefully disappeared into the clouds and returned safely to Boeing Field in Seattle. The flight will kick off almost a year of FAA tests on six 787s to perform an array of tests prior to commissioning for public transport. This is undoubtedly a day of excitement and anticipation, not only for those directly involved in the project, but also for the complete organization.

The flight test program is running behind schedule but Boeing[30] management continues to claim that the first delivery of a Dreamliner 787 to All Nippon Airways Co. will occur by year-end 2010. The certification process by the FAA has yet to begin. Minor delays have been acknowledged by management but manageable. The 787 is now two and a half years behind schedule. Boeing[31] expects to deliver its first Dreamliner by the end of September 2011, but by that time, will have 35 Dreamliners requiring many modifications prior to delivery. The fifth 787, requiring modifications, recently entered the hangar and CEO, Jim McNerney, noted that additional space will be required at Paine field through the end of 2012. He also reiterated his plan to deliver 20 Dreamliners in 2011.

Trying to move the Dreamliner back on track, Boeing[32] decides to bring in some old timers from retirement. Jim Albaugh, Chief Executive of Boeing's commercial airplanes business, tapped eight former senior Boeing executives to form a Senior Advisory Group (SAG) for the 787. Albaugh noted; "I was concerned that we had retirees who were worried about the company, and I wanted them inside the tent. They've got some very strong ideas." The SAG will brainstorm, with current Boeing engineers and managers, on issues related to Boeing's inability to get the product out the door.

The *WSJ* article also reveals some comments by John Roundhill, former Vice President of product strategy and development; Joe Sutter, 89, the unofficial leader of the SAG and leader of the design team that developed Boeing's jumbo jet; Lars Anderson, former program manager of the Boeing 777; and others. The article notes that

"others are not slouches. They are decorated engineers and were involved with every commercial jet Boeing has built since 1945. They aren't afraid to speak their minds or jump into the minutiae of the aircraft business."

The SAG did not couch their words. They were vocal about Boeing's efforts to outsource key parts of the Dreamliner when the "bean counters were running the place." Sutter noted that if you're going to rely on partners to supply components, "you better damn well have a high percentage of Boeing guys there looking over their shoulders." Boeing executives are evidently taking this suggestion seriously as it brought some outsourced work back in-house and "flooded suppliers with Boeing employees."

Boeing[33] announces another setback; no deliveries of the Dreamliner prior to mid-February 2011. The schedule change occurs because of a failure of the Rolls-Royce jet engine; and engine on the test-stand broke apart while undergoing tests. Rolls-Royce and Boeing declined comments.

Peter Sanders[34] reported, in the May 9, 2011, edition of the *WSJ*, that the FAA has given Boeing and Rolls-Royce its approval of the Trent 1000 jet engine for long-range nonconnected cities. The Dreamliner can also be equipped with a GE jet engine.

On November 7, 2010, a 787 test aircraft forced the pilot to make an emergency landing at Laredo airport in Texas, after smoke filled the main cabin. Boeing[35] claimed it, identified the source of the problem, and was working on a solution: a power panel in the aft electronics bay failed and ignited the insulation blanket. Each of the six test aircraft is uniquely configured to evaluate particular aspects of the 787. Jim McNerney admitted that the 787 development plans, involving significant outsourcing, had been "too ambitious." He continued with; "While game-changing innovation of this type is never easy, we've seen more of the bleeding-edge of innovation, than we'd ever care to see again. So we're adjusting our approach for future programs."

The *FT*,[36] on December 9, 2010, reports that the fire was sparked by a piece of foreign debris. Mr. Albaugh, head of Boeing's commercial aircraft business, did not believe the engineers. He said, "Come on guys, that's too easy an answer." The engineers eventually satisfied Mr. Albaugh by simulating what happened on the 787. Keep in mind that the delivery of the first Dreamliner was scheduled for May 2008; it's now December 9, 2010.

Seattle Times[37] report that Boeing Chief, Jim McNerney, said that the company is scheduled to deliver 20 Dreamtimes by the end of 2011. McNerney commented that it was *nothing new* that rework was required on some assembled planes. McNerney suggests that the press reports describe what Boeing has planned for. Current construction schedule calls for building 2.5 planes per month by the end of 2011, scaling up to as many as 10 per month sometime in 2013.

Federal Aviation Administration[38] reports that it has approved production of the Boeing 787 Dreamliner. The final tests to measure "function and reliability and extended-operations" will begin in June according to Scott Fancher, the program chief. Boeing will have built 40 Dreamliners before the first plane will be delivered and all those planes will be altered to meet FAA requirements. Boeing continues to struggle with suppliers to meet requirements and schedules.

A Boeing company supplier, Alenia Aeronautica,[39] a unit of Italy's Finmeccanica SpA, was surprised by a report that Boeing plans to take over production of the Dreamliner's horizontal stabilizer section on future models. This was confirmed by Mark Birtel, a Boeing spokesman. Alenia also builds two sections of the fuselage. Such issues create potential problems when a company works with "risk-sharing partners."

Boeing CEO, Jim McNerney,[40] declined to say when the Dreamliner would become profitable, but that it would be some time in the future. The now 3-year delay in scheduled delivery of the first plane was a result of labor strife and "glitches in the supply chain" according to McNerney.

Larry Dignan[41] reports that Boeing is ready to harvest its R&D efforts now that most of the issues with the Dreamliner are resolved. McNerney acknowledged that Boeing went through some rough times bringing the Dreamliner to the marketplace, but also believes the technical hurdles have been resolved. McNerney noted

> "This is a matter of taking technology we used on the 87, where we went to hell and back getting it done. Now that we have done it, it is a matter of—not yet inventing another whole new way of building an airplane."

McNerney has his eye on China which represents real competition at some time in this decade. He noted

> "This is one of the reasons we have to keep on innovating. Refurbishing an airplane when we can build an all-new one, we have got to be mindful that a Chinese airplane is going to be around, if not in this decade, the next decade. It's pretty competitive. But they will get there."

COMMENTARY

The Dreamliner was certified by the FAA in the summer of 2011. Problems began to occur with its power supplies, brakes, a fuel leak, and faulty wiring which created production scale-up problems. The major problem involved malfunctioning of the lithium-ion batteries which overheated and caught fire. This situation raised serious questions about the FAA's certification process. The FAA issued an emergency airworthiness directive that grounded all 787s in the United States on January 16, 2013; Boeing completed its tests on an improved battery design, and the FAA approved the revised design changes on April 19,

2013, and lifted the grounding on April 26, 2013. The 787 was then free to begin passenger service on April 27, 2013.

Boeing's difficulties with bringing the Dreamliner to the marketplace must be a major disappointment not only to the executives, but also to all who have either directly or indirectly participated in the program: it's a Boeing organizational disappointment. It is not difficult to realize the levels of frustration that must have existed in the organization after a 3-year delay. Those thousands of engineers, technicians, and support people who fought the problems 24/7 must be frustrated with the poor results thus far. Yes, they cherished that moment when the Dreamliner made its first flight, but that was just the beginning of a series of technical and management problems that further delayed urgent deliveries. This section deals with the decisions made regarding the following issues:

- Acknowledging the Reality
- Boeing's Management Principles
- Outsourcing
- Supply Chain
- New Technology
- Cultural Differences
- Technical Capabilities
- Retirees' Concerns
- Decisions
- Dreamliner Knockouts

Acknowledging the Reality

It took Boeing executives several years to acknowledge that perhaps their over exuberance in focusing on extensive outsourcing may be the major reason for the 3-year delay in bringing the Dreamliner to the marketplace. Jim Albaugh,[42] BCA Chief, spoke about the *lessons learned* at Seattle University, where he admitted that Boeing may have gone too far with its outsourcing strategy. The negative impact on Boeing's financial and operational performance continues to present new problems. Albaugh noted that

- The extensive outsourcing strategy backfired
- Boeing spent more money outsourcing than if the work had been done in-house
- Boeing was forced to compensate its partners, support or buyout the partners who shared in the 787's development costs

- The outsourcing strategy was put in place by Harry Stonecipher, then Boeing Chairman and Alan Mulally Chief of Commercial Airplanes and now CEO at Ford.
- Albaugh was not part of the decision at the time and noted that in retrospect things could have been done differently
- Justification of the extensive outsourcing was guided by financial considerations known as Return on Net Assets (RONA)—RONA involves doing less work in-house which reduces employee and facilities assets

Albaugh continued to relate a story where a decade ago, a senior Boeing and world-renowned airplane structural engineer John Hart-Smith, predicted the risks and outcomes of extensive outsourcing in a paper presented at an internal company symposium—Hart-Smith was not allowed to join the 787 program and no one from Boeing's leadership contacted him for further discussion about his concerns. Albaugh admitted that he read the paper and conceded that it was perceptive, if not prophetic.

Boeing's Management Principles

Evidently, someplace in the recent history of Boeing, William Allen's Principles of Operation lost their significance and were replaced with a bureaucratic management and cost-focused approach that McNerney now attempts to bring under control. As I read through the Boeing history and from various news releases and other sources, I gather that Boeing may be facing problems, similar to General Motors, except that the changes may have been created when Boeing and McDonnell Douglas became the new Boeing.

Perhaps Boeing transitioned in recent years in the same way as many major organizations: emphasis on cost-reduction programs and relegation of the business to the finance department. Did Boeing transition from a once very-proud engineering and technology organization to one managed primarily by the bottom line? Did Boeing operate as the US auto manufacturers? Bob Lutz,[43] a former General Motors Vice Chairman, who is certainly not antifinance, relates some of GM's problems in his book, *Car Guys vs. the Bean Counters*. He notes in a recent comment in the *WSJ*

"Detroit got a serious case of scientific management disease," he told CFO Journal in an interview. "Let's run everything by the numbers, let's do everything analytically, let's pretend that that such things as emotion for cars...excitement, beauty, all of the non-quantifiable things don't exist. And let's run this as a rational business. Well, the problem with

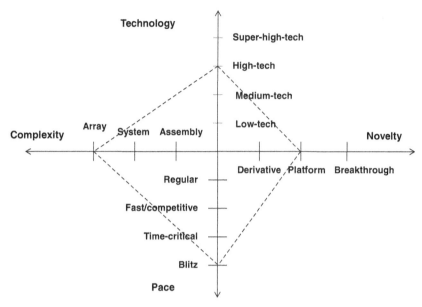

Figure 9.1. Diamond view of 787 Dreamliner at time of approval.

the automobile business is, it's a lot like the movie business, it's not rational. People either like the stuff or they don't like it."

Is Boeing[44] facing the similar internal culture problems that General Motors now is attempting to change? Mary Barra, now GM CEO and former head of Vehicle Development at General Motors, is making some progress in attempting to move "its stifling bureaucracy" into constructive action. Ms. Barra has a reputation of speaking her mind and moving the action forward. After taking responsibility for product development, Ms. Barra eliminated a string of executive positions that came between her and the top engineer responsible for product programs to speed up decision-making. In 2014 Ms. Barra was named CEO of General Motors.

Figure 9.1 shows how Boeing executives probably perceived the four factors in bringing the 787 Dreamliner to the marketplace. The dotted lines indicate how Boeing viewed the project as it took shape in evolving from concept to reality. Was this a realistic view, from the story as presented here, management certainly underestimated the complexities. The use of reinforced plastics required *innovation* as did the assembly process and the outsourcing strategy and the supply chain. Innovation would be required for successful launch of the Dreamliner. Boeing management assumed the company possessed sufficient knowledge and competence in the use of reinforced composite materials so no major obstacles should have been foreseen. The total assembly process, while complex and involving innovation would not create major difficulties if compo-nents and assemblies met quality standards. The supply chain, while extensive and across international boundaries, required added expertise in communication, not an issue that is unsolvable. FAA qualification was nothing new to Boeing; no major issue would prevent achieving timely FAA qualification. The Dreamliner certainly has a major *impact* on the organization's financial performance and the *risk* was moderate. After all, Boeing did not come to the Dreamliner as a neophyte in the aircraft industry: they have had tremendous success with the 747 as well as other aircraft. The *complexity* of the Dreamliner, however, surpassed any prior activity on which Boeing embarked, in all areas.

Someplace along that chain of human effort, the decision process broke down. Perhaps, too much emphasis was placed on spreadsheets, algorithms, computer modeling, simulations, and unsubstantiated assumptions, but without sufficient effort directed at physical prototyping and testing. Did Boeing rely too much on the advanced management tools in favor of the knowledge gained from hands-on experience? Who provided the input to the assembly simulations and the supply chain models; people who understand aircraft assembly or neophytes with up-to-date technical knowledge but without the operations knowledge and experience? Management took on an overly ambitious program, without the necessary due diligence. Keep in mind that Boeing was going to produce the Dreamliner in about half the time it took to deliver the 747.

Boeing made the decision to outsource not only the production, but also the design with partners sharing the development cost. Those major structural suppliers plus several thousand other suppliers presented a major management problem for Boeing. How did Boeing executives plan to manage this complex network of different cultures, different languages, different work methods, dif-ferent management styles, the long-term vacation shutdown of operations, con-flicting government regulations, unions, financing, interrelated design require-ments, interpretation of requirements, and then bring all the pieces together in one location and produce a Dreamliner every 3 days? Think of not only the number of decisions, but the number of different interests that required rationalization; decisions that will be made with input from all levels of execu-tives, managers, projects managers, professional specialists, technicians, and all associated people in the process from concept to implementation. Did Boeing executives understand this complexity? The results indicate they did not. Boe-ing executives should have viewed the Dreamliner project as shown in Figure 9.2. The 787 was, without any doubt, probably mid-way between a *high-tech to super-high-tech project.* Keep in mind that Boeing also introduced new commu-nication systems, eliminated thousands of feet of copper wire, included a new navigation system, and the list could continue, but all within the possibility of achievement. The Pace was certainly a *blitz* project since Boeing decided that the Dreamliner could go from concept to the marketplace in 2 years less than

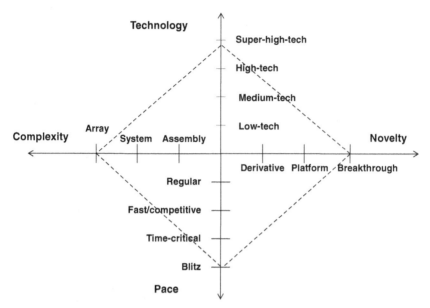

Figure 9.2. Realistic diamond view of the 787 Dreamliner.

their famous 747 aircraft. As for Innovation, the Dreamliner fits a *breakthrough* project description when considering the project from conception to successful delivery and operation of the Dreamliner. As for Complexity, there is little doubt about placing it in the *array* category: a system of systems project involving complex issues. However, Boeing people probably misread the fact that successful completion would require some breakthrough processes; not only in production, but also in logistics; in managing the outsourcing and the supply chain; in integrating the parts and assemblies from many suppliers into a functioning aircraft; in working with a multiplicity of cultures; and whether or not Boeing had the required experience in place to move forward. Those prior buyouts, layoffs, and terminations most likely created a loss of hands-on expertise.

Outsourcing

Outsourcing is not new to the airplane manufacturing industry and certainly not to Boeing; it has always outsourced production of parts and assemblies in the past. The difference, with Dreamliner outsourcing compared with past Boeing practices, lies in the extent of the outsourcing and the type of outsourcing without an apparent workable plan to meet the requirements. There is little doubt that extensive outsourcing created many problems in the development and production of the 787. Figure 9.3 shows how outsourcing was viewed by management and how it should have been viewed.

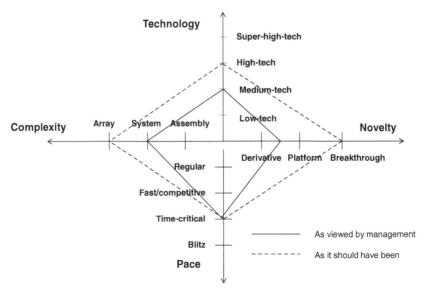

Figure 9.3. Diamond view of the 787 Dreamliner for outsourcing.

Boeing executives failed to listen to the dissenting voices? Hart-Smith[45] was a senior technical fellow and one of Boeing's eminent engineers and a world-wide respected airplane structural engineer. Hart-Smith presented a paper at the 2001 Boeing internal technical conference, in which he challenged Boeing's management to reconsider its approach to extensive outsourcing. Hart-Smith raised two major issues (1) excessive outsourcing, and (2) the uses of RONA as an operating strategy. In respect to excessive outsourcing, Hart-Smith discussed three objectives in this paper and their impact on performance.

1. Why selective outsourcing can be beneficial, but results in *added cost* and not *cost reduction.*
2. Why excessive outsourcing fails to take into account *total cost.*
3. Why, if outsourcing is the strategy, parts and assemblies must be designed keeping the assembly process in mind. This requires additional up-front effort to avoid situations where parts and subassemblies do not fit together in final assembly and add significant cost in rework.

Hart-Smith also raised the question; can an organization continue to operate if it relies primarily on outsourcing the majority of its work. In essence, the company becomes a system integrator. He asserts that a company cannot control its destiny if it creates less than 10 percent of the product it sells. Boeing management chose to disregard Hart-Smith.

Supply Chain

Supply chain management includes just about all the activities related from approving a concept for a new product or service, delivering the product to the customer, and bringing back the customer's comments regarding quality and meeting performance requirements. Every organization will probably implement supply chain management in very different ways, although fundamental guidelines must be followed. The chain includes supply chain planning and forecasting; developing sources for raw materials, component parts, assemblies; procurement; capacity planning; inventory storage and control; identifying economic shipping routes; implementing a communication plan; meeting the legal requirements in many different nations; and in Boeing's case with the Dreamliner, modifying aircraft to ship fuselage sections manufactured in Europe and Japan.

There's much more, but this gives a perspective of what's involved in managing the supply chain. With the emphasis on *just-in-time* inventory control, organizations exacerbate their exposure to unforeseen circumstances such as late deliveries or quality issues. Such initiatives have their unintended consequences when environmental or other issues arise to limit access to the required parts and assemblies. However, the supply chain is not managed solely by someone defined as the supply chain manager. The function requires input from many different organizational units. Figure 9.4 illustrates the Dreamliner supply chain both as originally estimated and what the real needs required. The solid lines indicate the estimated levels and actions that take place among technology,

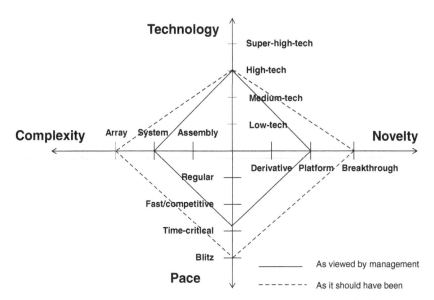

Figure 9.4. Diamond diagram of the 787 Dreamliner supply chain.

innovation, pace, and complexity. The dashed lines show what was required. The process required a breakthrough in thinking of the complexities in managing the activities of several thousand suppliers effectively and efficiently. Perhaps, Boeing in its attempts to accelerate the Dreamliner schedule either oversimplified or disregarded the complexities of the supply chain. There is certainly no doubt that management of the supply chain somehow failed to produce the desired results. The Dreamliner supply chain included a control system, but it evidently failed to meet requirements. Supply chain management requires more than tools; it involves not only judgments but human interfaces and interactions. Someone or some group at Boeing made a decision as to how the supply chain was to be managed; something was missing from their algorithm. Yes, the supply chain was complex; there were interlinked activities of multiple organizations; it included many different cultures; but it lacked an adequate hands-on control system.

We need to keep in mind that the Dreamliner involves more than the airplane's structure. The Dreamliner employs many technologies that span a continuum that includes materials, design, process, manufacturing, assembly, documentation, supply chain, information, communications, management, and others. Each of these technologies interacts with the others and requires more than computer systems to make them a reality. In this chain of technologies some judgment calls will affect the outcome negatively; that's the real world. How an organization manages the negative judgment calls determines the project delay time. Boeing, now by its own admission, recognizes that many of their assumptions did not meet requirements. Figure 9.5 shows the Dreamliner technologies

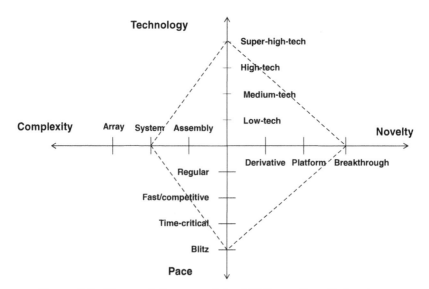

Figure 9.5. Diamond diagram of the 787 Dreamliner Technology.

as a composite for illustrative purposes only, recognizing that each technology diagram would be quite different.

New Technology

As we look at the Dreamliner technology we find it includes many technologies and the integration of those technologies require breakthrough thinking. This was demonstrated by FAA's desertification of the Dreamliner. While from a materials perspective, the use of reinforced substrate technology is a vital piece of the Dreamliner's success, the others mentioned cannot be disregarded. Design, as a function, has its own technologies, both in terms of tools and problem solving. Every major activity requires an approved process; otherwise activities become random and degenerate to a culture that suggests that any *process will do* which is not acceptable in the aircraft industry. Manufacturing has its set of technologies that provide quality components that meet requirements. Assembly, and especially in the Dreamliner case, requires technologies to meet the scheduled deliveries expected of Boeing, and those technologies involve more than those related to the structure. Documentation brings its own share of problems to any project; seldom is there time to document at the time a change occurs, not an excuse, but reality. Documentation for the Dreamliner becomes doubly complicated in spite of the available technologies. While some input may be generated without human interaction, most will require human intervention. The previous section dealing with supply chain needs no further elaboration; the technologies that are implemented must take into account the interrelationships of the parts and assemblies to guarantee timely availability on the assembly floor.

Cultural Differences

All nations including the United States have their distinctive cultures. In the United States, our cultures vary from east to west, north to south and every place in between. Cultures vary in different industry sectors as well as within the various organizational units within an organization. Work methods differ from one country to another. Consider the differences between the United Kingdom, France, Germany, Italy, Japan, China, Russia, and China. Promoting our US approach to working, without long-term educational programs, will yield one result, disappointment and disengagement. Boeing should have been sensitive to these issues, but the problems they faced with managing the supply chain indicate that preparation for foreign assignments and the impact of working with different cultures was not exactly a priority issue.

Boeing failed to follow some well-established principles related to outsourcing to non–English speaking countries. Oh yes, I know some of the foreign team members spoke English, but words have different meanings when translated. We even incur some of the same communication problems when speaking with other English-speaking countries. Communication presents a problem and must be understood and dealt with; it belongs in the project plan, it is an element that often determines success or failure. Mathematical models and algorithms do not resolve communication problems, they complicate the problems. It's also necessary that the host organization's people be embedded in the subcontractors operation on a full-time basis, for as long as necessary. Boeing would probably argue that its employees were embedded and communications were well organized. The history shows that, with the need for the CEO to make seven different apologies for major project delays, communications were not integrated. This is not to be critical of Boeing, but to demonstrate the importance of communication. The fundamentals are simple, the implementation difficult.

Technical Capabilities

The downsizing, over the years by Boeing, had some negative impact on the 787 program. An organization doesn't downsize 20 or more percent of its people without losing some of its intellectual knowledge and operational capabilities and experience. Not everything resides in reports, even though we live in a digital age. Someplace along the line someone implemented a fix that was never recorded and that person's expertise and experience are no longer available. Someplace there were managers who fulfilled their responsibilities as leaders and managers whose expertise no longer is available for problem solving. So, did Boeing lose its sense of *managing technology*? No research is necessary to demonstrate the loss of experienced talent; untried knowledge is not a substitute for experience.

Retirees' Concerns

The press, the blogs, and the comments of retirees in the Boeing engineering community suggest that Boeing lost its core competency: the ability to manage large projects successfully. Boeing has experienced a decade of bad habits that have embarrassed the company, doubted its capability to meet requirements, and questioned its credibility. It appears that Boeing faces what any organization faces when problem-solving principles are bypassed in favor of public relations responses. Supplier problems did not erupt in one instant of time. In the Dreamliner project, they were not acknowledged, although they may have been identified, no one pushed the button to force a timely decision. Disregarding these early warnings exacerbated the undisclosed consequences and jeopardized the integrity of the program. Here is a list of issues compiled from various retiree sources as to what actions or inactions created delays in the Dreamliner delivery schedule.

- Lack of accountability
- Confusion over responsibilities
- "Yes Man" approach parading as "Teamwork"
- Discarding decades of system knowledge in favor of unproven computerized systems
- Disregarding value of experience
- Senior management without technical skills
- Embracing the McDonnell Douglas culture
- Promoting people without execution capabilities
- Insufficient effort to build next generation capabilities
- Inability to manage a complex supplier base

The foregoing issues are common to any organization dealing with a lack of performance in meeting targets, regardless of the industry. Most of the items would apply to the US auto industry. Over long periods of time, in one way or another, all organizations find themselves facing these problems. Few organizations will go through a 50- or 100-year history without, at some time, losing their direction: those principles established by the founding fathers no longer seem viable and are disregarded until someone new arrives with a different focus. As noted previously, William M. Allen, Boeing President from 1945–1972 laid down the organizations operational guidelines, but those guidelines became corrupted over time.

Decisions

How many decisions were involved in bringing the Dreamliner to the position of being almost 3 years behind schedule is nothing but a guess even for Boeing. Was it one million, two million, or more millions? Probably several millions from the time Boeing decided to move forward on the Dreamliner. That principal decision, made by the Boeing Board, lost its significance when the program became operational and the visions required managerial and technological decision-making discipline for successful execution. The decisions required to implement what had been approved, took center stage and the executives who made the macro decision will now mainly rely on reports as to the project's progress. Now, many thousands of people will provide their knowledge, skills, experience, and capabilities to design and build the Dreamliner to meet the requirements, schedule, and costs cited in the proposal. But even with the best of intentions problems will arise. Once an organization begins to change managers and project managers and begins to announce a continuous chain of delivery extensions, the project is in serious trouble. In the Dreamliner's case, seven such formal announcements and the final announcement about delivery of the first aircraft by year-end 2011; even this date was not firm. Why a well-respected organization like Boeing allowed itself to become involved in repeated changes in schedule is difficult to understand. Boeing is not a neophyte in the airline business, it is a leader. The actions lead to the conclusion that Boeing executives and their managers were not willing to listen to those with the knowledge, skills, and expertise. As engineers, we know what occurs when inadequate designs are implemented; when design services are outsourced without proper input and quality control; when production processes are not tested prior to scale-up; and when realistic timelines are disregarded in favor of pleasing Wall Street.

Looking back on Boeing's past history, while the Dreamliner is not "a walk in the park," its people should have had the talent to move forward in an effective and efficient manner. Somehow Boeing just couldn't get its act together. Building airplanes is a complex process. Integrating a million or more individual parts, many with critical tolerances, where failure of any one part may result in a tragedy, involves more than reliance on spreadsheets, modeling, and simulation. While these tools are essential, they only provide guidance, not the answers. There comes a time where understanding and witnessing results, using all five senses, must take precedence.

After the first schedule change was announced, especially on a program with the Dreamliner's business promises and publicity, one would expect that management would have scrutinized the program details to avoid notifying their customers of any further delays. When I refer to management, I mean the highest executive levels in the organization; they must have believed all the information on those PowerPoints and spreadsheets. There was a significant lapse in time before anyone made the decision to analyze the problems from A to Z and back from Z to A, with a focus on the total program. As noted in the summary of events leading to delayed delivery, Boeing faced supplier problems; lack of and improperly installed specialized fasteners; delamination and cracking of composite materials created by fasteners; and a continuous stream of difficulties while claiming publicly that everything was under control. Executive management will not resolve these issues. Anticipating, identifying, and making provisions for resolving problems belong to the operations managers and their technology specialists.

Dreamliner Knockouts

I have previously identified what I refer to as *project knockouts:* those unknowns that if not resolved, will either create major difficulties in meeting requirements or in many cases lead to total project failure. If Boeing management and its professional specialists had taken the time to identify the project knockouts they would have identified the following:

- At the time of Dreamliner approval, what was the confidence level that the use of 50 percent reinforced composites would prove a viable concept? It was not just a matter of determining the viability of using reinforces composites, but also reviewing all of the issues related to manufacturing and its methods of fabrication. With the large investment involved, one would assume that sufficient experimentation and physical modeling validated the concept of substituting reinforced composites for aluminum and the associated million or more holes and rivets per plane. What tests were performed to determine machinability of composites? Only Boeing can answer this.
- Integrating the activities of partners Spirit, US; Kawasaki, Japan; Fuji, Japan; Alenia, Italy; and Vought, US for just the five fuselage subassemblies—this relationship should have raised the following questions:
  o How will these five partners integrate design and manufacturing—this should have signaled at least caution, if not a significant danger zone.
  o How will these groups communicate effectively in English, Japanese, and Italian? There's a general tendency in industry to disregard such issues, but they can seriously complicate not only the communication process but the results.
- These five partners must eventually produce assemblies that, when delivered, can be assembled without modification and retrofitting. Who was given responsibility for integrating the specifications, designs, material requirements, and production processes of five independent suppliers? From the available public information, the five partners are the major source of the delays. Evidently the decision-makers did not recognize this as a knockout at the time the project was approved.
- Providing home-office staffing in partner's operations to participate and monitor progress for the duration of the project and scaling-up in production as required. Are people with the required capabilities such as technical specialists, supervisors, and managers available and willing to accept and adapt to Foreign Service requirements. Can they be identified, are they available? People and their families must be willing, not only to accept a foreign assignment, but adapt to its culture. These are not 1-week sit-ins, they're full-time responsibilities.
- Delivery delays have been associated with issues of the partners involved in production of the 787 structure. But Boeing also projected the final

assembly goal of 3 days: that means one Dreamliner coming off the assembly line every 3 days. However, final assembly is only the initial step in the process of delivering a ready-to-fly aircraft. The assembled aircraft must now go through a series of tests for meeting requirements. The787 includes more than a structure with its appendages. It includes a navigation system, pilot control system, displays of various types, communication systems, internal power distribution, sensors of all types for controlling not only the aircraft but the cabin environment, fire and safety protection, water and waste system, lavatories and associated hardware, software of many descriptions, 40–50 thousand fasteners, a hydraulic system, and the list could go on. Each of these subsystems must now be verified that they work properly within the aircraft as a system and not as individual sub systems. Eventually the aircraft goes through FAA tests before delivery. Did Boeing identify the potential knockouts?

- Boeing faced a problem during assembly of its first 787s from a shortage of fasteners. These are sophisticated titanium and difficult to manufacture and are produced one at a time; they do not come off an automatic machine. The shortage of fastener manufacturer occurred after the September 11, 2001 terrorist attacks and hundreds of orders for jetliners were canceled. Boeing furloughed 35,000 people and of course that cascaded throughout Boeing's suppliers. Alcoa, one of the major producers of these fasteners, furloughed 41 plus percent of its workers. This was certainly known to Boeing people. Evidently someone or some group chose not to take into account the departure of these people in their planning. It wasn't in their algorithm.

- Why Boeing failed to perform a critical analysis once the delays surfaced is difficult to understand. We're not talking about delivery of the morning newspaper. Customers have made plans based on scheduled deliveries and Boeing could have protected its credibility by announcing, after a total appraisal of the project, a 2-year delay; a one-time major delay would have been preferable to an accumulation of seven delays. The 787 includes many "firsts" in the aircraft industry. Some very bold attempts to move many different technologies forward. Keep in mind that in June 2007 Boeing projected delivery of no more than 112 Dreamliners in 2008 and 2009 because of such unforeseen events as the fasteners. This was not a very realistic appraisal and yet McNerney, Boeing Chairman and Chief Executive noted; "The worst thing we can do for our customers is to over-promise and under-deliver." Somehow, the information and effort required to support such a statement was not available or disregarded.

- Boeing's situation is not uncommon; Chrysler, General Motors, Kodak, and others that have been cited. They suffer from a form of management myopia. As has been stated many times, less than 10 percent of projects meet requirements, schedule, and cost. That's not a very exemplary record of performance. But, while there is little doubt that, at Boeing, the global extent of the operations, cultural differences, and work-methods played a major role in the delays, there is no one single action that caused the need for announcing seven formal delays. It appears that these were self-inflicted wounds occurred because of the failure of many people and many decisions. However, within the time frame of the seven delays, there must have been some disturbing and dissenting voices that urged for a full review of the project. Either these voices were not heard or they did not exist: if they were not heard then probably no one was listening. It's difficult to believe that some engineers and managers would not have gone to the mat to oppose what was happening. I raise the issue of the disturbing and dissenting voices because, in reality, they would determine the future of the Dreamliner. They look to the future; they rock the boat, mostly diplomatically; they are the constructive mavericks; they are the thinkers and doers; they are the innovators. Moving their message up the hierarchy, and receiving either a positive or negative response, becomes a major challenge and requires courage to convince executives on the projects periphery about the problems that need to be resolved. Changing that mindset to acknowledge reality only occurs when someone continues to push for a decision based on the available facts.

KEY POINTS

I want to emphasize, that in spite of the delays in bringing the 787 Dreamliner to market, the effort represents a major accomplishment and one of the most complex projects ever attempted. The Boeing 787 Dreamliner demonstrates the management complexities involved when new technologies, new organizational processes, new manufacturing methods, global communication, extended supply chains, extensive outsourcing, project management, all interact in order to meet requirements, schedule and cost.

- Introducing new technologies becomes more complicated as the number of different and unproven technologies increases, when designs involve making tradeoffs to meet requirements, when various processes must be integrated into the system, when changes are made to original require-ments, and when levels of product specialization, as an example occur, in introducing a new-to-the-market product.
- Organizational processes, not only in manufacturing, but throughout the whole organization will change where a project such as the 787 is

approved. Such projects require conscious efforts to develop a workable approach to integrating the all the various functional Units that cross geographical boundaries.

- Manufacturing and all of its subdivisions from materials, standard hardware, special hardware, component parts, subassemblies, assemblies, assembly techniques (joining, welding, riveting, adhesives, etc.), need to be designed into the system; some even need to be prototyped. The Boeing Dreamliner required extra attention; the Dreamliner was not just another aircraft, it was a totally new aircraft. Just think of the objective, when reaching steady state, a Dreamliner every three days! The problems Boeing faced probably came from many areas; one reason, too often not acknowledged, is organizational knowledge Mergers create problems when the organizations come with a totally different mindset.

- Outsourcing has become an industry practice, but outsourcing using financial considerations only, without acknowledgment and an understanding of the dependence on human interactions for executing the details, creates unwanted problems that eventually need to be resolved, but cause delays and additional cost.

- The questions as to what to outsource and to what extent are critical decision points. The Dreamliner outsourcing approach disregarded the undocumented intellectual property and experience gained through prior major aircraft projects developments.

- Supply chain management involves more than just managing the flow of materials and sub-assemblies to be available at the appropriate time: it begins, when we start collecting information to make a case for a major investment of organizational resources and ends when the customer service department can be eliminated. Managing the supply-chain requires more than searching through documents to determine status; it requires face-to-face interchange with an emphasis on frankness and integrity.

- Management needs to pay attention to the discordant voices that warn against excessive outsourcing. Those voices often receive little consideration with final negative consequences.

- Beware of jumping on the bandwagon of every new management panacea. An organization cannot be managed solely by the numbers for long-term sustainability.

- Generally the larger the project the more difficult to manage the supply-chain. Advanced management tools such as use of spreadsheets, algorithms, computer modeling, and simulations provide significant benefit, but prototyping, physical testing, and knowledge gained from past experiences cannot be ignored.

- Managing a project that involves a system of systems requires greater emphasis on communication and integration of activities. Ambitious programs require additional due diligence on the part of all cooperating entities; the professional knowledge workers have additional responsibilities in guiding such a project.

- Organizational cultures present different problems based on geography, type of industry, product line, and age. Cultures also differ within organizations. Differences in culture need to be accommodated or resolved. When not resolved people will disengage. However, we know the consequences when well-intended failure is punished by various means.

- Work methods differ across the international community and while difficult to change, must be understood and rationalized. Attempting to dictate resolution yields failure; appreciate the differences as long as the work effort meets expectations. Just think of the work methods involved in the Dreamliner.

- Language differences are difficult to resolve; a simple word may make a significant difference in interpretation of a statement. Where projects cross international boundaries learn to appreciate the language differences and begin learning the language to demonstrate your interest. You will not master the language, but the effort will be appreciated.

- How many decisions were made after the initial decision the Boeing' Board of Directors passed; that one decision that gave authority for others to proceed. How many decisions followed; probably includes many thousands or millions of decisions, any one of which could cause delays in the project. CEOs and organizational Boards should understand what they're approving; it's more than looking at the *return on investment* figure.

- Managing the knockouts requires early attention. We have a tendency to delay resolving the inevitable problem, thinking that it might somehow go away; we usually pay a high price when we disregard doing what we know should be done but fail to do so because of the complexity. The Dreamliner body included components made of reinforced composites, so the problem is not only developing and manufacturing these components, but also developing the fabrication techniques for the components made from these reinforced d composites.

- Good communication determines level of success in any transaction. It becomes more so as the number of people involved and by several orders of magnitude if the communication requirements cross international boundaries. Even within a nation, the communication patterns vary from North to South and from East to West; the cultures vary. The difficulty is not in recognizing that a problem could exist, but accommodating the various interests before a problem arises.

- Time is of the essence—engineers provide input to determine total time—executives who approve projects, come back with "we can't take that long" and arbitrarily seethe schedule—engineers go along with the decision—when the day of project market launch arrives, the original time is exceeded: there must be a better way. Such actions are costly, not only in money values but also in customer satisfaction and reputation. Can you imagine how the Boeing CEO felt when forced to publicly announce seven times that the Dreamliner would be delayed. While management plays a role in this situation, as engineers we share as a group responsible for the delay. Perhaps, if engineers were more business oriented, such delays could be avoided; this would not absolve executive management from setting goals without thorough analysis of the issues involved.

NOTES

1. Boeing Co., http://www.boeing.com/boeing/commercial/787family/background. page Nov. 13, 2014
2. Gerard H. Gaynor, "Innovation by design or chance: challenges, rewards, and risks," NTC at Boeing, August 26, 2010.
3. Stanley Holmes, "BOEING: caught in its own turbulence," *Business Week*, December 8, 2003, p. 37.
4. Caroline Daniel, "Condit steps down as Boeing chairman," *Financial Times*, December 2, 2003, p. 1.
5. Boeing Media, "Boeing CEO Harry Stonecipher resigns; board appoints James Bell Interim President and CEO; Lew Platt to expand role," *Chicago*, March 7, 2005.
6. J. Lynn Lunsford and Jonathan Karp, "Boeing taps 3M's McNerney as chief," *The Wall Street Journal,* July 1, 2000, p. A5.
7. Kevin Done and Peter Spiegel, "New chief to build on Boeing's strengths," *Financial Times*, July 1, 2005, p. 1.
8. Stanley Holmes, "Boeing's strike: go figure," *Business Week*, September 25, 2005, pp. 112–115.
9. Alan Murray, "After the revolt, creating a new CEO," *The Wall Street Journal*, May 5–6, 2007, pp. A1 and A10.
10. Dominic Gates, "Zeal is real over 787's virtual rollout," *Seattle Times*, December 2006.
11. J. Lynn Lunsford, "Boeing scrambles to repair problems with new plane," *The Wall Street Journal*, December 7, 2007, pp. A1 and A13.
12. Doug Cameron, "Boeing reveals Dreamliner woes," *Financial Times*, October 26, 2006, pp. B14 and B17.
13. J. Lynn Lunsford and Paul Glader, "Boeing's nuts-and-bolts problem," *The Wall Street Journal*, June 19, 2007, p. A8.

14. J. Lynn Lunsford, "Boeing vows on-time Dreamliner," *The Wall Street Journal*, September 17, 2007, p. A8.

15. J. Lynn Lundsford, "Dreamliner nightmare gets worse," *The Wall Street Journal*, January 16, 2008, p. B4.

16. J. Lynn Lundsford, "Boeing acknowledges redesign work on Dreamliner," *The Wall Street Journal*, March 21, 2008, p. B4.

17. J. Lynn Lunsford, "Boeing CEO fights headwind," *The Wall Street Journal*, April 25, 2008, pp. B1–B2.

18. Monica Gutschi, "Boeing sticks to Dreamliner goal," *The Wall Street Journal*, July 16, 2008, p. B4.

19. J. Lynn Lunsford, "Outsourcing at crux of Boeing strike," *The Wall Street Journal*, September 8, 2008, pp. B1–B4.

20. J. Lynn Lunsford, "Boeing strike rattles key suppliers," *The Wall Street Journal*, September 12, 2008, p. B1.

21. J. Lynn Lunsford, "Boeing machinists run risk of drawn-out strike," *The Wall Street Journal*, September 25, 2008, p. B3.

22. J. Lynn Lunsford, "Boeing strikers dig in heels even as economy turns sour," *The Wall Street Journal*, October 23, 2008, pp. A1–A9.

23. J. Lynn Lunsford, "Fastener woes to delay flight of first Boeing 787 jets," *The Wall Street Journal*, November 5, 2008, p. B1.

24. J. Lynn Lunsford and Kerry E. Grace, "Boeing shakes up management as delays plague Dreamliner," *The Wall Street Journal*, December 12, 2008, p. B3.

25. J. Lynn Lunsford, "Boeing cuts forecast, jobs, but won't slow output," *The Wall Street Journal*, January 29, 2009, p. B3.

26. Dan Reed, "Yet another 787 delay puts Boeing's credibility at risk," *USA TODAY*, June 24, 2009, p. 1B.

27. Peter Sanders, "Boeing tightens its grip on Dreamliner production," *The Wall Street Journal*, July, 2, 2009, p. B1.

28. Daniel Michaels and Peter Sanders, "Dreamliner production gets closer monitoring," *The Wall Street Journal*, October 7, 2009, pp. B1–B2.

29. Peter Sanders, "At Boeing, Dreamliner fix turns up new issue," *The Wall Street Journal*, November 13, 2009, pp. B1–B2.

30. Peter Sanders, "Boeing's Dreamliner lags testing schedule," *The Wall Street Journal*, March 30, 2010, p. B3.

31. Christopher Drew and Nicola Clark, "Engine Problem Delays Delivery of Boeing's Dreamliner." *NY Times*, http://www.nytimes.com/2010/08/28/business/global/28boeing.html?_r=0

32. Peter Sanders, "Boeing brings in old hands, gets an earful," *The Wall Street Journal*, July 19, 2010, p. B5.

33. Dominic Gates, "Boeing says 787 delivery pushed back to February," *Seattle Times*, August 2, 2010.

34. Peter Sanders, "Dreamliner engine gets key FAA Approval," *The Wall Street Journal*, May 9, 2011.

35. Jeremy Lerner, "Boeing 787 risks further delays," *Financial Times*, November 12, 2010.

36. Pilita Clark, "Long wait for Dreamliner's arrival," *Financial Times*, December 9, 2010.

37. Seattle times, Dominic Gates, "2011 delivery target for Boeing 787 can be met, McNerney insists," http://seattletimes.com/html/businesstechnology/2014884764_boeingearns28.html?amp Nov. 13, 2014

38. Les Dorr and Ian Gregor, "FAA Approves Production of Boeing 787 Dreamliner" http://faa.gov.news/press_releases/news_story.cfm?newsId=13064 Nov. 13, 2014

39. Susanna Ray, "'Boeing can't move 787 work without permission,' Alenia says," *Bloomberg,* May 25, 2011, http://www.bloomberg.com/news/2011-05-25/alenia-says-boeing-can-t-move-787-tail-work-without-permission.html Nov. 10, 2014

40. "Update 1-Boeing CEO says 787 program faces margin head winds," http://www.reuters.com/article/2011/06/02/boeing-idUSN0224472420110602 Nov. 13, 2014

41. Larry Dignan, "Boeing is set up to harvest its research and development efforts such as its Phantom Ray hydrogen-powered drone that can stay aloft for four days and ...," http://smartplanet.com/blog/smart-takes/boeing-with-787-almost-ready-its-time-to-harvest-rd-efforts/ Nov. 14, 2014

42. Seattle Times Business Staff, "A 'prescient' warning to Boeing on 787 trouble," *The Seattle Times*, February 5, 2011 and revised February 9, 2011.

43. Darren McDermott, *"Bob Lutz, I'm Not an Anti-Finance Guy,"* http://blogs.wsj.com/cfo/2011/06/14/bob-lutz-im-not-an-anti-finance-guy/ Accessed 11.13.2014

44. Sharon Terlep, "GM's latest change agent tackles designs, red tape," *The Wall Street Journal*, June 16, 2011, pp. B1 and B4.

45. L. J. Hart-Smith, "Outsourced profits – the cornerstone of successful subcontracting," Boeing Third Annual Technical Excellence (TATE) Symposium, February 14–15, 2001.

10

COMMUNICATION IN DECISION-MAKING

Decisions has emphasized the need for improving project performance and provided the research and data to justify the conclusions; the data relates to academia, government, and industry. Too often we have a difficult time *doing it right the first time* on major projects, so we do it over and at times more than once. I'm not referring here to what I have described as "well-intentioned" failure that occurs in developing new products and services; support for this "well-intentioned" failure determines the organization's future. Lack of adequate and responsive communication plays a major role in the decision-making process, which in turn affects performance. The late Chester I. Barnard,[1] an AT&T top executive, in 1938, and author of *The Functions of the Executive*, considered communication as the central theme of management and the dominant factor in the structure of complex organizations. He raised the issue of irrelevant information and primarily irrelevant data in the management process. Was 1938 the beginning of information overload? Griffin and Hauser[2] examined communication patterns among marketing, engineering, and manufacturing in matched product-development groups and found communication a major contributor to performance. They also cite a survey (Souder 1988) that reported that 60 percent of new-product teams experienced disharmony. Moenaert[3] et al.

Decisions: An Engineering and Management Perspective, First Edition. Gerard H. Gaynor.
© 2015 The Institute of Electrical and Electronics Engineers, Inc. Published 2015 by John Wiley & Sons, Inc.

identified five requirements for effective and efficient communication in product-development teams; network transparency, knowledge codification, knowledge credibility, communication cost, and secrecy. William D. Jones,[4] *On Decision-Making in Large Organizations*, concluded that failure to solve problems is a result of poor communications and a lack of relevant and important information. Each of the four references in one way or another focuses on communication as related to decision-making related to project performance. Lack of adequate communication usually plays a major role in project failure. At the same time, adequate and appropriate communication does not guarantee project success. Nevertheless, communication drives decision-making and project execution. Engineers, and their managers, as part of the organization's decision-making body (DMB), must recognize that engineering represents only one piece of the continuum from idea to customer/user satisfaction. As engineers, we're only successful, when working with other discipline specialists and organizational units. An engineering success without a comparable business success provides little organizational value. Communicating is far more complex than generally considered; IBM's Silverlake Project and Boeing's 787 Dreamliner cases demonstrated the complexities. Tom Furey, at IBM Rochester, accomplished a successful turnaround because of his emphasis on communication; Boeing's 787 Dreamliner team faced many of its difficulties because of a lack of communication. Every decision creates some level of dissonance, because seldom does everyone agree with the decision, or how the decision will be executed. That single decision may have long-term implications as in Boeing's decision to design and build the 787 Dreamliner; it will impact Boeing's operations for several decades.

Chapter 10 does not provide a guide for developing competencies in communication. If you need to develop competencies in speaking, writing, making presentations, and listening, you'll find many sources available from academic institutions and commercial providers that will meet your requirements. As you consider communication in the decision-making process, keep in mind that we have established previously in Chapter 2 that engineers and other discipline specialists participate in the management of the organization; their input now drives the decision process. As Drucker[5] noted

"… those knowledge workers, managers, or individual professionals who are expected by virtue of their position or their knowledge to make decisions in the normal course of their work that have impact on the performance and results of the whole."

Chapter 10 focuses on the *communication* required to meet the requirements of the *decision to execution continuum*. Chapter 10 topics include

- New-to-the-Market Product
- What is Communication?
- Types of Communication
- Organizational Context
- Barriers to Effective Communication
- Ethical Issues in Communication
- Eliminating the Communication Barriers
- Key Points
- Notes

NEW-TO-THE-MARKET PRODUCT

A New-to-the-Market Product involves integrating not only the required talent from the whole organization but also from external resources. While engineering plays a major role from research through production and distribution, it depends on support from all other organizational functions to meet its challenges. Figure 10.1 shows the generalized and simplified information flow in the decision-making process for major projects. An idea is presented; inputs are requested from managers of Engineering M_e, Marketing M_m, Production M_p, and Others M_o. Information flows from the various discipline specialists E, M, P, and O to the managers of those functions and then up to some DMB. The DMB may go back and forth for more information or clarification with the E, M, P, and O, their respective managers, and eventually reach a decision. The back and

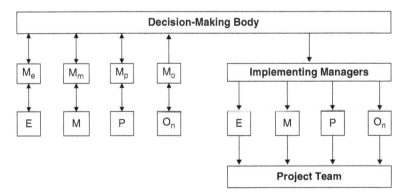

E, Engineering; M, marketing; P, Production; O, Others—Discipline/Functional Specialists. M_e, Manager Engineering; M_m, Manager Marketing; M_p, Manager Production; M_o, Manager Others.

Figure 10.1. Inputs and outputs of the decision-making process.

forth iteration may also include other management levels and selected internal and external sources. When the DMB reaches a decision, it is communicated to the implementing managers of M_e, M_m, M_p, M_o, and then to the project team. This is an oversimplification; it describes the idea to implementation process. Proposals can originate from anywhere in the organization and flow through the levels of functional managers and discipline specialists and then through the process as shown in Figure 10.1.

Many different models describe the elements of project flow. These models will be similar and include five basic activities; (1) define the requirements, (2) investigation, analysis, synthesis, (3) develop the plan, (4) execute the plan, and (5) close the project. The real-world implementation process of bringing an idea to its fruition does not follow such a dogmatic approach and involves significantly greater challenges. These five stages take on very different and expanded constructs based on the scope of the project. Project definition begins with a *raw idea* that someone considers worthy of pursuing. That *raw idea* will undergo much iteration before agreement will be reached to pursue it in some form. The idea will be challenged from many different sources and perspectives including complexity in implementation, marketability, available technologies and user benefits, protecting the current product base, capital investment, available resources, and infrastructure.

Figure 10.2 expands on some details that must be considered while bringing a new-to-the-market product to the marketplace successfully and the role of communication in that process. The four-stage process t includes the idea/concept stage, pre-project stage, project stage, and marketplace execution. The idea/concept and pre-project stages are what I refer to as the *up-front* work. A *new-to-the-market product* includes all the organizational disciplines and functions: in essence, it includes every internal organizational unit, plus external sources of competence and capability. A *new-to-the-market* product is one that does not exist at the current time. It is not a current and improved product with added features. The product does not exist. Such a project requires input from many functions involved in engineering, plus other organizational units involved in the idea to customer/user continuum.

As shown in Figure 10.2, a new-to-the-market product begins with an idea. Someone presents an idea that appears worthy of consideration. The source of the idea, at least theoretically, is unimportant. However, we do know that executives, managers, engineers, and their colleagues include their share of bias in the decision process. But, here is where many project problems begin and they come about because of a rush to judgment. By this time you know, I spent a major part of my career at 3M where, "never kill an idea, just deflect it," was embedded in the culture. Employees suggest many ideas that do not meet the organizations purposes or strategic direction, at least not at the time they're suggested. Ideas are abundant, taking the time to develop them into a discussable

Figure 10.2. Basic new-to-the-market product process.

IDEA/CONCEPT STAGE	PRE-PROJECT STAGE	PROJECT STAGE	MARKETPLACE EXECUTION
1. Idea	1. Identified Concept	1. Project Launch	1. Financial Review
2. Concept	2. Value Added	2. Project Definition and Scope	2. Product Tests
3. Known	3. Preliminary and Design Iterations	3. Finalized Plan	3. Go
4. Unknown	4. Prototypes	4. Project Proposal and	4. Production
5. Unpredictable	5. Validating Design Concepts	5. Approval	5. Marketing
6. Uncontrollable	6. Reduction to Practice	6. Competencies and	6. Sales
7. Strategic Fit	7. Models and Simulations	7. Capabilities	7. Distribution
8. Resources	8. Resolving Knockouts	8. Assignments	8. Customer Service
9. Infrastructure	9. Team Assignments	9. Communication Plan	9. Feedback
10. Knockouts	10. Project Plan	10. Project Management Team	
11. Deliverables	11. Preliminary Business Case	11. Logistics	
12. Metrics		12. Project Reviews	
13. Pre-Project Proposal			
a) *Research*	a) *Research*	a) *Research*	a) *Research*
b) *Product Development*	b) *Product Development*	b) *Product Development*	b) *Product Development*
c) *Manufacturing*	c) *Manufacturing*	c) *Manufacturing*	c) *Manufacturing*
d) *Marketing*	d) *Marketing*	d) *Marketing*	d) *Marketing*
e) *Distribution*	e) *Distribution*	e) *Distribution*	e) *Distribution*
f) *Finance*	f) *Finance*	f) *Finance*	f) *Finance*
g) *Information Technology*	g) *Information Technology*	g) *Information Technology*	g) *Information Technology*
h) *Human Resources*	h) *Human Resources*	h) *Human Resources*	h) *Human Resources*
i) *General Administration*	i) *General Administration*	i) *General Administration*	i) *General Administration*

concept requires work, work, and more work making sense of contradictory evidence. An idea is a suggestion. Developing the idea into a concept involves exploring the possibilities for eventual commercialization or implementation. That process emphasizes the need for constructive communication. I differentiate idea and concept because too often ideas are suggested, with no intention of the originator to pursue it: pursuing it is left to someone else. The originator doesn't even take the time to write it down and it dies. Developing the *idea* into a *concept*, forces one to consider many issues, before jumping into the fray of promoting the idea. This applies, whether the idea is generated at the executive level or at some other level in the organization. Since this is a new-to-the- market product, it will involve input from all of the functions listed from (a) to (i) in Figure 10.2, and consider all of the 1–13 representative items.

Pursuing a potentially successful idea comes after much reflection on what this particular product accomplishes, that cannot be accomplished by products currently in the marketplace. If this idea is coming from a group of engineers, they may need to subordinate their enthusiasm for the technology and replace it with understanding what the product actually accomplishes and for whom. What problems does it solve? What is the added value? What benefits will it provide me as person, my family, my organization, the community I live in, and the betterment of society? These topics will be considered through discussion with selected colleagues in the (a)–(i) category. Developing an idea into a concept also includes identifying the known, the unknown, the unpredictable, and uncontrollable. The known and unknown can be identified, it just takes time and applying the 80/20 rule shortens the effort; the rest is judgment. While we cannot identify the unpredictable and uncontrollable items, we at least need to be cognizant of them and recognize their possible impact. We can at least take them into consideration by asking "what if" and not assuming that the economic and business environment will continue in an upward trend for the next 2 or more years. We should have some intelligence of what competitors are doing. We should know what advancements are being made in technology and their associated processes: that's what we call *forward thinking* and it's a moving target.

This new-to-the-market product must promote the organization's strategic direction or, if sufficiently important, alter the strategic direction in some way. The resources and infrastructure must support this new effort. The potential knockouts identified, deliverables must be catalogued as what and for whom, metrics evaluated, and a pre-project proposal put together to socialize the concept.

You may conclude that this approach becomes too structured. You may prefer to begin experimenting immediately. You may conclude there's insufficient information to make a logical decision to proceed. But remember, precision is not expected at this stage. You may conclude that the idea/concept stage consumes too much time. However, in developing an idea into a concept, engineering precision is not required, major studies are not required, application of knowledge and judgment are required. The objective of the idea/concept stage is to identify the potential for further investigation. If the proposal requires experimenting, fine, but you're not building a prototype in this stage, you're attempting to identify if the proposal is worthy of further consideration. Too often a team is put together to begin working and accumulating data. The preliminary work, suggested here, provides an opportunity to identify issues that too often are identified after major investment of the organization's resources. The idea/concept stage deliverable; a proposal that sets forth conditions for further consideration, and most likely will involve input from the organizational units listed in Figure 10.2 from (a) to (i).

The pre-project stage involves investment of the organization's resources. What was speculative now must be confirmed and resolved. It's time to begin the nitty-gritty process of identifying the details and resolving the unknown elements and being diligent in monitoring situations that arise from the unpredictable and uncontrollable elements. The concept has been identified. The value added by this product now must be identified; that includes specifics that can be validated. Engineering now engages in all the activities from product development through manufacturing. Those potential knockouts must be resolved now, or mitigated in a way as to lose their impact. Resolution of knockouts cannot be delayed pending some unknown solution. The Boeing 787 Dreamliner provides an excellent example, where the up-front work was either viewed as unimportant, or possibly disregarded for the complexities involved in pursuing such an ambitious program. The end result of the pre-project stage: A detailed project plan making a business case for not only a financial investment, but an investment of all the organization's resources to fulfill the mission.

If the *up-front* work results in approval the organization can proceed to applying the well-known fundamentals of project management. Project management principles are clearly documented in many publications, academic programs, and independent organizations such as the Project Management Institute (PMI). There are no mysteries, just knowledge, experience, dedication, and strict attention to detail. But, organizations and their project managers seldom put the effort into, what I refer to as a Project Launch. Why, a Project Launch? Embarking on a project involving millions of dollars; multiple organizational units; requirements, schedules, and cost; 2 or more years to date of market launch; and dedication above and beyond, deserve more than someone mouthing, OK guys, let's get to work. Such comments are an invitation to disregard the interactions that will be required to develop a successful product. A product launch involves more than a discussion by a few top-level managers from the various organizational units, the project manager, and the various team leaders. A project launch brings together all the people involved in the project for whatever time is required to fully articulate the scope and purposes, objectives, critical issues and relationships, expectations, impact on the organization, and all the factors related to this particular project. It's an opportunity to bring everybody together to understand the interrelationships in bringing the project to a successful conclusion.

The marketplace execution stage involves more than what's shown in Figure 10.2. Further, while I have set it out as a stage, in the real world, these stages overlap each other. The role of engineering changes and may be considerably reduced when the project reaches the market execution stage. However, engineering should not consider its job completed. As the product enters the production stage, different types of engineers will be required. Scaling-up production of a new-to-the-market product does not occur in zero time; it is usually a slow and laborious process to reach the desired production rate of acceptable quality products. Although many engineers may be out of the loop at this time, it's absolutely essential in the majority of situations, that engineers receive those users' field reports, review them carefully, request more information if necessary, and make appropriate recommendations. These user reports often point to potential problems and also include valuable comments related to further product expansion. These situations require communication among all the interested participants, based on facts, to resolve the immediate and long-range user concerns.

A new-to-the-market product or service will die or result in something less than expected, without an adequate communication plan. Figure 10.2 shows more than nine different groups from "(a)" to "(i)" and their many subdivisions that must communicate, often in real time, to produce a positive result.

WHAT IS COMMUNICATION?

Previous chapters of *Decisions* have considered who makes decisions, why they are made, how they are made, and how those decisions are communicated to those with the responsibility for implementation. The theoretical framework for communicating decisions does not exist. Perhaps the context in which decisions are made limits the opportunity for a sound theoretical base that operates in all situations. By theoretical framework, I mean like theoretical in physics $F = M \times A$ (Force = Mass × Acceleration) kind of definitiveness. The research in communication does not provide guidance for the practitioner manager and engineer.

Communication can be defined in many different ways. A composite dictionary definition would consider *communication as a process by which information is exchanged between individuals through a common system of symbols, signs, or behaviors*. The means can be oral, written, and visual, those means that may arise in the future, and through any available media. But communication involves more than an exchange of information; it also involves an understanding of what is being communicated: without understanding the essence of the communication, information has not been communicated. That seems obvious, but unfortunately, we falsely assume that our communications are understood. You only need to reflect on your personal experiences, where the communication and the interpretation were not aligned by the sender and the receiver, both may have totally different interpretations. Our discussion focuses on communication in making decisions.

Communications from the executive suites often arise in *executese* language. As an example; we're all familiar with how organizational strategic plans, various strategic directions, and strategies are communicated from the executive suites. Those communications provide little if any guidance for engineers and other discipline specialists. Stating that the organization will gain "x" percent of market share provides no guidance to the engineer at the bench. Promoting that audacious goal provides no guidance; it anything it causes confusion, because the expectations of those audacious goals are seldom defined in terms of a measurable performance criteria. Those executive communications must be translated in such a way to have meaning at different operating levels.

For practical purposes, executives basically ratify the decisions of others; this does not in any way minimize their roles as executives. Many executives have recognized this change in decision-making with the growth of the multinational organizations and the role that technology plays in organizational sustainability. Andy Grove[6] of Intel noted

> "To be sure, once in a while we managers in fact make a decision. But for every time that happens, we participate in the making of many, many others, and we do that in a variety of ways. We provide factual inputs or just offer opinions, we debate the pros and cons of alternatives and thereby force a better decision to emerge, we review decisions made or about to be made by others, encourage or discourage them, ratify or veto them."

The communication process becomes more complicated whenever people are added to the group. Let's face it; some people have difficulties communicating with themselves. There are "$n!$" ("n" factorial) ways to arrange "n" distinct objects into a sequence. Figure 10.2 provides an example showing nine major organizational units (from (a) to (i)). The total possible sequences ($9 \times 8 \times 7 \times 6 \times 5 \times 4 \times 3 \times 2 \times 1 = 362,880$ theoretical combinations. I use the word theoretical because in the real world of decision-making, all those combinations would not be used. However, I use this to demonstrate how quickly combinations occur with each additional person. Adding the 10th person to the example would increase the number of combination from 363,880 to 3,628, 800. The concept of

$n!$ (n factorial) may be easier to comprehend using smaller number. Two people have a possible two exchanges; (a) to (b) and (b) to (a); three people, 6, (a) to (b); (a) to (c), (b) to (c), (b) to (a), (c) to (a), and (c) to (b). Once we reach four people, the visualization becomes more complex; four people, 24; five people, 120 possibilities. These conversations take place where words are interpreted differently, codified by regional language differences, and the special discipline languages. While using "$n!$" may appear unrealistic, we need to keep in mind that every time an additional person is added to the communication, the number of possible combinations increases significantly. If we add the communication that takes place in the pursuit of global markets worldwide, we add an additional dimension to the communication process.

TYPES OF COMMUNICATION

We communicate in many different ways and through many different means for different purposes. The subject matter may be the same, very different, or complementary. The following section considers:

- One-on-One, Face-to-Face
- Communicating in Groups
- Up, Down, Laterally
- Organizational Context

One-on-One, Face-to-Face

Over the past decade much face-to-face communication has given way to email and other electronic means. A worldwide survey[7] showed that 67 percent of senior executives and managers claim their organizations would be more productive if there was direct personal contact. From personal experience, I find a considerable waste of time and delays in decisions because of the total dependence on various forms of electronic communication. Managing the decision-making process solely through use of email requires multiple starts and stops that result in delaying the decision. This does not suggest that face-to-face must be used at all times. On the contrary, email has its place, but seldom for design sessions.

There was time when we didn't know the person on the other end of the telephone or telex. Not knowing complicates the communication process. We don't need theory to prove it. Once we know something about the other person, that relationship changes for better or possibly worse, but in most circumstances it at least provides an opportunity to understand the other person. Sharing experiences often brings people together in resolving an issue. When we identify the shared experiences, we find it easier to communicate. Some common experience from one person or the other creates a breakthrough: recognizing some common interest about national origin, travel, family, schooling, sports, academic disciplines, or the arts, somehow changes the environment. It was easy to disregard a caller's request on the telephone; it's easier to do it through an email. A good start would begin by leaving those cubicles and stop communicating with the person in the next cubicle using email. You might find some common interest.

Communicating in Groups

Groups meet for many different reasons. They meet for (1) project review meetings, (2) they meet for brainstorming design sessions, and (3) they meet to resolve specific problems by developing solutions. Project review meetings need to be face-to-face. There's something about telling the group face-to-face that you either resolved the problem or didn't. It's difficult enough to gain an understanding of the actual status of a project, without visibly engaging the participants. Using various brainstorming techniques on technical sessions, except for very minor design changes, seldom provides an effective way of reaching a conclusion. My technical brainstorming sessions on design projects usually included no more seven people and ran for a week 24/7 (as many times as necessary), and away from the office. This type of brainstorming should include people who come to explore new initiatives and not to push a favorite concept or some agenda. Sessions scheduled to resolve specific issues, probably not as lengthy or requiring offsite facilities, may be supplemented by outside experts with the required expertise. In today's digital world, I often find little in-depth thought in reaching a conclusion. There appears to be a rush to judgment without exploring alternatives. Remember those "shovel ready" projects in 2008; Washington didn't know the meaning of "shovel ready." The engineering community faces similar issues. It's insufficient for one group of engineers to consider a problem resolved, if their solution has not been communicated to every group whose work effort depends on that solution.

Up, Down, Laterally

Communicating in the process of reaching a decision of major consequences involves the competence to communicate up, down, and laterally. The competence to persuade, to focus attention on the requirements of the decision-makers, and to integrate information from many different sources, comes from knowledge and experience. An idea that cannot be clearly communicated has a slim chance of being implemented. A proposal, that fails to focus on the requirements of the organization and the decision-makers, has little chance of approval. The inability to integrate information from many different sources leaves an idea in limbo.

To develop an idea into a concept that can be supported by a proposal to some level of management, usually involves information from multiple disciplines and functions. Even a proposal for a major investment in exploring a new technology will not be made solely by the technical organization. That technology will somehow morph itself into a product at some time in the future, so marketing and finance may well have a voice in the decision. This is an exploratory stage and Eisenhardt's research (Chapter 1) showed the differences between slow and fast decision-makers. Fast decision-makers

- Take 2–3 months to reach a decision as contrasted to the slow who take 12–18 months
- Use more information than slow decision-makers
- Develop more alternatives
- Recognize conflict management as a critical element in making decisions

This information to reach a decision comes from many sources from the bottom to the top of the organization.

Organizations that fail to understand the relationship and interaction of the role of information that arises from up–down–lateral continuum demonstrate a misunderstanding of organizational behavior. Each of these three areas of involvement provides different sources of information and guidance. "UP" provides the business perspective, the economic, the organization's strategic directions, and the ultimate responsibility and accountability for performance. "DOWN" provides the discipline information from the scientific organization if one exists; the many discipline and subdisciplines from the engineering community; the process requirements from manufacturing; the marketing information related to customer interest; the eventual product distribution requirements; and all other activities from the idea to satisfied customer/user chain. "LATERAL" pertains to those working with Colleagues at all levels and provides the means for clarifying issues: the issues that define the proposal. This first level of integration of analyses from others clarifies the originators thought processes. At times these analyses essentially find the idea not worthy of consideration. At other times, input from colleagues modifies the idea to the point where it has little of the original idea. The sooner idea originators involve their colleagues, the sooner they begin the process leading to a decision. At times, colleagues are known to disparage any new idea, so idea originators need to recognize constructive criticism from negative comments by the naysayers.

ORGANIZATIONAL CONTEXT

Discussing the issues regarding communication in relation to decision-making must take into account context. Context includes factors such as the vision, values, and value proposition of the organization. Decision processes differ significantly among organizations depending on the users they serve, the industry involved, and the organizations' strategic directions. The decision processes will be quite different at organizations such as Boeing, HP, Intel, P&G, and 3M. Henry Mintzberg[8] isolated 12 factors from Fondas and Stewart[9] and summarized the evidence into five major areas of context in the fulfillment of managerial responsibilities. They include

1. **External context:** considers national culture; industry sectors organizational sectors; government; commercial organizations; and the not-for-profit organizations
2. **Organizational context:** form of organization such as entrepreneurial and innovative; professional; and also with respect to age, size, and stage of development
3. **Job context:** level in the hierarchy, the work or function; length of service and competencies; and human behavior requirements as differentiated between an engineer and other discipline specialists
4. **Temporal context:** temporary pressures dealing with the issues at hand; managerial style; managing practice; moving the product to the customer
5. **Personal context:** background of the appointee; tenure in the job, the organization, or the industry; and personal style.

Understanding context is fundamental to effective communication. Just think back of past communications, whether up, down, or laterally, and reconstruct them as to their contextual alignment. Each of these five contextual areas takes on greater significance, when we begin to communicate across international boundaries that involve different cultures, work requirements, and behavioral patterns.

The context would be quite different for organizations predominantly managing top-down and those managing bottom-up as a matter of policy. Organizations, managing predominantly with a defined combination of managing top-down and bottom-up, as policy presents a different context. The use of these terms top-down, bottom-up, and some combination of top-down and bottom-up requires clarification. No organization manages at a 100 percent level in these three categories. In organizations that manage from the top-down, activities begin at the top of the organization. The CEO and senior executives play a major role in directing organizational activities. The TOP, not only defines directions, but manages them: ideas originating at the TOP take preference in many situations: the organization approaches a *command and control* environment. TOP level executives, knowledgeable in their disciplines, set direction and basically direct activities. HP, under CEO Carly Fiorina, provides an example that was unsuccessful with a top-down strategy; a long way from the organizational culture under William (Bill) Hewlett and Dave Packard. This does not suggest that executive management is deaf to new ideas from suborganizational units, but generally manage from the TOP. As I followed the history of industry icon Eastman Kodak for several decades, I concluded that the organization was managed mostly top-down. Their attempt to replicate 3M's intrapreneurship program essentially failed. One Kodak entrepreneurial leader noted that he was supposedly in control, but was forced to use engineers assigned to him: he had no control in the selection. He also noted that, Kodak people would take their 8-hour day and go home. Entrepreneurship does not succeed when participants watch the clock. Entrepreneurship does not occur by assigning someone the title of "entrepreneur" or establishing an entrepreneur department.

No organization operates solely bottom-up. While many organizations, primarily in Silicon Valley begin managing from the bottom-up, their success will depend on using the approach judiciously as they grow and bring more employees on board. There comes a point in an organization's growth where it needs to focus its resources on success, and while freedom to do one's thing is a commendable approach, building an organization requires discipline. Not very many people can accept total freedom. Expectations need to be defined and that process involves guiding the organization by providing workable options. We need to recognize that even in the technologically oriented organizations, many jobs are routine and will continue to be routine. Steve Jobs has been considered as an anomaly according to Roberto Verganti[10] because he did not fit the orthodox perspective of a CEO. Verganti notes that Jobs put people at the center where ideas "flew from the bottom up." Jobs never listened to users. Jobs added meaning to employees, by working on visionary products. Verganti describe Jobs' "leadership style as vertical, top-down approach, often harsh. At new product launches, he, not the team, was the protagonist."

The bottom-up/top-down organization provides opportunities, both for the employee and the organization: it provides opportunities to release individual initiative with executive management guidance, but depends on the organization's products and structures. The BU/TD organization opens the communications capability across the organization. Level in the organization does not in any way inhibit open communication. 3M Company provides an excellent example: it continually raises its target for the number of new products providing a large percentage of revenue that have not been available in the previous 5 years. That type of strategy usually requires a top-down/bottom-up approach. 3M's current target, generate 40 percent of revenue from products not available in the past 5 years. To introduce this type of culture to the auto, aircraft, or chemical industries may be problematic, unless directed at devices and components as parts of the total package.

The 3M culture was defined by William McKnight[11] in 1948 when he challenged management with the following statement

"As our business grows, it becomes increasingly necessary to delegate responsibility and to encourage men and women to exercise their initiative. This requires considerable tolerance. Those men and women, to whom we delegate authority and responsibility, if they are good people, are going to want to do their jobs in their own way. These are characteristics we want, and people should be encouraged as long as their way conforms to our general pattern of operations. Mistakes will be made, but if a person is essentially right, the mistakes he or she makes are not to tell those under its authority exactly how to do their job. Management that is destructively critical when mistakes are made kills initiative, and it is essential that we have many people with initiative if we are to continue to grow."

It's interesting to note that McKnight was an accountant by profession and that he included men and women in this statement; this was in 1948.

Other CEOs have also established organizational principles to guide the organization's future. William M. Allen,[12] Boeing President from 1945–1972 established the following basic principles of operation to guide the company's operations that focused on decision-making. Boeing was basically an engineering organization at the time dominated by engineers. Allen's first 7 of 16 principles involved decision-making.

1. Avoid hasty decisions or actions when angry or under emotional stress.
2. Base decisions on merit alone. Apply rules uniformly.
3. Keep the promises you make. Avoid making any you can't keep.
4. Acknowledge your own mistakes and refrain from buck passing.
5. Avoid decisions or actions before all facts are in and carefully considered.
6. Avoid delaying decisions and actions after all the facts are carefully weighed.
7. Explain reasons back of your decisions and actions.

The last nine focused on behavioral issues related to colleagues at all levels in the organization.

3M's approach utilizes personal initiative guided by a supporting management for developing ideas into useful product. Not all ideas are supported and 3M executives have acknowledged when they made the wrong decision, but they have always supported *well-intentioned* mistakes and what could be learned from them. Introducing 3M's approach in Boeing would be most likely related to components, assemblies, and devices as parts of an aircraft and not the aircraft. The contexts in which 3M and Boeing operate differ, if no other reason, from the fact that 3M produces thousands of products with life span measured in years, Boeing produces a limited line of products with a life span of decades. The operational contexts are different, and communication must meet the five contexts as described by Mintzberg: external, organizational, job, temporal, and personal.

Communicating effectively, whether up, down, or laterally, presents more difficulties than normally anticipated. We assume the content of the communication has been interpreted correctly. That assumption may or may not be correct. Communication channels, while viewed as coherent and direct, include significant barriers for understanding.

BARRIERS TO EFFECTIVE COMMUNICATION

Much has been written about the barriers to effective communication, with little of the content grounded in research that is translatable to the practitioner. Perhaps, it is a topic, because of its scope and direct human involvement, and with an expansive range of variables, to allow for scientific research. This section considers the problems and interventions associated with communicating an idea, concept, directive, or result. These are the issues faced daily in various combinations of senders and receivers and significantly impact organizational performance.

The major barriers to effective communication in developing a *new-to-the-market* product involve the following issues and will be considered individually.

- Content in Context
- Language
- Noise Level
- Listening
- Judging
- Feedback
- Technology
- Communication Plan

Content in Context

The message begins by developing the content so that it can be understood by all for whom it is intended. When the content must be received by multiple levels within an organization and also to external users, the communication becomes more difficult. As an example, when a decision is passed down from the executive level to those involved in the project implementation. That decision, if positive will most likely say, project approved. In other words, the operational level provided the majority of information to reach the decision, so now, implement it. Here is where mid-level managers often fail to communicate effectively. Multimillion dollar projects are started without an operational project launch. The work is selected and distributed to the various organizational units, their functions, and their disciplines without an opportunity, for those who will be intimately involved, to see the total picture. Such actions create the first major barrier. The project begins, not with a broad perspective of the objectives, but a mindset that allows every group to work in its own silo.

As the implementation of the project begins, communication takes place among individuals, individuals within teams, groups, task forces, and so on, regarding countless issues. We could assume that one engineer communicating with another would have no difficulty providing the required content and in context. Unfortunately, that's not necessarily true. I suggest you review your past experiences in communicating details with some of your colleagues. Messages, either written or spoken, considered by the communicator to be clear, concise, and complete, continue to be misinterpreted. Sometimes, only part of the message is heard. At other times, some interruption momentarily distracts a colleague from the topic at hand. The majority of miscommunications do not result in disastrous events, but very often require extensive physical as well as mental rework. This rework reverberates throughout the chain of individuals and organizational units that depend on timely performance of others.

Here is another example of what can occur among a group of engineers involved in developing very sophisticated equipment. As manager of an instrumentation laboratory, one of our projects involved using x-rays for measuring certain parameters. Since this was a one-of-a-kind specialized measuring device, the engineers who developed it were responsible for preparing the maintenance manual. The operation of the device required knowing how to turn the device on and off, calibrate it, and do normal x-ray, electronic, and mechanical maintenance. When I saw the installation and maintenance document, I was surprised to see several pages of differential equations. Including such information for maintenance on the factory floor goes beyond what is required. In communicating technical information we need to be cognizant of the user. What do you think of the operating and maintenance instructions that accompany your purchases? Were they meant for the user?

Language

It's difficult to realize that we do not have a common language of technology. It is also difficult to realize that we do not have a common language in the engineering community except, perhaps, in one of our most fundamental equations, $F = MA$. David Whyte,[12] philosopher and poet, suggests a few thoughts for our consideration to communicate more effectively.

- "You cannot enter any world in which you do not have the language."
- "What is the conversation we're not having?"
- Cutting off the "conversation" too early.
- The language we use is influenced by the world we're facing.
- "Will"—is an elaborative mechanism—once you decide to build a house and where, that's when "will" comes in—until that time it is "conversation."

I selected these quotes since they eloquently describe the requirements for usable language: if we fail to understand the communicator's language or the communicator fails to convey the content at the appropriate level, we arrive at barrier one. If we fail to consider the required issues either directly or indirectly, and face up to the requirements, we begin the downward slope to some level of failure. If we stop the discussion too early, without considering associated issues, we jeopardize not only our activities, but those of others. If we fail to consider the operational environment and the people involved in a specific discussion, we fail to make use of the organization's competencies and capabilities. Finally, searching for facts and knowledge, analyzing opportunities, developing scenarios, and reaching an acceptable decision is just *conversation* until someone demonstrates the "will" to make it happen.

We live in a highly technical society compared to the agricultural and even the industrial age. In spite of our emphasis on technology, we do not have agreement on what the word "technology" means. We also fail to have agreement on the meaning of the word "innovation" which is on the tongues of every reporter, pundit, and politician. W. Brian Arthur,[13] technology thinker and economist, in *The Nature of Technology*, raises many questions about technology that remain unanswered. As an example, the word "technology" carries several meanings. Arthur begins by asking what technology is. He notes that we have studies of how technologies come into being; analyses of design processes; adoption processes; diffusion; how society shapes technology and how technology shapes society; but we have no agreement on what the word *technology* means and no overall theory of technology—an "ology" of technology. Definitions matter according to Arthur and "how we think about technology will determine how we think of it coming into being. Arthur[14] continues by noting; if technology originates as knowledge, it must originate in some way as knowledge; if technology is a practice, it arises from practice; if applied science, it must somehow derive from science. Arthur concludes that if these definitions define technology, then they must be fused together in some manner. Arthur proposes three definitions.

1. Technology is a means to fulfill some human purpose. His examples include oil refining, the diesel engine, computers, chemical processes, and materials.
2. Technologies as an *assemblage of practices and components*. He refers to these as bodies of technologies and includes electronics, and biotechnology that are collections of technologies.
3. Technology in this sense includes the entire collection of devices and engineering practices available to a culture. In essence, a collective or as Kevin Kelly defined it, the "technium."

Each of these three descriptions considers technology in a different sense. So, when we use these words, that have multiple meanings, we need to define what aspect of the word we're considering.

The word "innovation" likewise takes on many different meanings. It is unfortunate that policy makers have difficulty recognizing the differences between invention and innovation, science and engineering, and other dualities that leave the listener wondering about the message content and context. Consider innovation. To some, innovation is equivalent to invention. To others, innovation begins in the research laboratories. A recent review in *The Wall Street Journal*[15] of *The Idea Factory* notes that the author Jon Gertner makes the common mistake of confusing invention and innovation. The author considers Bell Laboratories the most innovative scientific organization in the world during the period 1920–1980, yet Bell Laboratories never commercialized its inventions. There is no argument that Bell Laboratories was a leader in invention. Bell Laboratories did not commercialize the transistor and even though it invented the silicon solar cell in 1950, solar energy remains uneconomic today. In the past decade, even the financial community speaks of financial innovation with its extensive negative consequences on the economy. Here are a few descriptions of innovation for your consideration by Gaynor[16] in Innovation by Design.

- Innovation is controlled chaos. James Bryan Quinn, Professor
- Innovation is creating a new idea and getting it to work. Theodore Levitt, Economist
- Innovation is not science or technology. Peter Drucker, Professor

- Innovation creates new wealth rather than knowledge. Peter Drucker, Professor
- Innovation is turning an idea into a business success. Gifford Pinchot III, Co-founder Bainbridge Graduate Institute
- Innovation = Invention + Exploitation. Edward B. Roberts, professor
- Innovation is newness, in the sense that it has never been done before. Theodore Levitt, Economist

As an engineer, technology executive, innovator, and author, I have promoted a modified version of the description suggested by Roberts.

Innovation = Invention + Commercialization or Implementation

There's a caveat associated with this description; *no commercialization or implementation, no innovation.* This description also embodies the descriptions by Drucker, Levitt, and Pinchot III. It also includes Bryan Quinn's suggestion that innovation is *controlled chaos.* If you question Bryan Quinn's conclusion, I suggest you become an innovator and experience the chaos. However, I suggest that the least we can do as we discuss innovation or any other topic, is agree on a *situational definition.* Meaningful discourse cannot emerge when what is being discussed is not defined. A group discussion, where some members consider innovation equivalent to invention, will not reach any viable conclusion. Words are important and have meaning. If everyone uses their personal dictionary, problems will arise. If in doubt, make sure everyone is in agreement.

Noise Level

In this discussion of noise I take a practitioner perspective. I do not discount the academic and important discussions related to the theories that back up the conclusions related to psychological noise, physical noise, physiological noise, semantic noise, and cultural noise. I'll focus my comments on the *noise* that generates problems in the decision-making process: the pre-decision process, the discussion of alternatives to reaching a decision, and the execution of the decision. Noise can be defined as anything not relevant to the discussion. There are many factors related to noise that hinder reaching a decision: (1) irrelevant information, (2) opinions instead of facts, (3) unnecessary interruptions, and (4) environment. Keep in mind that while I have tried to categorize each of these noise factors, they're all interrelated.

Irrelevant Information. Assuming that every discussion, whether one-on-one or in groups, begins with a defined purpose, may be naïve. However, for purposes of discussion, I make this assumption. Further, if no purpose exists, then, perhaps the discussion is not necessary. There is a note on our refrigerator and I don't know where it came from, but it states: "Speak only if you can improve the silence." That may be going a bit too far, nevertheless worthy of noting. The same dictum may apply to written communication. It appears that today's written and oral communications span from the tweets to the multi-page documents with much of the information irrelevant to the decision-making process. The same applies to oral conversation.

Discussions take place at different levels in the organization and with distinctly different purposes. For our purposes consider two types, (1) strategic and (2) operational. When I refer to strategic sessions I'm not referring to the annual strategic planning sessions, but to discussions that arise during the normal work cycle that need an organizational perspective. Each type of meeting includes different levels of competence and capability. The composition of a group discussing a major investment in technology differs greatly from a group resolving a specific technical issue. In such strategic discussions, bringing in extraneous minutiae contaminates the discussion and detracts from resolving the major issue. There's a tendency usually for some members of the group to focus attention on their particular problems that represent unnecessary noise and detract from the discussion. Discussions at the operations level do require consideration of the minutiae, because it's the lack of concern for the minutiae that often leads to some level of failure. But, the minutiae must apply to the solution of the issue on the table. Every organization faces problems with *meetingitis*. At times some people are booked solid with one type of meeting or another. At your next meeting, have someone clock the amount of time spent on irrelevant information. This action is not to improve efficiency, but to bring some discipline into the discussion process, and thereby provide adequate time for considering alternatives.

Discussions among engineers and other discipline specialists, about information to be provided to upper management, involve a significant amount of unrelated information. You've been to those meetings where hours are spent discussing minutiae, of little importance at the time, instead of the strategic issues. You've probably participated in those discussions where someone is insisting on 100 percent compliance in their requirements. How about the presentation that focuses on the technology, rather than on how the technology provides significant user benefits and improves the organization's competitive position. You most likely have been involved in those discussions, where those private conversations disturb the whole tenor of the discussion. And of course, the group always finds itself fighting with those multitaskers who need sections of a presentation repeated. Too often participants bring the cubicle mentality into the discussion, their needs are the only ones worthy of consideration. This irrelevant information allows the discussion to not only go off topic, but also often fails to consider important issues. These same situations occur after a decision has been approved, and the work effort begins with some of these same people responsible for implementation of the decision focusing only on their needs. Information prepared by engineers and other discipline specialists for upper management must demonstrate to decision-makers that it is verifiable, that it includes general agreement among the providers, and represents their best judgment.

Opinions Instead of Facts. Some people are entitled to opinions, others are not. That statement may be presumptuous on my part. People with knowledge have a right to an educated opinion; people without knowledge might apply, "Speak only if you can improve the silence." You've heard the statement, managing with data, and it's difficult to argue with the statement unless you define "data" as nonessential data or too much data. We might ask questions such as: what are the sources of the data; what was the methodology used to develop it; is data of the past useful in projecting the future; is the data relevant to the situation under discussion; does the data take into account demographics, and similar questions that often determine the validity in using the data in the context of the topic under discussion. Answering such questions determines the usefulness of the information and subsequently the knowledge to be derived from the data.

As engineers we can argue that engineering decisions are based on facts. As noted, engineering depends on more than $F = MA$, $E = IR$, or knowledge of the Periodic table. The engineering function goes beyond just doing the engineering. The engineering functions decide whether customer's buy the product or service. The success of the effort depends on whether or not the users find the product or service useful; does that product or service allow them to compete more effectively in the marketplace. Does that product or service improve their internal effectiveness and efficiency: does it enhance their performance with external entities on which the organization depends? So the engineering solution must take into account more than engineering.

The number crunching in any engineering design provides a significant amount of information, but is that information sufficient? Engineering design, as an example, involves selecting a design after considering the requirements and the requirements include more than engineering requirements. Designs may involve problems in user competence; safety and environmental issues which the designer may not possess sufficient knowledge; different international market requirements; and costs associated with raw materials which will affect choice of a design. These issues can be resolved by selecting an appropriate design which will be some combination of alternatives that have been considered. The design will balance many different needs and will not be optimum for many different applications. The Boeing 787 Dreamliner, made up of thousands of parts and assemblies and subassemblies, no doubt posed many different solutions: some based on past experience, but many others in the unknown and untested territories. Every technical discussion requires negotiating tradeoffs.

Seldom does a perfect solution present itself. As engineers, we select the most appropriate solution based on the available information and judgment on the impact of the unknown.

Engineers and managers work in the quantitative information; information that can be described with numbers. Those complex algorithms provide quantitative results. However, algorithms are based on certain assumptions. If the algorithm assumes some future impact from technological advances, those assumptions are qualitative. We might even refer to them as, the *best guesses*. Hopefully, they involve judgment based on knowledge and experience. But, the technical decisions include more than the quantitative, they also include qualitative information; the decisions that relate to quality in operation, style, color, ease of use, and customer satisfaction. Some years ago a group of colleagues questioned my mental state, when I suggested that qualitative data could be quantified at some level: understanding could be gained by applying semiscientific methodology to provide direction. Assume you need to make a choice between (a) and (b). It doesn't matter what (a) and (b) refer to. The quantitative information can be examined and a decision rendered assuming there's agreement on the importance of each of the parameters under consideration. However, providing a figure of merit, as an example, for the characteristics such as perceived quality, reliability, and user satisfaction for (a) and (b), poses a critical problem. Each of these three characteristics is quantifiable, at the point of production. The production quality records may show that (a) meets all the quality standards (quantitative), but what about the input from the user (qualitative), where the product is perceived as not meeting user requirements. The user information will be qualitative and integrating all the user information provides some level of quality as viewed by the user in practice. The same applies to the characteristics associated with (b). The *production results* for (a) and (b) are quantitative, and can be codified. The user responses for (a) and (b), are qualitative, but that is not sufficient reason to disregard them; in the final analysis these qualitative responses determine success of the product.

Conclusions can be drawn from qualitative information. As an example: The decision to pursue an idea for a new product, in the initial stages, will involve qualitative information. Exploring the products utility through surveys and focus groups produces qualitative information, but that information can be discovered through appropriate scientific methods. The decision of 3M's marketing group to dismiss Post-it Notes as a nonviable product was based on qualitative information. The determination of the engineers and product champion used qualitative information to demonstrate its possibilities—let people try them. The decision to invest in a new technology will be based on qualitative information. The facts are not available. Experts in the field may be asked to comment on its potential, but there responses are qualitative information based on their knowledge of the technology.

Consider the following example: the telephone rings and the customer on the other end of the line raises issues about the quality of the product. What is the response, how do you communicate with the customer; a rush trip to the customer or an attempt to determine the scope of the problem through appropriate questioning. If the issue is resolved after a discussion, what is the next step, wait until the next customer calls or determine whether other customers, using similar processes, are experiencing problems.

Here is an example of how two well-qualified people communicate. Please note that I refer to "user" rather than "customer," since the customer may be the procurement department, which most likely is not the user. Come back with me to the 1950s when telephones were our primary source of oral communication. This is the story of two competent salesmen trying to convince organizations to expand their communication capabilities. Each had a different way of communicating. You may recall those days involved telephone operators who switched calls manually by "pulling and plugging." Major organizations hired hundreds of telephone operators who sat at rows of switchboards.

This situation involves Salesman "A" and Salesman "B" working for a supplier of telephone equipment and services. Both "A' and "B" knew the products and services. The story was told to me by Salesman "A." Salesman "A" and "B" were not competing for the same orders; they were friends and colleagues working in different territories for the same company. Salesman "A" went about his work very methodically. He spent time in every department, observing and interviewing every person, to determine the problems associated with the current telephone system. He then did an analysis and made specific recommendations in a neatly bound document and presented it to the organization. Salesman "A" closed about 3 in 10 accounts.

Salesman "B" used a different approach. He somehow managed to gain access to the switchboard room, where many operators were doing their pulling and pushing of those connecting cords. He entered switchboard room with an appropriate-sized box of candy. You should be aware that at that time candy stores seemed to appear on every corner and occasionally at all four corners of an intersection. Salesman "B" observed what operators were doing, the frequency of the calls, length of hold time, level of operator frustration, and other actions and operations. When some took their break, he managed to engage in individual conversation for further elaboration. Generally, Salesman "B" made two to four calls to a location, each time bringing the candy. His reports and recommendations usually included a formal letter of two to three pages. Salesman "B" made the Company's Top Salesman's List every year by obtaining orders from over 90 percent of his calls.

Salesman "A" had difficulty understanding why salesman "B" was so successful. Salesman "A" did his work meticulously; documented everyone's needs and also their dissatisfaction with the phone system; he had all the facts, wrote excellent documents by any standard, and was a dedicated employee. Did he really need all that data to make a recommendation, probably not: he was data driven in the mid-1950s to the extreme? He could have acquired all the required information to make a recommendation by contacting some small percent of the users. We can discuss whether the operators or the users are the best source of information, the fact is that salesman "B" found a much easier way. Sometimes we have to step away from those policies, procedures, and recommended practices and demonstrate some individual initiative. There is no doubt that salesman "B" had a more interesting challenge to acquire the needed information in a much shorter period of time.

Unnecessary Interruptions. How long does it take to recall a thought after you've been interrupted? Losing a thought during a meeting may not be detrimental, but losing the thought by a process engineer in a nuclear power plant could present a catastrophe. This topic should be of interest to the academic and the practitioner. Sometimes you never resurrect that thought until months later, and it may have lost its value. Interruptions, whether occurring while writing or speaking, create the same effect. Engineers, other professional disciplines, and managers when working in groups often display similar behaviors that appear on the Television talk shows. Questions are asked of one person and others respond. The group Chair asks a question and answers it; doesn't give the person an opportunity to respond. When such actions continue, not only do many participants stop listening, but more importantly, they have, for all practical purposes, become disengaged from the discussion. As a young design engineer I paced myself, so as not to be in a position of stopping at some important point in my work. That usually meant staying after hours to reach a certain point where it would be easy to recover the next morning: I didn't have to spend time trying to consider where I left work the previous day.

Interruptions occur from many different sources. Our 24/7 mentality, with its array of electronic devices and the belief that we must respond immediately, generates much unneeded discourse and a significant waste of time. This does not suggest that at times it may be important to respond immediately. Today, most engineers do not have secretarial help available to request a hold on all email requests and phone calls for the next 2 hours. Group meetings usually include a laptop at every position with every participant checking email at one time or another. And of course, we can't disregard the interruptions from those cellphones, and the disruptions that occur when the recipient leaves the room, and then rejoins the group and attempts to pick up the thread of the conversation. The cost of such interruptions depends on the complexity of the topic under discussion. The impact, on a group of software engineers developing a program for a Numerical Control Machine or a group of mathematicians involved in developing an algorithm, could have more serious consequence, than for a group discussing the upcoming department picnic.

Nonrelevant information has been considered previously, but it also provides unnecessary interruptions. Obviously, different interpretations can be given to the appropriateness of the information. I'm not suggesting that stories that help demonstrate a point should not be included. I'm not suggesting that an appropriate amount of levity should not be introduced to demonstrate a point or to relieve what appears to be building to a high level of frustration. I do suggest that we need to consider the relevance of the information being brought forward. This leads to the question of how much information is required to reach the decision. As engineers we tend to seek precision while a project that involves a new-to-the-market product requires significant amounts of personal judgment; third decimal point accuracy is not required, 10 or 20 percent may be acceptable. There are no algorithms that integrate the engineering constraints, individual user requirements, market segments, disparate worldwide economies, and the organization's capability to execute new product programs. Integrating all of these information becomes a matter of judgment: a judgment based on the knowledge, experience, and respect for logical reasoning in making the appropriate decision.

Environment. The information that engineers feed to the ultimate decision-makers involves problem-solving and brainstorming sessions. We should recognize that problem-solving sessions in one sense resemble brainstorming sessions, although not necessarily following the rules. Problem solving includes generation of alternatives and selection of the appropriate alternative, if one exists. Those problem-solving session usually require pursuing new avenues and acquiring new knowledge, probably not available at the time. But how the participants communicate determines the outcome. There is a reluctance to "tell it like it is," it's not polite to freely express what may be considered critical thoughts. All the information doesn't come forward and some falls in the "unknown" column.

Too often we speculate on the "unknown" rather than make an attempt to develop it. Whether we speculate or find the information obviously depends on its importance to resolving the problem. Information regarded as important to the decision must be rationalized in some way to go forward. This becomes especially important when engineers provide recommendations to upper management. If the information is not available or cannot be verified by inferential means, it becomes incumbent upon engineers to advise those responsible for making the ultimate decision accordingly. I'm well aware that "kill the messenger" often comes into play, but your integrity becomes more important than taking some immediate criticism. Maintaining integrity applies not only to information going up the organization, but perhaps more importantly, with your colleagues. Whether "you're killed as the messenger" depends on how you present the message. People with management responsibility generally disdain responses as to why some activity is not achievable, they prefer a response to the question, "what's required to accomplish it." They'll decide whether or not to go forward.

How can organizations find appropriate means for resolving differences related to either strategy or operations? Engaging participants in a discussion often becomes difficult and produces more heat than light. Anyone who attended or chaired a meeting where it became very difficult, if not impossible, to engage the participants in rational discussion searches for ways to move the discussion forward. Is it time for the leader to introduce some *cognitive dissonance*?

Festinger[17] speaks about the issue of deciding between two mutually exclusive and attractive alternatives. Some level of dissonance will occur; regardless of which alternative is selected. The question is how to minimize the dissonance, keeping in mind that the proposal of one group has been rejected and requires resolution. Probably no amount of explanation will resolve the issue. Adams[18] notes that such dissonances build up over time and the organization is fortunate when someone has the insight to bring the issue into the open. Such an action allows the dissonance to be resolved, rather than being swept out of sight only to fester dissatisfaction among a group of colleagues whose proposal was not accepted. In such circumstances the communication must be very clear and coherent. Were both proposals equally attractive and if so why was one selected over the other? Was there an attempt to pacify the group whose proposal was rejected?

I also want to consider dissonance, in the sense of directly introducing dissonance, into the conversation to stir people to think. Festinger[19] approaches cognitive dissonance with the notion that we try to establish internal harmony, consistency, or congruity among knowledge, opinions, attitude, and values: that we drive for *consonance*. He breaks down dissonance into elements, pairs, or clusters of elements. Festinger defines these elements as "knowledges." Elements include knowledge about ourselves; what we do, what we feel, what we want, and who we are. Other elements include the world in which we live; what things are painful, inconsequential, or important.

1. Pairs of elements can exhibit irrelevant, consonant, or dissonant relations.
2. Two cognitive elements are in an irrelevant relation if they have nothing to do with one another.
3. Two cognitive elements are in a dissonant relation if, considering these two alone, the obverse of one element follows from the other.
4. Two cognitive elements are in a consonant relation if, considering these two alone, one element follows from the other.

Listening

An issue of the McKinsey Quarterly[20] provided *The Executive guide to better listening*. The article notes that: "Strong listening skills make a critical difference in the performance of senior executives." I have rewritten this statement that states: "Strong listening skills make a critical difference in the performance of every person who contributes information to the decision-making process." The addendum[21] to the article considers six of the more common archetypes of bad listeners.

- The Opinionator: Listens to others to determine agreement with personal views. Generally not listening with an open mind. Can intimidate others.
- The Grouch: Grouches are poor listeners. Approach the conversation with your approach is not worth considering. Takes perseverance and a lot of energy to get through to them.
- The Preambler: Begins with a long lead-in commentary intended to restrict discussion. Ask questions intended to generate a specific answer. Comments lead to one-way communication.
- The Perseverator: Perseverators spend a lot of time without advancing the conversation; they reiterate what others have said to support their ideas or biases.
- The Answer Man: The Answer Man provides solutions before a consensus has been reached about the formulation of the problem under discussion. Point out a flaw on the Answer Man's thinking, and a string of ready answers follows.
- The Pretender: Pretend engagement and possibly agreement but aren't interested in what you're saying. They have made up their minds before the conversation begins.

We have met people who demonstrate these characteristics to greater or lesser degrees. The intent is not to demean or embarrass them in any way when they participate but to recognize their impact on the conversation. So what is required to be a good listener? The article suggests that showing respect, keeping quiet, and challenging assumptions lead to conversation that resolves issues.

1. **Show respect.** In recent times the emphasis on "I" has replaced the "we." Not often can anyone say, I did it, implying that I did it all by myself. Accomplishing anything of significance usually requires input from many different disciplines and constituencies. The article suggests that being a good listener simply involves, *helping to draw out critical information*

and put it in new light. Respect also requires accepting insights of colleagues in other disciplines, regardless of *position in the organization.* In essence, respect for other professions and their contributions to the organization.

2. **Keep quiet.** The purpose of any conversation usually involves gathering information and making a decision. Ferrari[21] invites us to consider using the 80/20 rule. He suggests that his partner in the conversation speak 80 percent of the time while he speaks 20 percent of the time. Ferrari prefers to spend his 20 percent of the time asking questions. However that is not an easy discipline to follow. As humans, we have the urge to make our thoughts known even though they may be irrelevant to the conversation; even if they're responding to an irrelevant conversation. The fact remains that you can't listen if you're talking. Perhaps the dictum, *speak only if you can improve the silence* may be a guideline to developing good listening skills.

3. **Challenge assumptions.** How dare you challenge the assumptions? That's the way we do it here. That's the way an organization dies. Listening involves challenging the basic assumptions regardless of the owner. As professionals that's one of our major responsibilities. It's easier to go along with the crowd than to raise an issue that no one is interested in considering yet vitally important to the discussion. It's not easy to ask a group that has decided on a path to some nirvana, why are we doing this? What's the validity of the assumptions? There's no problem in speculating or even blue-skying the results, but is there any evidence, even inferential evidence, that justifies the conclusions. The question might also be asked; what's the impact on the organization, if we decided to delay discussion and assemble more information.

Organizational units often decide to focus on some specific aspect of their business, let's say generating additional revenue; that's the primary interest and certain programs are established that could meet the goals. This will require all the resources of the organization. Very quickly expectations are added that have absolutely nothing to do with increasing revenue. What is your response? Say no or go along. You know you're overcommitted to meeting the revenue goals. It might take some courage to say no and it could be detrimental to your career, but if these added expectations continue, the revenue goals will not be met.

Ferrari[22] provides an example of a discussion between a group of engineers and the Chief Marketing Officer (CMO) of a large industrial company dominated by engineers with strong product-development competencies. The CMO was concerned about a new product introduction that "had fallen flat."

The CMO agreed the product was unique and she was struck by the engineers "passion and excitement." The CMO listened intently, but then noted they didn't sell as many units as they thought they'd sell in the first 3 months. She then asked for customer comments and the reply was that they haven't spoken to any customers. The engineers assumed the product benefits would speak for themselves. The CMO could have belittled the engineers for their naiveté of not speaking with customers, but she chose to give them responsibility by raising targeted questions. She didn't give sermon on *marketing for engineers*. There is a tendency in management literature promoting the idea of asking the *tough* questions: it's really not a matter of asking the tough questions as some tough questions could be relegated to the stupid questions column, but as the CMO noted, ask targeted questions. It doesn't matter whether the questions are tough or simple; the questions must elicit responses that provide insight.

Judging

There are no algorithms that eliminate judgment especially when people are involved. The numbers may tell the complete story when dealing with mathematical constructs, but the discussions about those mathematical constructs will be accomplished by people; different conclusions will be drawn from the same set of data. The implementation of those mathematical constructs will be accomplished through people, not all from the same perspective. So, personal and group judgment comes into play and cannot be avoided. However, many engineers and other discipline specialists, managers, and executives show various levels of discomfort when making a personal judgment. Judgment about performance, either organizational or people, provides the greatest amount of agony and indecision. Yet, personal judgment enters into every decision regardless of the level in the organization in which it is made or in relation to a particular topic.

Michigan Engineering,[23] a publication of the University of Michigan College of Engineering published an article, "Errors in judgment: engineering's great teacher." Engineering at its best involves judgment and the associated risk. The demise of Deepwater Horizon in the Gulf of Mexico, the Challenger explosion, and Columbia's disintegration illustrate three tragic events that psychologists have attributed to groupthink: groupthink is defined as a state in which mental efficiency and judgment deteriorate under pressure. We may argue if all factors relate to groupthink but that's really immaterial: engineering was involved and somehow didn't make its case with final decision-makers. The article notes that

"The Deepwater Horizon incident was confluence of multiple errors in judgment made by people in various positions of authority, with different objectives, in different locations—Transocean owned the rig and was drilling for British Petroleum, Halliburton was responsible for engineering. Investigating experts concluded that the companies compartmentalized information; engineers reported possible collapse under high pressure, but companies kept information to themselves; drilling engineers recommended installing redundant barriers to keep oil from escaping; companies opted for fewer barriers; operators were asked to cancel a cement test; crew alerted the bridge of what was referred to as 'well-control situation' without response; crew failed to activate emergency shut-down system; at 9:45 p.m. Deepwater Horizon lit up the sky."

The article reports that the Companies cited reasons, one of them being human judgment. Mineral Mine and Management (the responsible oversight Federal Agency) repeatedly declined to act on advice of its own experts. The Columbia and Challenger disaster involved similar actions. Thomas Zurbuchen, a Michigan Engineering Professor of Atmospheric, Oceanic, and Space Sciences who happens to be a proponent of empowerment noted that many mistakes are found by people who work with a project, hands-on. These people need to be empowered and we need to listen to them. Lack of empowerment creates negative incentive; making an independent decision that could result in punishment. The safer course for the workers is to do nothing. When management proclaims *empowerment* as an operating principle, it opens the organization to various levels of risk. Successful *empowerment* programs require communicating its limitations until participants understand their limitations.

In the same article Jennifer Macks, a Project Director at Barton Mallow Company, provides some guidance for the engineering community. She warns engineers that just because they can design something doesn't mean that somebody can build it. She argues that engineers need to have a practical sense of what's achievable. Mack also warns that engineers must be aware of the system's potential; she said computers are great at identifying issues and checking out special cases, but judgments are human: do I stop an integration process and test it if I'm concerned about it, or do I make our customer happy. She raises the issue of her frustration with people who believe they're capable of becoming project managers after 1 year of experience, but have no clue as to how to engage in resolving a serious problem or anticipate that something is going wrong. The engineering profession involves making judgments either pro or con on a daily basis. No formula decides which alternative to select, or which direction to take when you come to the fork in the road. Engineers learn to make these judgments, mostly from failures because as a community we celebrate successes, but seldom ask ourselves, why were we successful.

Feedback

Give me some feedback! What's the purpose of providing feedback? Do you really want it? Are you willing to accept feedback that might be negative or instructive? If you receive feedback, what will you do with it? Are there limits to the amount of feedback? How do you give intelligent feedback without destroying the person? Do people generally want feedback?

Feedback is difficult to give as well as to receive. Those with an intense desire to provide feedback often display the characteristics that we described for The Opinionators, The Grouch, The Preambler, The Perseverator, The Answer Man, and The Pretender. Giving feedback requires work: it involves more than receiving an answer to the question, what do you think. If I'm going to provide you with feedback on a proposal you're preparing, I better have knowledge of what's in the proposal; that takes time and effort depending on the scope. It can't be provided by reading the executive summary. If I'm going to provide feedback on a new technology you plan on implementing in a particular program, I'd better understand the technology and its role in the organization's future activities. Such requests also require thoughtful consideration or else they become useless gestures.

Technology

Communication is not limited by tools and techniques: it's limited by our ability to use the appropriate tools. Those tools include verbal; written correspondence in many different forms; the telephone; email; conferencing tools; websites; other types of electronic devices; and flip charts, white boards, and Post-it Notes. Email appears to be the favored means of communication when considering important issues, tweets only go so far. We cannot disregard the benefits of using email for communicating. It's fast and effective if used properly. However, email is also a time waster and a distraction to work that requires longer-term thinking time. Effective use requires personal discipline. It is not my prerogative to tell anyone how to use the internet, but a little thought might improve the effectiveness of this most valuable tool. My major concern arises when multiple exchanges of emails could be resolved more effectively by a phone call or a conference call. Selecting the proper tools for communicating depends on the context and need for the communication. As engineering practitioners you are aware of the issues related to email communication.

Managers of the engineering function and their engineers and their counterparts in the other discipline specialties spend a great percentage of their time involving work that requires thinking. Thinking requires uninterrupted periods of time; otherwise the thinking stopwatch starts and stops and the rethinking process begins. I know from personal experience the cost of these interruptions in creating additional problems. As an example, design involves a thinking process whether by individuals or groups. Forgetting what might be considered a minor detail often produces negative consequences someplace in the cycle toward completion.

Communication Plan

Writing a formal project communication plan is a relatively simple task if the plan focuses on reporting. There's no difficulty in identifying who should receive reports, from whom, and at what intervals. This type of communication deals with the past, what is being reported has already occurred. If the report outlines future actions, the receiver has an opportunity to reflect and comment if necessary. Such communication plans identify the stakeholders, the frequency, and the method of reporting. The stakeholders may include a broad range of interests depending on the project scope: the original decision-makers, the sponsor, the project work team, suppliers, an advisory group, any special interest groups related to governmental issues, the major organizational units, and in a variety of combinations. To the project manager, there appears to be an almost unlimited number of requests for some type of reporting and it usually is more than the project's status. Any group, that even has a tangential interest in the project, will request some type of reporting. Communicating, or perhaps more appropriately reporting and receiving feedback, follow routine processes and procedures. Project status reports are difficult to manage; they require input from many different organizational units; project team members do not accord them a high priority; so organizations often assign a responsible agent to manage the reporting process. The more critical project communication plan involves developing and understanding the communicating processes and procedures at the operational levels during the execution stage. These communications arise when necessary, and not according to some predetermined schedule.

Every major project (no accepted definition of *major*, depends on the organization) begins with a defined scope and purpose. The decision to proceed usually comes down with a somewhat terse *Project Approved*, and a request to advance the completion date if possible. At this time, if the project was considered a fait accompli, the project manager/leader may have been appointed. The project manager could be appointed from any level in the organization, and it's not inconceivable that it could be senior vice president. Someone must be responsible for project performance; it cannot be "we" since "we" results in no one accepting responsibility.

Communicating becomes complex at the operational level, it's not reporting, it's about gaining understanding of the requirements among the organizational units and negotiating the tradeoffs. It's not just about internal communication, it includes the external entities that in one way or another influence performance. Communication at this level is about the interactions among diverse units with many different disciplines. Units may speak the same language, but understand the content differently. The discipline terminology, often referred to as jargon, enters the conversation and misunderstandings begin to occur.

The formal communication plan requires the freedom to communicate. If the organizational culture fosters a military type chain of command based on level and hierarchy, there's no reason to expect that the project communication plan will relate a realistic picture of impending problems. The silos exist; the project team will be drawn from those silos, their managers will guard their silos. How do the team members respond to questions not only posed by their silo manager, but also possibly from other silo managers and upper level management? Several options are available: (1) follow the chain of command, avoid contact with people above your level, especially from cooperating groups; (2) offer no more information about the project than absolutely necessary, discuss only the specific area in which you are involved; (3) never reveal any project difficulties, or discuss other people; (4) couch your responses in such a way as to be noncommittal, you may pay a price for this action sometime in the future; and (5) tell it like it is. If the three project parameters (requirements, schedule, and cost) are not being met, the response to known problems often is continually delayed.

Consider each of these five options. Option 1: Chances are slim that you will not meet someone above your level and will ask about the project. After all, it is a major organizational investment and others not directly involved may have an interest in the project. If you accidently met the CEO on the elevator and she asked, how the project is going, what would be your response? You can't remain silent without jeopardizing your career. What if the CEO asked you to come in immediately and give your perspective on the project, how would you respond? Option 2 might be away, but show that your interests in the project are limited to your own cubicle and that could limit future opportunities. Your integrity would be compromised in Option 3, if in the near future, reports emerged with contrary opinions; you could try to change the topic, but that might be quite difficult. Option 4, couching your comments to be noncommittal, could get you in trouble with certain types of executives and senior managers. You would most likely not be on their list of promotable engineers. I suggest that the only viable option is No. 5, not necessarily the easiest option, but the best for the long term, but must be presented in a nonaccusatory manner of others. You might suggest that if you responded in such a manner, you might be terminated. I suggest you take a chance and if that is the situation, why do you want to continue to work in the organization. I'm not suggesting you quit the organization without sufficient thought before locating another position, but think about your career. Unfortunately, too often we fail to communicate until it's too late to do anything about it.

ETHICAL ISSUES IN COMMUNICATION

In this section on ethical issues, I am not concerned about the dealings in the financial markets that have landed some high level executives in the penitentiary; my comments focus on the ethics of engineers, other discipline specialists, and their managers. I find most dictionary definitions related to ethics unsatisfactory. So instead of a definition I propose a composite description: ethics deals with human behavior. In its simplest form, it involves honesty in all dealings regardless of the circumstances. That simple word *honesty* encompasses significant responsibilities: it includes avoiding actions like lying, deceiving, cheating, stealing, embezzling, sneaking, and appropriating intellectual property as one's own. Being ethical does not follow the laws of physics; it's matter of judgment and unfortunately, as humans we probably pay greater attention to the ethics of others, than our own.

Most professional disciplines follow some defined code of ethics that defines the obligations of the profession and professional conduct. As an example, the IEEE Code of Ethics[24] which is similar to those of other engineering professional group's states

1. accept responsibility in making decisions consistent with the safety, health, and welfare of the public, and to disclose promptly factors that might endanger the public or the environment;
2. avoid real or perceived conflicts of interest whenever possible, and disclose them to affected parties when they do exist;
3. be honest and realistic in stating claims or estimates based on available data;
4. reject bribery in all its forms;
5. improve the understanding of technology; its appropriate application, and potential consequences;
6. maintain and improve our technical competence and to undertake technological tasks for others only if qualified by training or experience, or after full disclosure of pertinent limitations;
7. to seek, accept, and offer honest criticism of technical work, to acknowledge and correct errors, and to credit properly the contributions of others;
8. treat fairly all persons regardless of factors such as race, religion, gender, disability, age, or national origin;
9. avoid injuring others, their property, reputation, or employment by false or malicious action;
10. assist colleagues and co-workers in their professional development and to support them in following this code of ethics.

These ten points lay down the principles for ethical conduct in most engineering communities, regardless of disciplines.

William J. Daughton[25] identifies four ethical principles for balancing the self-interest in the decision-making process that include (1) Utilitarian Rule, (2) Moral Rights Rule, (3) Justice Rule, and (4) Practical Rule.

1. **Utilitarian Rule**: produces the greatest good for the greatest number of stockholders
2. **Moral Rights Rule**: protects the inalienable rights of people affected by the decision
3. **Justice Rule**: based on equitable distribution of benefits or injuries
4. **Practical Rule**: can the decision undergo public scrutiny? Would you want this decision to be headlined on the morning newspaper or the internet?

A major ethical problem occurs at the operational levels, when engineers and other discipline professionals appropriate the work of others as their own. Managers and executives are subject to the same foibles. Such actions raise serious ethical questions and not only create problems for the organization by raising legal issues, but also challenge the integrity of the individual when the action becomes known. Proposals from external sources often request design information, and the responses to those proposals present designs that are then attributed to the requestor: the source is not identified appropriately. A similar situation occurs when internal discussions take place and someone in the group disseminates information indicating the writer originated the idea. These two examples, which some may consider inconsequential, can destroy unity of a group that depends on new ideas for its survival.

The 1986 Challenger disaster provides another more serious example, where interpretation and meaning of a phrase, and lack of understanding of a disaster in the making, took the lives of seven astronauts. The problem involved the ability of the O-rings in the booster rockets to function properly at 38°F. Six months prior to the launch of the Challenger, a Morton-Thiokol engineer sent a memo to management suggesting that all flights cease, until the O-rings issue was resolved. Management disregarded the advice. On the eve of the launch, 15 Morton-Thiokol engineers agreed that NASA should not launch the Challenger. The Thiokol Executive Vice President told one of the 15 skeptical engineers to "take off his engineering hat and put on his management hat." Four other top executives vetoed the engineers' recommendation. NASA subsequently launched the Challenger according to schedule, in spite of the fact that the engineering staff recommended a delay in the launch. We all know the result of that decision: seven crew members perished when the Challenger exploded.

Thiokol and NASA manager evidently did not understand the meaning of the phrase, "take off your engineering hat and put on your management hat." Putting on the business that does not allow managers to ignore the safety, health, and welfare of its employees. Evidently the NASA and Morton-Thiokol managers must have misplaced their business hats; had they worn their management hats, they would have delayed the launch until the O-ring problem was resolved. Of course, there's another side of this story. Edward Tufte[26] suggests that, had the engineers displayed their data more clearly, the seven astronauts would not have perished. That statement is difficult to uphold. At best, managers may not have launched Challenger. However, Tufte does raise the issue as to how engineers present information. It's not just the information, but how it's presented to demonstrate the point. Just because we have almost unlimited capability in data acquisition and analysis doesn't mean it must be presented; what the data tells us becomes far more important than the numbers. I have mentioned several times in this book, the need for engineers to communicate to meet the requirements of the person or group to whom the message is directed. Avoid the technical jargon when communicating with the less-technically competent. The same applies to all professions; technospeak does not translate into understandable communication.

ELIMINATING THE COMMUNICATION BARRIERS

The barriers to communication included discussions of context in content; language; noise level considering irrelevant information, voicing opinions versus facts, and unnecessary interruptions; listening, judging, feedback, and technology. So how do we make progress in mitigating the consequences of these barriers? There is a simple answer but difficult to implement: introduce operational discipline and develop a mental attitude that focuses on pursuing excellence. The process begins with whoever happens to be responsible for performance, it includes anyone on the continuum, from the head of the organization to the many discipline specialists in the organization, in essence anyone who has responsibility for the actions of others.

Content in context: Organizations assume that all employees know how to communicate. The ability to communicate involves more than making Power-Point presentations. Remove the PowerPoint slides and we quickly realize the failure to communicate effectively. You've heard about the 30 second elevator speech. Think about that for a moment, describing an idea so that it can be fully understood in about 60 words. Perhaps that is why so few projects met requirements. The importance of communication in the decision-making process does not require justification; the academic and commercial suppliers provide many options. A large percentage of employees come unprepared to communicate effectively. Communicating effectively is hard work, it isn't learned by taking a course, and like developing any skill it requires practice and more practice. Removing this barrier poses many problems. A major organization will not begin teaching every employee or even a small segment of employees how to communicate, but there may be an opportunity to establish a group that screens major communications, this is not public relations, this is a group of writers who know how to communicate.

Language: We assume we speak a common language and that words have the same meaning to every listener. Several years of Foreign Service develops sensitivity to different interpretations of the same words or phrases. How can an organization improve the appreciation for different interpretations of the same words and phrases? If executives and managers can be convinced that interpretation can be a problem, the solution can be relatively simple; bring the problem to the attention of the organization, and take the time during a conversation or in preparing written document, to present the message in language suitable for the user.

Noise Level: Eliminating the noise level in the conversions requires courage to bring some level of discipline into the conversation. Four types of noise level were identified (1) irrelevant information, (2) opinions instead of facts, (3) unnecessary interruptions, and (4) environment. Each of these four types of noise levels can be, if not eliminated, brought under control with some discipline. The leader of the conversation has a choice, allow the noise level to continue or curtail it. In our politically correct society, a certain reticence and fear prevails in limiting the conversation. When adults begin acting as juveniles, it's time to act but in a civil manner. Participants who continue to generate noise should be dealt with in private. Under extreme circumstances, it's your conversation, invite those who contribute and respect the time of others.

Environment: Creating the appropriate physical environment for conversation should not provide any obstacles. What occurs, in that environment and the results of the conversation, depends on the competencies of the leader in establishing the mental awareness of the participants. The objective of the conversation is to elicit responses from the members and reach a conclusion. The leader must be forthright, speak less, think more deeply, challenge assumptions and conclusions, and create the dissonance necessary to develop a response to the issue under discussion. Not an easy task, but a competency that must be learned.

Listening: Do we need any more admonitions about the need to develop listening skills? Some groups communicate effectively, others with disastrous results. The answer depends on who's participating. The IBM and Boeing case studies provided excellent examples of not listening. The McKinsey article demonstrated clearly that listening continues to be a major factor in organizational performance. Listening requires patience, becoming a good listener requires practice. How do you learn to focus on the speaker or author to the exclusion of all other stimuli? How can you learn to focus on an uninteresting or even boring speaker? Learn the fundamentals and then practice. In today's electronically connected world, we have so many visual stimuli. It was easier to learn to listen, when we only had radio. The authors and the performers were required to set the stage and the rest was left to imagination.

Judging: There's an inherent aversion to make judgments (to judge), especially when the judgment relates to people or issues that in some manner may reflect on our character. Yet we make countless judgments every day on rather significant issues such as while driving, purchasing property, or engaging in the stock market. We make these judgments for ourselves. Using judgment in relation to work activities presents a more complex situation; the exposure to failure may pose more severe consequences. The failure now involves the organization and colleagues. But a successful engineering career, as an example, requires judgment. Today will not be the same as yesterday, and if it is, perhaps it's a job rather than a career. The ability to use judgment comes from experiences, experiences that involve success and failures and the competency to deal with both.

Feedback: Before you ask for feedback make sure you really want it. We need feedback but we need to understand the person or group providing the feedback and their motivation. Feedback should be given with absolute integrity and it can either motivate to greater accomplishment or to despair. Even positive feedback can create a negative impact if given in a flippant manner or viewed as being insincere. We live in a period where all feedback should be positive; no room for recommending correction. Learn to accept both positive and negative feedback, if it is given with integrity. If you're giving feedback, it's not enough to make some mindless comment that is viewed as insincere. If you like the idea or design approach, be specific and say what you like about it. If you have questions about the idea or design approach, be specific about what you like. If you don't like it, also be specific, explain your concerns. Perhaps, a few comments regarding options may be appropriate.

Technology: We have all the tools we need to communicate effectively. Let's learn to use them appropriately and focus on using them effectively and efficiently.

Communication Plan: There is no doubt that the level and quality of communication has an impact on project performance. We need to treat it as any other competency. Do you need a communication plan on a major project? Yes. Do you need a general communication plan for the organizational unit? Yes. But, let's not complicate the plan to the point that it limits rather than enhances communication. If you reach a point where you need to appoint someone to manage project communications, you may think of replacing some people obstructing the free flow of information. If you placed unnecessary restrictions on the project team, by limiting open communication, consider the negative impact on future performance. Make sure the communication loop is closed, one way communication seldom results in the desired action. Functional managers perform a dual role of providing the competence and at the same time not interfering with the project manager; there's a fine line between interference and providing guidance. Open communication allows team members to voice their technical concerns, but concerns need to be investigated, assessed, and structured in a way to allow for disciplined discussion. Finally, for managers, reading reports in any format provides information, but communication requires face-to-face exchanges: for engineers, expand your horizons by learning what's going on in those cubicles that surround you.

KEY POINTS

There should be no disagreement as to the importance of communication in the decision-making process. Unfortunately, communication involves people, many people, and those people do not come out of a mold. They bring different perspectives to the same set of word combinations. Today's 24/7 society does not lend itself for deep thought before communicating information, that should have been interpreted, to provide meaning to those who need to act upon the communication. As noted even in engineering, we do not have a common language, except when dealing in numbers. So here are a few points to remember, whether you're an engineer or other discipline specialist or manager, or in the lengthy chain that converts executive decisions to customer/user products and services.

- Effective communication requires effort, whether the sender or the receiver—it requires work
- Communication becomes complex with the addition of every additional person in the chain—"$n!$" requires consideration
- Formal communication channels need to be defined in a way as to not restrict bringing major issues to the appropriate level for resolution—drive for open communication
- Informal communication in resolving technical issue, either one-on-one or in groups of various sizes, up or down or laterally, determines project success. Boeing's design engineers could not disregard the assembly of the aircraft—engineers need to consider many issues beyond their own work effort for successful project implementation
- The barriers to effective communication need to be neutralized in some way and that requires managerial discipline: David Whyte's comments should be noted as a guide to communicating more effectively

- Listening may be more important than talking for managers and executives; they depend on the engineers and other discipline specialists, especially in technology-based organizations—Ferrari's four points provide an excellent guide between listening and speaking
- Whether engineer or manager, you'll make judgments based on limited information—there's no algorithm—it just requires using your personal and the organization's resources and acceptance of failure—you won't be right 100 percent of the time
- Accept feedback for what it's worth but recognize that feedback comes with its pro and con biases—pay particular attention to the negative feedback for its authenticity, but don't fight it, accept it for what it is and don't brood about it
- We have more technology than we need, so use it where applicable—you need time to think so organize your time in spite of the boss-imposed time—develop the courage to challenge your colleagues and your management, it's your future
- Ethical issues will arise in the normal execution of any project—observe them, but be cautious about accusing others of unethical conduct—facts only, not opinions
- Finally, if somehow your education shortchanged you on learning good communication skills, whether written or orally, take the time to become proficient—good communicators receive more opportunities

NOTES

1. Chester I. Barnard, *The Functions of the Executive*, Harvard Business Press, 1938.
2. Abbie Griffin and John Hauser, "Patterns of communication among marketing, engineering, and manufacturing—a comparison between two product teams," *Management Science*, 38(3): 360–373, March 1992.
3. R. K. Moenaert, F. Caeldreis, A. Lievens, and E. Wauters, "Communication flows in international product innovation teams," *Journal of Product Innovation Management*, 17: 360–377, September 2010.
4. William D. Jones, *On Decision-Making in Large Organizations*, Santa Monica, CA: Rand Corp., 1964, RM 3968 PR.
5. Peter F. Drucker, *The Essential Drucker*, New York: Harper-Collins, 2001, pp. 10–13.
6. W. Brian Arthur, *The Nature of Technology*, New York: Free Press, 2009, p. 61.
7. Chuck Martin, "The Importance of Face-to-Face Communication," CIO, March 6, 2007, http://www.cio.com/article/print/29898 Accessed 11.11.2014.

8. Henry Mintzberg, *Managing*, San Francisco, CA: Berrett-Koehler, 2009, pp. 97–121.

9. N. Fondas and R. Stewart, "Understanding differences in general management jobs," *Journal of General Management*, 1992, Vol. 17, No. 4, pp. 1–12.

10. Roberto Verganti, "Steve Jobs and Management of Meaning," October 7, 2011, HBR, http://hbr.com/cs/2011/steve_jobs_and_management_by_meaning.html.

11. Ernest Gundling, *The 3M Way to Innovation*, Tokyo: Kodansha International, 2000, p. 58.

12. David Whyte, Personal notes from a radio broadcast.

13. W. Brian Arthur, *The Nature of Technology*, New York: Free Press, 2009, p. 13

14. Ibid., p. 27.

15. Jon Gertner, *The Idea Factory*, London: Penguin Press, 2012. See "Where the future came from," *The Wall Street Journal*, March 17, 2012.

16. Gerard H. Gaynor, *Innovation by Design*, New York: American Management Association, 2002, pp. 14–17.

17. Leon Festinger, *A Theory of Cognitive Dissonance*, Stanford: Stanford University Press, 1957, pp. 18–24.

18. D. K. Adams, "Conflict and integration," *Journal of Personality*, 22: 548–556, 1954.

19. Leon Festinger, *A Theory of Cognitive Dissonance*, Stanford: Stanford University Press, 1957, pp. 9–18.

20. Bernard T. Ferrari, "The executive guide to better listening," *McKinsey Quarterly*, February 2012, pp. 3–9.

21. Bernard T. Ferrari, "The executive guide to better listening," *McKinsey Quarterly*, February 2012, pp. 12–13.

22. Bernard T. Ferrari, "The executive guide to better listening," *McKinsey Quarterly*, February 2012, pp. 3–6.

23. Bill Clayton, "Errors in judgment: engineering's great teacher," *Michigan Engineer*, June 13, 2011.

24. IEEE Code of Ethics, www.ieee.org

25. William J. Daughton, *The Engineering Management Handbook*, American Society of Mechanical Engineers, 2010, pp. 15–18.

26. Wade Robinson, Roger Boisjoly, David Hoeker, and Stefan Young, "Representation and misrepresentation: Tufte and the Morton Thiokol engineers on the challenger," *Science and Engineering Ethics*, 8: 59–81, 2002.

11

EVALUATING DECISION-MAKING PERFORMANCE

Evaluating decisions made in the past and learning from what occurred during actual implementation of those decisions, provides organizations with information to prevent repeating past mistakes and focusing more realistically on the means to determine its future. But that evaluation must go beyond evaluating the macro decision since it only reveals what every macro analysis reveals; an average of the many thousands of subsidiary decisions that led to some level of success or failure. Evaluating the macro decision teaches little about what actions might be taken to improve organizational performance.

Chapter 11 topics include

- People
- Purposes
- Processes
- Strategic Thinking
- Culture
- Products and Services
- Resources

Decisions: An Engineering and Management Perspective, First Edition. Gerard H. Gaynor.
© 2015 The Institute of Electrical and Electronics Engineers, Inc. Published 2015 by John Wiley & Sons, Inc.

- Leadership
- Innovation and Entrepreneurship
- Organizational Readiness
- Policies and Procedures
- Employee Benefits
- Downsizing
- Going Global
- Government Regulations
- Offshore Operations
- Integrating Organizational Units
- General Governance Issues
- Key Points
- Notes

PEOPLE

Decisions regarding people performance, whether related to internal staff or outside supporting staff present a major challenge for those required to make those decisions. Success in any activity involves a continuum of talents and levels in the management hierarchy. Research, however, has not identified an algorithm that leads to identifying the best candidate and the follow-up requirements to maintain the required organizational competencies. In the final analysis, we identify people based on a specific set of requirements for the position: it is a judgment call and all judgments include both facts and emotions subject to interpretation and personal biases. So how can organizations measure their *decision-making success*?

People decisions begin with the CEO; executives in different organizational functions and operational scope; managers from entry level to very senior level managers, with significant operational responsibility; project managers with responsibilities that may exceed those of the CEO at some point in time; the discipline professionals in the sciences and engineering, marketing, and manufacturing; and the organizational support services such as finance, information technology, and human relations. The following list of generic questions provides a means for determining the organization's decision-making practices in relation to people.

1. Do the organization's executives and managers understand the competencies required from both internal and outside sources to meet the requirements for the decision under consideration?

2. Are the major people decisions that led to various degrees of success and failure identified and evaluated?

3. Do the candidates, selected to fulfill key positions, possess the required knowledge and experience or were they starting on a new learning curve?

4. Were the job requirements spelled out with sufficient due diligence?

5. Were appointments made to critical positions based on knowledge and experience to meet the requirements; a track record of past performance that demonstrates competencies; favoritism of some sort or lack of due diligence?

6. Does the organization listen and resolve people issues as they arise? Identify the situations in which appropriate action did take place or did not take place.

7. On major issues that require resolution, what were the timelines to reach a conclusive decision and resolve them; timely, muddled, drawn out, resolved by itself, or no action?

8. Were the occurrences, where nonperformance was not dutifully recognized and not addressed, identified and resolved?

9. Did the person making people assignments really know the candidates, or was the selection based solely on performance reviews by others? Did the questions asked during the interview process dig deep into the individual's capabilities: capabilities defined as a group of specific competencies?

10. Did the skills and competencies of individuals and groups meet the requirements to fulfill the decision's requirements?

11. What specific programs were initiated and supported to provide adequate competencies and capabilities in decision-making?

12. What knowledge, attitudes, competencies, and experiences in decision-making does the candidate bring to this specific appointment?

13. Does the candidate have a solid grounding in management fundamentals; either self-taught, from experience, or formal academic program?

14. What was the track record of successful performance and subsequent growth in accepting greater responsibilities over a period of years?

15. Has the candidate demonstrated good judgment in making some critical decisions?

16. Does this position offer growth and stretch opportunities for the selected candidate?

17. What is the candidate's understanding of other related disciplines involved in the work effort?

18. Did the candidate, even though lacking some requirements, have the potential to take on the responsibilities for managing the group's activities?
19. Did the candidate possess the competencies required to develop an organizational unit vision and purpose, and then bring the participants together to fulfill the requirements?
20. Does the candidate's past performance show competence to execute the proposed activity's requirements?
21. Our age of ultraspecialization in science, engineering, technology, marketing and management has developed few people with multidisciplinary competence; does an active program exist to develop people to function as integrators?
22. Were all the required competencies in engineering and other related disciplines identified at the time of the macro decision approval?
23. Did the engineers and other discipline specialists understand each other's roles in the project? How did they negotiate their differences?
24. How was interdepartmental and interdisciplinary decision-making managed? Was there a comprehensive plan?
25. Did the project include a comprehensive communications plan? Were levels of authority in decision-making identified?

PURPOSES

Organizations involve many different yet integrative purposes. There's the corporate purpose, those of the various suborganizations, the various project purposes, and then the individual purposes of each participating internal and external entity. And finally, each organizational entity depends on how individuals see their purpose in the organization. Measuring decision-making in relation to fulfilling the organization's purposes involves exploring how those purposes were fulfilled.

1. Identify where the organization's leadership has promoted its purposes to the employees.
2. Are the purposes of the organization published and promoted by the organization's leadership?
3. Identify the organization's programs to determine levels of employee satisfaction.
4. Identify how the organization measures levels of contribution by employees?

5. Why do customers buy the organization's products? Those products evidently meet the buyer's purposes. But, does the organization know why their customers buy its products? Customer alignment depends on personal understanding of the customer's problems and providing solutions: if the next order was given to a competitor, regardless of the reason, alignment probably did not exist.

6. Suppliers play a major role in an organization's success: are the suppliers' purposes aligned with the organization's purposes? Is alignment of purposes with suppliers required? If it is, it's important that it be recognized.

7. Are the organization's purposes aligned with the community? We're familiar with the "not in my backyard" attitude that constantly surfaces when considering nuclear power plants and their storage of spent materials, and more recently with wind farms for generating electricity. In most situations total misalignment drives the conversation. Environmental issues are important and a response cannot be disregarded. How has the organization responded to these community environmental issues?

8. Establishing a base for employee alignment with organizational purposes relies on qualitative analysis. No quantitative data are available to measure employee alignment. However, a positive response from employees, when the organization is challenged in any sector of its business provides a good secondary measure.

PROCESSES

Follow the process and you're assured of success; sometimes "yes" but mostly "no" except for very routine activities. Organizations define processes for many activities, some more important than others. Generally, besides the official organization's processes, others exist to fulfill specific needs of the many organizational units. There are two major process types: (1) administrative processes and (2) production processes that include the continuum from product concept through its development and test; the design and development of production equipment; the factories to manufacture the product; others to bring the product to the marketplace; and finally processes for meeting customer requirements.

Questions related to evaluating administrative processes and production processes would include

1. Who developed the process—operational users or other entity? What did they know about process?

2. Was the process validated as to its effectiveness in meeting requirements?

3. Was the process tested in the work environment?
4. Is there general agreement on the process?
5. Are deviations from standard monitored?
6. All processes reside someplace on the compliance continuum (such as related to safety, security, environmental hazards, toxicity, etc.). How does the organization manage those that require absolute compliance?
7. Is latitude in compliance an individual judgment call, or defined in the process?
8. Does a process exist for recommending changes? Are the processes monitored for compliance, value to the business, functionality, and cost?
9. Are deviations from requirements monitored on a regular basis?
10. When deviations are found, is there a standard process for resolving the deviation?
11. How does the organization verify adherence that requires absolute compliance?
12. Is latitude in compliance allowed for an individual judgment call?
13. Does a process exist for recommending changes?

STRATEGIC THINKING

Most organizations have lived through the period where strategic planning consumed incalculable resources to prepare a book that once approved was seldom referred to. Those pompous statements and financial projections seldom materialized. It's interesting to note how executives became enamored with 5-year plans and forgot that strategic plans assumed an essentially steady-state environment and disregarded the business dynamics that affect implementation of the strategy. Seldom were these strategic plans supported by an operational plan.

Unfortunately, strategy too often is treated as though it's fixed in time for a period of years. Yet, we know that whether we look at strategic directions related to marketing, technology, or other organizational functions, the next 24 hours may require a change in direction. Fortunately some of the strategy mania has disappeared. In 1993, Henry Mintzberg,[1] a well-known management scholar at McMaster University, authored the *Rise and Fall of Strategic Planning* and in the following year authored *The Fall and Rise of Strategic Planning*. Mintzberg raised a controversy when he recommended that the term *strategic planning* be dropped in favor of *strategic thinking*. He considered strategic planning as a bureaucratic process that focused on analysis and disregarded the essence of strategy which involves synthesis. So to evaluate decision-making related to strategy, an organization may begin by asking some questions as to its reality.

1. Does the organization measure performance against its strategic plan or its defined strategic direction?
2. Do the organizational units measure performance against their strategic plan or the organization's strategic plan?
3. Does the organization continue to think, that in a global environment, the 5-year strategic planning approach meets the requirements? If so, compare the operational results to the strategic plan.
4. Were the strategic decisions implemented not only for the current year, but also for those scheduled for the future approved, funded, and on schedule?
5. If your organization chose to do strategic thinking, what has been accomplished in relation to the developed strategic direction?
6. If you're a professional specialist in any discipline or function, what was your contribution to fulfilling the organizational unit strategy?
7. Does the strategy include decisions related to scientific direction, technology and engineering, and information technology?
8. Does the organization's strategy show any departure from past practices or pursuit of new targets; new initiatives in organizational innovation across all functions beginning with the executive levels on the organization.
9. If the strategic direction lacks creativity and innovation, does it provide a viable and workable strategy?

CULTURE

Organizations make various pronouncements about their culture: those shared values, beliefs, rituals, legends, past history, the intellectual and operational traditions, pride in past accomplishments, rules of conduct, the organization's general operating principles and practices, and other artifacts that define the organization. However, those posters of "what we stand for" take on many different meanings. They're all important. But, culture is more important than developing and promoting a consistent description of culture for all organizational units within an organization.

The required culture may vary from one organizational unit to another within the macro organization, depending on their purpose. Supporting organizational units, likewise, may require totally different cultures. Consider the different cultural requirements in the organizational functions like research and development, manufacturing, innovation, entrepreneurship, sales, and order processing. Each of these organizational units will operate with different levels of freedom and judgment.

Industries operate in very different cultures. The railroad industry may require a totally different type of culture than an organization that prides itself on bringing new products to market. So, here are some of the decisions that affect organizational culture and more specifically the *organizational unit* culture.

1. Obviously, respect for people, opportunity to advance according to one's competencies and interests, and fair treatment cannot be compromised.
2. Does the culture support freedom to act on one's personal initiative?
3. Does the culture provide for flexible enforcement of policies and procedures?
4. Does a set of established norms exist regarding acceptable performance?
5. Does the business system enforce a spirit of accountability for results—both individual and collective?
6. How does the organizational culture adapt to changing functional, business, or economic requirements?
7. Does the culture encourage cooperation and build trust?
8. Are problems approached through open discussion without threats, that is, an open discussion of issues—everything on the table?
9. Is there a general understanding and appreciation for cultural differences in global negotiations and operations?
10. Does the organization value its constructive mavericks, nonconformists, and eccentrics?
11. Are successes celebrated and failures resolved without accusations?

Each of the above actions will provide both quantitative and qualitative results. As an example: If decisions in the organizational unit provide *for freedom to act*, those actions can be identified. However, that does not imply that total freedom reigns. *Freedom to act* must be coupled with discipline.

PRODUCTS AND SERVICES

Decisions related to products and services determine organizational success. In essence, products and services provide the income stream. As noted, IBM lost out to Apple on the personal computer; Kodak lost out to Sony on digital cameras; and Xerox never capitalized on the inventive spirit in the 1970s of its Palo Alto operations. IBM, Kodak, and Xerox somehow failed to recognize the future. Why did management neglect to do the critical thinking and how did management allow it to happen? How could their executive management levels be so isolated from the technological advances that were taking place and refusing to understand the marketplace? An evaluation of decision-making effectiveness, related to Products and Services, would raise the following questions.

1. Does the organization have a strategy for promoting new products and/or services? Does that strategy include the technologies relevant to the particular product or service? Compare the last five-year performance against the strategy.
2. Identify the return on R&D investment, product development, manufacturing, and marketing over the past five-years. What was the value-added as a result of these investments?
3. What was the impact of introducing new-to-the-market products on the organizations financial performance during the previous three years?
4. What was the impact of introducing improved products on the organizations financial performance during the previous three years?
5. Does the organization evaluate its processes; processes involved in the continuum from idea to product introduction in the marketplace?
6. Describe the methods used to introduce improved products and new-to-the-market products; determine what needs to be done to improve.
7. Does the organization evaluate its project performance; how many product related projects meet requirements, schedule, and cost? Are measures being taken to improve performance?
8. Achieving new product development goals involves more than nine to five work schedules as the project approaches market launch. What is the track record on meeting original launch dates and what conditions helped or hindered meeting launch dates?
9. Introducing new-to-the-market products or making major improvements to current products involves integration of many functional units and outside resources. What factors prevented integration and what was the impact on organizational performance.
10. Introducing a new-to-the-market product or making major improvements to a current product line involves making many decisions. Which decisions, at what time during the project cycle and at what level affected project performance and how?

RESOURCES

An organization's resources[2] involve more than people and money. Those resources include intellectual property, access to information, managing technology, marketing, time, distribution, customers, suppliers, and production capability. The integration of these resources with the organizational infrastructure determines organizational effectiveness and level of success. Evaluation of the decisions related to resources includes the following.

Access to Intellectual Property

Organizations invest significant financial resources in information systems, yet too often what's needed is not available or at least easily available.

1. Who owns the organization's intellectual property?
2. The organization or the individual organizational units where it might have been developed! Who has access to it?
3. Who makes the decision to provide access? Are there any limitations? Open the intellectual property resources to those who need it and avoid the extensive duplication of effort that costs organizations time and energy.
4. Not everyone needs to start at the bottom of the learning curve.
5. How many reports are published that no longer provide value?
6. How many reports are much longer than needed?
7. Are strategic plans and directions translated for the various needs within the organization?
8. An information access caveat, make it available for those who need it.

Managing Technology

Managing technology links engineering and science with management; it's multidisciplinary and involves managing from a systems perspective. It defines the organization's technical capabilities. In evaluating technologies, organizations too often overemphasize what they consider their proprietary technologies. Technologies, in common use by competitors, cannot be considered as proprietary; they may be support technologies, but not proprietary. So, evaluating organizational proprietary technologies involves facts and not opinions.

1. Does the organization understand what managing its technology involves?
2. Does the organization clearly understand the meaning of proprietary technologies?

3. Has the organization identified its proprietary technologies?
4. What role do the proprietary technologies play in the organization's business performance?
5. In what areas of the concept to market product cycle are the proprietary technologies recognized by the competition; research, development, process, production, distribution, and management?
6. Are the proprietary technologies based on technology platforms or stand-alone technologies?
7. Is the organization actively managing its technologies with a holistic perspective?

Marketing and Sales

Successful product/service commercialization involves providing consumers products/services that they're willing to purchase; those that provide a benefit whether real, personal, emotional, or social. Marketing finds the market areas to pursue and sales build the organization's income stream. Decisions in these two areas ultimately determine an organization's financial success. If marketing makes the wrong decision, sales may not follow. If marketing makes the right decision, there's no guarantee that sales will meet expectations. Integrating, yet recognizing the different functions of the two groups, can lead to conflicts between marketing and sales. The marketing–sales relationship presents the same difficulties as that which exists between product development and production; what marketing suggests must be sold, what product development proposes must be built.

1. List the new products introduced during the period under consideration. Classify them as (1) *new-to-the-market*, (2) major additional features to current product, and (3) minor improvements. What was the impact on business performance of each?
2. Evaluate the product/service opportunities where marketing identified the opportunities and sales either met or did not meet expectations.
3. Evaluate the product/service opportunities where sales identified market opportunities and marketing failed to do due diligence in evaluating business opportunities.
4. Identify the creative/innovative opportunities proposed by marketing.
5. Evaluate how sales changed its approach in dealing with customers and users.

6. Satisfied customers determine an organization's sustainability. How has the organization managed customer relations? Identify the decisions that advanced and those that hindered customer relations.

Time

Lost time is not retrievable; it's a vital resource that cannot be reclaimed or recycled. Lost time in decision-making creates the man-made problems we inflict on ourselves. The number of hours in a day is fixed. It's time to take a serious look at work practices. Perhaps, we may need to bring back Frederick Taylor's time and motion principles and review them for use with knowledge workers. As one who has been always sensitive to effective use of time, I suggest that we have not found a way to work effectively in our digital age. We continue to have people, with salaries in excess of $100,000 annually, hunting and pecking on a keyboard. We continue to spend 3 months or more reaching a conclusion that could be reached within a week by personal contact. We continue to appoint people with questionable qualifications to perform the duties assigned after gathering volumes of information. These actions affect time-to-decision.

1. Where organizations spend the available time doesn't require developing massive big data or analytics. Just analyze the time-to-decision, from initial proposal to approval and providing the resources on projects that affect organizational performance.
2. Identify those individuals or groups that advanced the decision process and those that delayed the decision process. Determine the circumstances for each case.
3. Identify the factors that delayed or accelerated decision-making.
4. What was the impact on the organization's performance of the delayed or accelerated decision?
5. What actions were taken to resolve the delays? How were the accelerated decisions recognized?

Distribution

The distribution system includes four basic components; (1) means by which an organization sells its products and services, (2) the physical resources required to move the product from the production plant to the warehouse and then to the customer, (3) the order entry and processing through billing activities, and (4) customer service. The decisions in each of these four operations can be evaluated on performance.

1. How does the organization sell its products? Changes regarding sales occur continually; sales territories change; sales personnel are moved from one organizational unit to another; new products enter the marketplace; and headquarters imposes itself in regard to product priorities. Examine how the decisions related to the aforementioned issues affected individual behavior and organizational performance.
2. Products must move from the production floor to the warehouse to the customer. Identify the delays that have occurred because of ineffective decision-making; gross and minor delays in decision-making can occur anywhere by anyone involved in moving the product from production to the warehouse and seriously affect negatively with the customer.
3. Order entry through billing may be considered a routine and repetitive process, that's an extensive process especially where customization is involved. Do you know the gaps and what are you doing about it? Is the process effective and efficient? Where are the problems, how do you eliminate them?

Customers

Arguments have been made, pros and cons, about customer involvement in product development and as a source of new product ideas. However, don't expect a breakthrough from a customer. The source of the breakthrough may be initiated by the customer, but there's a significant difference between bringing the idea forward and implementing it.

1. How does the organization make decisions related to customer input?
2. Is there formal acknowledgement of customer concerns?
3. How do those professionals in engineering and marketing use customer input? Do they claim credit or acknowledge the source?
4. What does the organization know about its customers, and what decisions arise from that knowledge?
5. How are decisions made in relation to meeting customer needs? How does the organization use the customer's intellectual property?

Suppliers

Suppliers have always provided valuable input related to all aspects of organizational processes, and often more importantly, because they have the specialized expertise. In essence, suppliers market their intellectual property. How does the organization work with its suppliers? I'm not referring to what's in the policies and procedures manual, but in real everyday relationships beginning with the proposal and bidding stage.

1. Evaluating the decisions that determine contractor–supplier relationships determines whether on the next request for proposal, the organization will begin to search for a new supplier and goes through a new learning curve.
2. At a minimum check how often the organizational unit contacted a supplier before the scheduled delivery date.
3. Did the supplier meet the requirements, schedule, costs, and quality requirements?
4. How did the supplier engage other suppliers who were depending upon it for their performance?
5. When problems were found, what actions were taken? Were they taken in a timely manner?
6. Did your decisions support the suppliers? If so, how?

Production Capability

Providing production capability usually involves significant investment in capital. This is true regardless of where the organization falls on the continuum from start-up to one of Fortune's 500 companies. These decisions eventually determine an organization's return on investment.

1. Evaluating the decisions related to production requires answering a single question—did the investment yield the expected results? Results measured against product quality, waste, costs, and return on capital. The question though needs to be asked; how those decisions were reached, was there a negative or positive impact on the organization's culture.
2. Many production processes are totally automated. The questions—were the processes automated too far? Were sections automated, which would have provided a better cost-benefit had automation been limited to certain types of operations?
3. Generating some level of waste cannot be eliminated, but it requires attention. Just about every punched hole generates waste. Products that use solvents as carriers vaporize and go up the stack or through some type of recovery system to limit the amount; an infinitesimal amount remains in the product, the remainder is waste. How much attention is given to

decreasing waste at the time of design, rather than providing ways to minimize it in production?

Finance

Finance, including all the activities related to authorization of funding capital as well as special projects, becomes the ultimate broker in decisions that involve a request for funding. That does not imply that they always make the right recommendation.

1. Evaluating financial decision performance involves a simple comparison of estimates used to make the decisions to actual results accomplished.
2. Allocating costs often becomes a game in order to demonstrate some particular positive aspect of a project and thus promote someone's agenda. Too often, such actions leave the participants in dismay; it then demotivates those who dedicated themselves to meet the requirements. Examine such activities and take the required action.
3. The more important decisions relate to how organizational units work with the various functional groups within the finance department to reach those decisions. Are financial departments active participants in the project process, or judges of the actions of others? Are they involved in the project from day one providing their advice and counsel? Or do they become involved after the proposal has been developed and given the task to put together a justification of the investment. As noted, time cannot be reclaimed or recycled. Time is of the essence.

LEADERSHIP

How does an organization evaluate its leadership? The answer depends on how the organization describes leadership. If the organization looks for leadership solely from the CEO or the executive levels, much of the organizational talent may be underutilized. While this situation may not occur as an identified practice, it can be detrimental to an organization's future, if it is perceived to be so by the organization's members. Peter Drucker[3] reminded us that

"To expect every manager to be a leader is futile. But, as a member of the leadership group, the manager must practice an ethic of responsibility."

I extrapolate Drucker's statement where he uses the word *manager* to include all organizational participants from the executive offices to the mail room. Leadership, like innovation is not a choice, but an expectation from all organizational units.

1. Does the organization's educational program include leadership development? Did the program focus on the full scope of leadership requirements; the risks, the commitments, the self-sacrifice, and the responsibilities?
2. What is the attitude of top management regarding leadership; actively promote and recognize the importance of leadership, or assume that leaders will arise when the need requires?
3. How does the organization promote leadership?
4. Does the organization take notice of the leadership that emerges from the organization's non-leadership community?
5. Does the organization provide a culture that supports freedom-to-act response from employees?
6. Has the organization identified the invisible leadership in the organization?
7. Does the organization appoint its supervisors, project managers, and managers?

INNOVATION AND ENTREPRENEURSHIP

Innovation lives in the marketplace, not the research laboratory. Innovation is often confused with ideas and invention. Entrepreneurship, while touted in the media and the political community as the primary link to competitiveness, fails to be fully understood by the groups that promote it. Peter Drucker[4] reminds us that

> *"Every organization—not just business—needs one core competence: innovation."*

Engaging in innovation and entrepreneurship, too often misses the mark because of a lack of due diligence and a failure to be realistic in evaluating the organization's competencies and looking beyond its business and management traditions. Innovation involves more than new products and services; it includes innovations related to performance, quality, total cycle time reduction in all activities, reduction in energy consumption, elimination of bureaucracies, simplification of administrative requirements, and every activity in any organizational unit.

> Innovation = Invention + Commercialization or Implementation. No commercialization or implementation, no innovation.

Innovation does not involve any mysteries; there are no 10 easy lessons; there are no seven-step panaceas for becoming an innovative organization. It doesn't require genius; it does require initiative, ingenuity, focus, hard work, and accepting the risk. So how does an organization measure the impact of its innovation and entrepreneurial ventures on performance?

1. Does an organizational spirit exist that supports the innovators, stifles the naysayers, and provides for open communication?
2. What effort does the organization put forth in educating its professional community about business realities? Do the potential intrapreneurs know what's required to put together a business plan for a project?
3. Organizational entrepreneurship often described as "Intrapreneurship" is an extension of innovation; the culture allows the innovator to take on the responsibility for developing a new business. Has the organization promoted intrapreneurship or some version of it, as a means for developing executive level management?
4. People who focus on innovation, entrepreneurship, and intrapreneurship possess a *put-it-all-together* competence. Identify the people who have these competencies, if none are apparent, begin a program to develop them.
5. Identify all innovative programs and describe the results from the time the program was given a "GO" to its current status. Evaluate the programs on meeting requirements, quality, schedule and cost from an operational and management perspective.
6. Decisions at all levels in the organization determine at what level innovation and intrapreneurship will drive the fulfillment of strategic directions.
7. Does management at all levels encourage the creative and constructive mavericks or just tolerate them? I use the word maverick in a very positive way and not pejoratively. You may prefer individualist or nonconformist.
8. Is support demonstrated by action and providing resources?
9. Does the organization tolerate well-intentioned failure? Does the organization have a process for learning from failure?
10. How does the organization recognize individual and group success? Does the organization know how innovation takes place?
11. Are expectations for innovation limited to the introduction of products and services or from all organizational units from the executive suites to the mail room?
12. Does the organization track its innovation history and use it as a source of motivation?

13. Does the organization provide the advocate or sponsor for the innovation at the appropriate time?

14. How does the organization measure its investment in innovation? Decisions in all of these areas determine whether or not the organization can develop a spirit of innovation.

15. Does the organization communicate its strategic direction in sufficient detail to move those organizational thinkers to anticipate future needs that meet the organization's technology and marketing platforms?

ORGANIZATIONAL READINESS

Organizational readiness consists of being able to anticipate both internal and external actions that may affect an organization positively or negatively. Obviously, not all events can be identified. Japan could not anticipate the 2011 tsunami that created significant loss of life as well as the destruction of part of the nation's infrastructure. I've seldom found organizations investing effort on examining and making provisions on what the impact might be on operations if certain people, at any level and in any position, decided to leave the organization or were unavailable for some other reason.

1. What decisions were made that disrupted supply chain, not only for a short period but an extended period?

2. Have decisions been made regarding disruption if a major production facility was destroyed or shut down for some reason?

3. What are the plans if a competitor introduced a product that provides significant benefits?

4. If any one of many government agencies revised regulations with detrimental effects, what are the available alternative solutions to be implemented?

5. If a product recall becomes necessary because of defective operation, is a plan available to manage customer concerns?

6. How would the organization manage patent infringement?

This list could continue but it provides the territory that needs to be considered as organizations attempt to define how they'd manage their organizational readiness. Every organization faces its own particular readiness issues and preparedness does not mean becoming fearful of how every possible unexpected incident could negatively affect operations.

POLICIES AND PROCEDURES

Policies and Procedures (P&Ps) aid as well as hinder organizational performance; they're essential for conducting business from the start-up entrepreneur to the megabusinesses. It's difficult to make an argument for eliminating them.

1. Do those shelves of policies and procedures overwhelm the organization, if so; it's time to reexamine their benefit to the organization.
2. Are those P&Ps up-to-date, continue to be applicable, and meet the needs of the organization?
3. An organization cannot sustain its viability through enforcing their many P&Ps: disregarding the P&Ps at times provides significant benefits; rigid adherence to P&Ps limits freedom to act and limits personal initiative. What is the organization's policy on by passing P&Ps? Are P&Ps that are necessary specific, short, and don't attempt to cover every possible action? You're asking people to make a judgment. Personal initiative requires freedom to act with discipline.
4. Do the administrative policies help or hinder in promoting the organization's objectives?
5. Don't spend hours analyzing and evaluating compliance, take the time to determine if the P&P meets its purposes. Take a look at the policy and reduce the length by at least one-half.
6. How many managers promote educational opportunities beyond what is stated in the P&P?
7. Forget about line-by-line expense report analysis; use applicable statistical methods.
8. Do the P&Ps provide flexibility in providing salary advances for exceptional performance beyond the limits stated in the P&P? Are limits required, yes, but not for the exceptional producers.

EMPLOYEE BENEFITS

Organizations, regardless of size, provide financial and social benefits beyond basic compensation. Financial may include some form of profit sharing, 401(k) participation, educational programs, financial planning services, and others. Other social benefits include such activities as travel, book clubs, discussion groups, photographic clubs, reduced theatre and sports tickets, golf outings, and at one time countless bowling teams. Quantifying the value of these financial and social benefits, continuing or extending them, or providing new and possibly different benefits determines the ability of an organization to keep its base of professional talent. What may have been acceptable in the past may no longer be of value.

- Employers tend to provide the same employee benefits to the whole organization. Are the general benefits applicable to all? If so, do they meet their purposes?
- What may be acceptable on the plant floor may not be valued by the scientific or research community. What may be valued by the sales department may be totally unacceptable to a group of highly skilled programmers. The expectations of the innovator may be quite different from those of engineers or marketers who obtain job satisfaction with lesser expectations. How does the organization meet the requirements of individual constituencies?
- While organizations cannot personalize all employee benefits, do managers and project leaders have flexibility in providing benefits based on individual performance?
- Do managers who recognize exceptional service to the organization have the full authority to act within the organization's P&Ps or does the process require engaging the organization's bureaucracy? In other words, do they take personal initiative to advance their staff?

DOWNSIZING

Organizations downsize usually because of economic reasons that force the reduction of personnel or as a result of productivity increases primarily due to automation and enhanced information systems. Downsizing does not occur because human labor was expected to work faster: the speed of the assembly line has not increased. Much across the board downsizing has had significant negative impact in some organizations, where knowledge of the past was a vital component for success. Much can be learned from assessing the results of downsizing. If downsizing was required,

1. What steps were taken to educate the organization about the need for downsizing?
2. Was the downsizing implemented with dignity and respect for the individuals involved?
3. Was any thought given to the net effect on remaining employees and what steps were taken to minimize any negative impact?

4. Were any specific actions taken to satisfy the needs of the retained employees?

5. Was the downsizing accomplished through a selective process or a blanket dictum to reduce by "x" percent?

6. How much talent was released and then rehired as consultants?

7. Was any thought given to assess the process by which additions were made to staff?

8. What disruptions occurred because of the release of critical talent?

9. Such information may force greater justification of adding staff in the future.

10. Can you quantify the costs associated with the loss of key people?

11. Were legal issues taken into consideration?

12. How were the downsized employees notified of their status, by email, in groups, or in person?

GOING GLOBAL

Going global requires more than an understanding of the financial implications of the actions taken; it's a strategic decision. While those global markets present opportunities, they also are subject to unprecedented and unappreciated challenges. The most important may be a lack of understanding of the cultures which is not gained by the 1-week trip to meet possible participants in some new business association. The initial association is only the beginning. The problems begin when two cultures come together to develop a working organization that depends on the integration of two or more different cultures.

1. Was the decision to engage globally a conscious decision based on opportunities or an *ad hoc* decision?

2. What steps were taken to prepare for entering the global marketplace? Who were the people who understood the full implications of the global marketplace?

3. What steps were taken to determine the acceptability of the product or service not only from the new customer's perspective, but also with compliance to legal requirements and regulations?

4. Were the financial issues related to international transfer of funds identified and understood?

5. What was the relationship with the partners in different countries?

6. Did both sides know how to communicate openly and understand each other?

7. Does the organization know how to operate in other cultures? Under-standing culture involves more than appreciating the country's cuisine and native beverages.
8. What were the consequences of going global?

GOVERNMENT REGULATIONS

Every organization is subject to governmental regulations from the international, national, and through a host of state and local ordinances. They include taxes from multiple governing bodies, environmental regulations from the federal to the local level, labor requirements that transfer personal responsibility to the organization, and others. While the federal government issues hundreds of safety requirements seldom are they enforced. As an example, every mine acci-dent somehow results from unenforced federal regulations without any negative consequences to those responsible for managing mine safety.

1. What is the record on meeting government regulations from the national to the local level, and in many situations today, those of foreign govern-ments?
2. Is there sufficient organizational oversight over the many different and often conflicting regulations?
3. In relation to, as an example, environmental or uses of toxic chemicals, does the organization depend on government regulations or recognize its responsibility of providing safe products?
4. Are designers and engineers grounded in safety requirements related to the area in which the organization functions? (This will be quite different for a power company operating a nuclear power generating plant and an organization manufacturing computer chips.)
5. Are the organization's facilities designed with the necessary safety fea-tures?
6. Does the organization enforce safety standards within its laboratories and manufacturing operations?

OFFSHORE OPERATIONS

Moving manufacturing operations offshore solely for purposes of taking advan-tage of lower labor costs has not always proved successful. Witness the product recalls for lead contaminated toys, toxic compounds in drywall, food additives, and pet foods. Add to these major problems, inadequate oversight of the general working environment.

1. Offshore operations require greater supervision of the environment from the parent organization. The responsibility does not end with the issuance of the contract. Moving operations offshore provides opportunities and benefits, but the process requires control. How does the organization manage offshore relations?
2. Does the organization track total costs associated with offshore operations?
3. What is the cost of the product recalls including the associated legal costs and subsequent loss of customers?
4. What is the negative impact on the organization's reputation?
5. What does the organization do to maintain the quality of its products and services?
6. Is moving some operations offshore accomplished on the cheap or staffed with adequate and knowledgeable management and supervision to guarantee quality products and services?
7. What is the organization's policy on offshore operations; set standards and depend on contractor to fulfill the requirements, or police activities at the contactor site? What decisions have been made to guarantee quality and safety requirements and also meet employee environmental requirements?

INTEGRATING ORGANIZATIONAL UNITS

Integrating organizational functions within an organizational unit provides its share of difficulties. What do I mean by integrating organizational units? Bringing a new product or service to market does not just include product development: it requires a team from research, product design and development, manufacturing, marketing, sales, customer service, and a host of staff services. In essence, it requires taking a systems approach. If that product involves participation from other international subsidiaries or other organizations, the process becomes more complicated. Integrating that chain of activities across the continents requires professional disciplinary competencies; an understanding of human behavior in different cultures; and the ability to accept, reject, or negotiate cultural differences.

- To what degree are the functional levels integrated?
- How do they communicate with each other?

- What is the status of cross-disciplinary understanding?
- How do marketing and technology functions relate, cooperatively or independently?
- What is the organization's goal, when multiple functions are involved; meeting the functional requirements or the project requirements?
- If one or more major global organizational units are involved, do the cultures support the interactions?
- If offshore operations are involved, do the people who interact know each other, not through the internet or twitter, but through sufficient face-to-face contact?
- Are the executive activities at the major organizational units integrated?
- Does the organization promote integration and use of the systems approach and how does it accomplish this task?

GENERAL GOVERNANCE ISSUES

Organizational governance receives little attention from both the academic community and industry executives. Most organizations emphasize the documentation and processes of governance. Organizational governance is a multidisciplinary field that includes organization theory, sociology, economics, psychology, political science, and industrial engineering. Organizational governance in the abstract has been described as follows.

> "Organizational governance concerns how agents, pursuing their own interests, and with different preferences, knowledge or information, and endowments, use instruments of control to regulate their transactions to avoid problems of coordination and motivation they confront when interacting within or through the purposely designed social system systems known as "organizations.""

What does this somewhat abstract description mean? Simply stated, corporate governance involves integrating all the "*stuff*" (substantive resources) that allows an organization to administer and control its actions to meet its purposes and satisfy its stakeholders. The question, does an organization allow decisions related to the "stuff" just happen or make them consciously in relation to and in anticipation of the organization's future performance? The "stuff" presented here in alphabetical order, so as not to suggest priorities, which may be different for every organization, requires evaluation based on the following comments and questions and the derivatives thereof.

Evaluating decisions related to project governance does not involve finding blame; the purpose is to identify the decisions that led to the successful or unsuccessful actions that in some way provided a benefit or hindered the operations. Project governance applies to all organizational projects, not just those related to the technological side of the organization. Project evaluation is based on facts. Did the project meet the organization's strategic intent and the criteria for approval? This assumes that the organization approves projects based on established criteria.

Alignment: Alignment includes a multitude of issues such as organizational vision with available resources and infrastructure and business objectives; strategy and operations; all organizational units with the organization's purposes; research with resources to capitalize on the investment in research; identified and specific talent requirements with project needs; product development; marketing with sales and product development; human resources policies with organizational ability to comply in the long term with realistic perspective; and finally alignment with all activities that affect performance with the organization's purposes. How is alignment accomplished and what has been the impact on performance due to alignment and lack of alignment?

Authority Formal: The organization's legal documents disclose formal authority and lines of authority in decision-making and in regards to financial issues. The "who" approves and at what level describe the limits of authority. The documents describe types of contracts that require specific signatures and related issues described in detail. But, those lines of authority when dealing with nonfinancial matters can become somewhat blurred and may lead to unfavorable consequences. In essence, the documents do not define the many areas where decisions affect performance. While there is no desire to institute another organizational bureaucracy, how does the organization manage the potential areas of conflict?

Authority Informal: What are the limits of informal authority? Acting with informal authority and not officially having that authority produces pros and cons. When used appropriately in the absence of formal authority, it can provide a benefit. However, if used without restraint, it can have unintended consequences. As an example; a senior design engineer may make a decision, because her manager continues to delay making a decision which affects the program cost and schedule. If the decision yields a positive result she may be recognized, providing the action and/or the results did not in some way compromise the manager. Not everyone can take such risks, but without them it's difficult for an organization to meet its objectives. Using informal authority should not become a standard operating procedure; it should be used judiciously and with judgment. Identify results where informal authority generated either positive or negative results. In today's complex organizations, promoting informal authority has become a necessity.

Boundaries of Operation: What decisions has the management made to reduce the silo effect that costs every organization not only countless hours of lost time, but also, in the process, fails to provide for avenues of understanding and cooperation between functions and disciplines?

What questions have managers posed regarding the negative impact on performance?

1. Is there any effort to broaden the scope of those working in the silos and expanding their horizon?
2. Has there been an emphasis on integration of activities?
3. Does the organization promote managing with the systems approach?
4. How does the organization focus its employees on cross-functional understanding?
5. Few people in any organization move beyond meeting the minimum requirements. Too often, the attitude "I do my job that's assigned to me and that's all I'm interested in" prevails. How does the organization manage such attitudes?

Bureaucracy: How does the organization deal with its bureaucracy? The word bureaucracy generally is used in a very pejorative sense. But unfortunately, in any major organization there are many functions that fall under the purview of *this bureaucracy*. There are routine procedures and demands placed on all employees beginning with the CEO. The objective is to make sure that the bureaucracy works for the organization, rather than hinders personal initiative and performance.

1. So, what decisions have been made at all organizational levels to make sure that the bureaucracy benefits rather than hinder operations?
2. Are the organization's bureaucracies effective and how is that effectiveness demonstrated and measured?

Community Participation: In one way or another every organization becomes part of the community in which it operates. An argument can be made that the organization should focus on its success and that success will satisfy its contribution to the community. A contrary argument can be made that organizations have a responsibility to the community. Most major organizations actively participate in community activities through their foundations or direct contributions to various social programs. Other than financial donations or sponsorship of activities, much of the participation comes voluntarily from the employees. These employees make up the front-line with the community; they become involved personally in areas of their own choosing. Is this employee outreach required? Yes! Is it beneficial? Yes! The organization's role involves keeping the volunteer contributions in perspective, but without negative effects on career growth. So, how does your organization and organizational unit support community efforts?

Competitive Business Model: In today's global economy organizations become involved in many different business models depending on their product lines and the customers they serve. While there may be an organizational business model, the more important model for engineers and other discipline specialists may be the organizational business unit model responsible for providing its share of the organization's income. In many cases the business unit model may involve several product business models. The organizational unit business model involves the activities of all the functional units in the continuum from research to customer satisfaction. This model involves all the various professional specialists in engineering and marketing. Do these professional specialists meet the educational and experience requirements of the global competitive marketplace? Identify the decisions that have been made about developing programs that foster continued growth and employee preparation; what worked and what didn't. Identify the decisions that changed the mindset that prefers the status quo to one that encourages change; can the specific actions and results be identified? Identify the decisions that brought the competitive issues to the engineer's work bench; quantify them.

Decision Rights: Decision rights at the macro and executive levels are usually defined by legal documents that identify the signatories to those decisions at different levels of the hierarchy. Those decision rights involve more than financial. They cover the gamut of all possible types of decisions related to such areas as appointments, salary schedules, customers, suppliers, government agencies, and others made in the course of doing business. However, as the decision process flows down through the organization there are, what might be considered minor decisions that have a significant impact on performance. As examples: The selection of a specific vendor's product as a component in an assembly; the field salesperson making a decision on an accelerated delivery without first checking availability; a manufacturing process engineer changing the production parameters without proper authority. Does the organization place strict demands on managing decision rights? How far and under what conditions can an employee act? Do current decision rights allow for use of judgment, but at the same time require a follow-up with adequate documentation.

Employment Contracts: Employment contracts involve written and implied conditions of employment. For practical purposes most employment contracts, except for upper level executives and certain specific assignments fall into a general category of employee agreements. An organization with 100,000 employees does not sign individual contracts. The organization makes an offer to a candidate and the candidate either accepts or rejects the offer. Candidates with years of experience and special sought after competencies do have some opportunities for negotiation. In such situations employee policies and practices guide the relationship between employer and employee. Organizations do have agreements related to patents and copyrights which are usually assigned to the organization that made the investment. The legality of such agreements varies from state to state in the United States. So, do the organization's decisions regarding employee contributions help or hinder overall job satisfaction?

Project Governance: Project governance involves more than the mechanisms associated with project management. Governance includes those basics of project management, but also issues such as leadership, structure, pre- and post-project processes, and customer satisfaction. I relate project governance to those organizational projects that make a difference, not all projects include governance issues. My comments here relate to those projects that meet the strategic and operational objectives of the organization. These will normally include projects related to introducing new-to-the-market products; major upgrades of current products; new facilities, manufacturing facilities, office buildings, sales offices, and warehousing operations; mergers and acquisitions; global expansion; and projects of similar scope.

1. Does the project under consideration meet the organization's criteria for success: success not only in financial terms, but more importantly in its strategic direction?
2. What was the buy-in level of all groups involved in the project? If there was no buy-in was the issue resolved with changes in personnel or other actions?
3. Commitments are often made by managers and often under some pressure from various constituencies in order to gain approval. Did such commitments affect the project outcome?
4. Were critical issues raised during the term of the project; were issues resolved or disregarded by either managers or the professional specialists? What was the impact on project outcome?
5. Putting the controversial issue on the table for resolution is often unappreciated; it takes a certain kind of courage.
6. Project postmortems are a common event and can provide some lessons learned, regardless of the level of project success; focus equally on the positive and negative.

7. At the time of approval were the project knockouts identified, and if not, why not? Were suggestions disregarded without adequate consideration?

8. Was the project driven from the top-down or the bottom-up?

9. Were decisions made to integrate the various functions?

10. Was there a planned modus operandi that included a communication plan that allowed participants to self-address their limits of responsibility and authority? What decisions either helped or hindered keeping the project on schedule and within cost estimates? Did any decisions alter the project requirements and as a result deliver something less than expected?

Organizational Structure: Organizational structure too often is used as a reason or as an excuse, for meeting or not meeting expectations. If you have the right people competencies, structure is not that important; if you do not have the required competencies, changing the structure will not deliver the expected results.

Organizational structure obviously plays a role in meeting requirements. Management might begin by asking questions along the following lines.

1. Has management analyzed its macro structure recently? Analysis requires more than identifying available internal and external talent.

2. What is the strategy for the organizational design?

3. How much freedom does the organization provide to the many suborganizational units within the organization? If freedom to organize as required to fit a situation exists, has it been successful? If not, why not.

4. Are considerations given to organizational difference for staff and operational units?

5. If the organization involves international organizations, what is the relationship to the base organization? What are the levels for acting independently? Are limits identified?

6. Does the organization understand the differences between how the formal organization functions and how the day-to-day informal structure required to move products/services from idea to the customer?

7. Does the organization understand the white spaces on the organization chart?

KEY POINTS

- **People.** People competencies translated into organizational capabilities drive an organization's performance and future sustainability. Decisions related to hiring, development, and assignment of, especially the knowledge workers, requires due diligence.

- **Purposes.** Working without a purpose, both individual and organizational, seldom provides opportunities for achievement. Clearly stated organizational and sub-organizational purposes provide the employees with a direction and opportunities for maximizing performance.

- **Processes.** Defined processes, both administrative and production processes provide organizational discipline among the many sub-organizational units. It takes leadership to find a balance in promoting the use of established processes and the opportunities that arise that require deviation.

- **Strategic Thinking.** Strategic thinking departs from the bureaucratic process of strategic planning that seldom includes an operational plan to fulfill the strategy. The essence of strategy involves synthesis of the organization's principle issues into developing a strategic direction.

- **Culture.** Culture impacts every organizational activity. It's all about people and how they interact within the organization and with associates outside the organization. Organizational culture is not monolithic; it may establish a norm, but every organizational unit develops its own culture.

- **Products and Services.** Products and/or services provide the organization's income stream, but the selection of the ideas in which to invest, involves decisions from many different constituencies in the organization. It is not solely a marketing or technology decision; it's an integrative process.

- **Resources.** Organizational resources include more than people and money and more than what's owned by the organization. Most organizational activities involve use of many different types of resources. Decisions related to providing the internal resources and also using the external resources effectively and efficiently set the stage for meeting the organization's goals.

- **Leadership.** Leadership can take on many different forms. Not everyone has the courage to take a leadership position; it usually involves some level of risk-taking. Leadership involves, at its most basic level, being accountable for one's actions.

- **Innovation and Entrepreneurship.** Innovation and intrapreneurship and entrepreneurship are interrelated creative acts that require *me* to come up with the idea and *we* to implement it; it is not a singular action by one person. It requires total dedication above and beyond the normal and willingness to disregard the naysayers.

- **Organizational Readiness.** Organizational readiness depends on an organization's ability to anticipate events; it also depends on the ability of the knowledge workers to anticipate events in their respective disciplines. Anticipation of potential negative events is not being fearful of the future, but realistic and prepared to manage it.

- **Policies and Procedures.** Policies and procedures are a required necessity in an organization; however, rigidly enforcing them can limit freedom-to-act and personal initiative. Too much emphasis on policies and procedures limits the opportunities for making judgments when required; judgment is always a requirement.

- **Employee Benefits.** Employee benefits play a major role in employee retention; they go beyond the social, financial, the educational, and the one-time company sponsored bowling clubs. A major benefit, usually forgotten or disregarded as nonessential, involves the ability of one to make decisions within the sphere of one's capabilities.

- **Downsizing.** Downsizing of knowledge workers negatively affects the organization's ability to meet project requirements, schedules, and cost. Too often loss of non-recorded historical knowledge and experience leads to negative consequences. Decisions become critical as evidenced in the daily business press.

- **Going Global.** Going global involves more than bottom-line performance. While expanding in global markets presents opportunities, it can also present unprecedented challenges. Success depends on understanding the differences in the cultures, cultural priorities, and finding ways to reconcile the differences.

- **Government Regulations.** Government regulations, at all levels of government, continue to increase. These regulations not only apply to the organization, but also and more importantly to the people within the organization who have responsibility for meeting the legal requirements. Decisions often deal with conflicting regulations.

- **Integrating Organizational Units.** On any major project individual organizational units only provide part of the answer. Major projects, however, involve many organizational units. These projects need to considered with a systems perspective and the people involved in those projects must also think and operate with systems perspective.

- **General Governance Issues.** Corporate governance involves integrating all the substantive resources that allow an organization to satisfy the stakeholders; it involves dealing with multi-disciplinary actions that include organization theory, sociology, economics, psychology, political science, and industrial engineering.

NOTES

1. Henry Mintzberg, *Rise and Fall of Strategic Planning*, New York: The Free Press, 1994.

2. Gerard H. Gaynor, *Innovation by Design*, New York: American Management Association, 2002, pp. 155–190.

3. Peter F. Drucker, *Management, Tasks, Responsibilities, Practices*, New York: Harper & Row, 1973, p. 788.

4. Peter F. Drucker, *The Essential Drucker*, New York: Harper-Collins, 2001, p. 65.

INDEX

Acquisitions and mergers, 49–52
  culture clash in, 50–51
  DaimlerChrysler merger, 50–52
  merger of equals, 51–52
Activities, Resources, and Infrastructure
  (ARI), 111–113
AHP. *See* Analytic Hierarchy Process
  (AHP)
Alenia Aeronautica, 200
Ambiguity, 157–160
Analytic Hierarchy Process (AHP), 93,
  177
Answer Man, 246
Appointments, 128–130
ARI. *See* Activities, Resources, and
  Infrastructure (ARI)
Assignment work, 135–136
Attitude questions, 165–166

Bad listeners, 246
BCAD. *See* Boeing Commercial
  Airplanes Division (BCAD)
BDSS. *See* Boeing Defense, Space &
  Security (BDSS)
Biscuiterie Nantaise (BN), 97–98
Bloomberg Business Week, 200
Boeing
  acknowledging reality, 201–202
  communication among staff, 209–210
  cultural differences, 210
  decisions on Dreamliner, 212–213
  787 Dreamliner. *See* 787 Dreamliner
  Dreamliner knockouts, 213–215
  Engineering, Operations &
    Technology, 191

  management principles of, 202–209
  management problems in, 192–193
  operation principles of, 192
  retirees concerns in, 211–212
  Shared Services Group, 191
  technical capabilities of, 210–211
Boeing Commercial Airplanes Division
  (BCAD), 191
Boeing Defense, Space & Security
  (BDSS), 191
Boeing Engineering, Operations &
  Technology (EO&T), 191
Bottom-up strategy, 232
Bottom-up top-down organization, 232
Brainstorming design sessions, 229
"Broken Bonds," 6
Bull Computer Corporation, 5
Business concept, 56

Car Guys vs. the Bean Counters, 203
1986 Challenger disaster, 254
Chief Executive Officer (CEO), 15
Chief Technology Officers (CTO), 36
Cognitive dissonance, 245
College recruitment programs, 120–122
Command and control environment, 231
Communication, 219–221, 226–228
  barriers to, elimination of, 255–258
  definition of, 226
  effective, barriers to, 234
    communication plan, 251–252
    content in context, 234–235
    feedback, 249–250
    judging, 248–249
    language, 235–238

Decisions: An Engineering and Management Perspective, First Edition. Gerard H. Gaynor.
© 2015 The Institute of Electrical and Electronics Engineers, Inc. Published 2015 by John Wiley & Sons, Inc.

Communication, (*Continued*)
listening, 245–248
noise level, 238–245
technology, 250
ethical issues in, 252–255
executive, 227
in product-development teams, 220
types of, 228
communicating in groups, 229
one-on-one, face-to-face, 228–229
organizational context, 230–234
up, down, laterally, 229–230
Communication plan, 251
as barrier to effective communication,
251–252, 257–258
Content in context, as barrier to effective
communication, 234–235,
255–256
Context, in decision processes,
230–231
Continuing education, 138–139
Corporate Pathfinders, 141
CTO. *See* Chief Technology Officers
(CTO)
Culture, evaluation of decisions related
to, 267–268
Customers, evaluation of decisions
related to, 272–273

DaimlerChrysler merger, 50–52
Dance of Life, 106
Decision-making
failed project, history of, 2–5
knowledge, sources of, 7–8
organizational, 9–11
organizational discipline and, 5–7
Decision-making competencies
dealing with ambiguity, 157–160
decision dilemmas, 144–148
deliverables, execution for, 160–164
attitude questions, 165–166
business strategies, support of,
160–161
characteristics questions, 166
experience questions and, 165
knowledge questions and, 164–165

marketing and sales, 164
people decisions, 164
project cost, 162–163
project importance, 161
project manager, choice of, 162
project objectives, 161
project scope, 161
project staffing, 161–162
research, investment on, 163
skills questions, 165
technology for, 163–164
education for, 151–156
learning to make decisions, 148–151
clear presentation of issues,
148–149
creating debate, 149
decisions by consensus, 150–151
intentional dissonance, creation of,
149–150
timely decision, 150
Decision-making, inputs in
acquisitions and mergers, dealing with,
49–52
entering new markets, 59–60
external decision drivers, 46–48
investment
in new technologies, 57–59
in new-to-the-market product or
service, 55–57
knowledge chain, 43–46
locating business operations, 65–66
product line, discontinuation of,
60–61
promoting innovation and
entrepreneurship, 61–65
restructuring organizations, 52–54
worldwide operations, expansion of,
48–49
Decision-making knowledge, sources of,
7–8
*On Decision-Making in Large
Organizations*, 220
Decision-making process
communication in, 219–220. *See also*
Communication
information flow in, 221–222

Decision-support system (DSS), 107–108
Defining Market Problems, 97
Deliverables, execution for, 160–164
  attitude questions, 165–166
  business strategies, support of, 160–161
  characteristics questions, 166
  experience questions and, 165
  knowledge questions and, 164–165
  marketing and sales, 164
  people decisions, 164
  project cost, 162–163
  project importance, 161
  project manager, choice of, 162
  project objectives, 161
  project scope, 161
  project staffing, 161–162
  research, investment on, 163
  skills questions, 165
Denver International Airport project, 76–77
  diamond diagram of, 77
  risks associated with development of, 76
Direction and style, setting, 131–134
Discussions at operations level, 239
Distribution system, evaluation of decisions related to, 272
Doing What Matters, 125
Doing What Really Matters, 6
Downsizing, evaluation of decisions related to, 279–280
787 Dreamliner, 83–84
  challenges of, 194–200
  diamond diagram of
    for outsourcing, 206
    real, 205
    supply chain, 208
    technology, 209
    at time of approval, 203
  documentation for, 209
  impact on performance of, 206
  outsourcing of, 205–206
  overview, 189–190
  scope and expectations of, 190

Senior Advisory Group, formation of, 198–199
  succession of problems, 194–200
  supply chain management, 207–208
  technology of, 208–209
  virtual rollout December 2006, 194
DSS. *See* Decision-support system (DSS)

Employee benefits, evaluation of decisions related to, 279
Employee performance, evaluation of, 124–126
  approach to, 125–126
  competent employees, 124
  exceed expectations or outstanding, 125
  nonperformers, 124
  self-esteem and, 125
Employee potential, assessment of, 126–127
Empowerment programs, 249
Engineers, 23–25
Entrepreneurship, promotion of, 61–65
Environment, as barrier to effective communication, 244–245, 256
EO&T. *See* Boeing Engineering, Operations & Technology (EO&T)
The Essential Drucker, 20
Evaluation of decision-making performance, 261
  culture, 267–268
  downsizing, 279–280
  employee benefits, 279
  general governance issues, 283–289
  going global, 280–281
  government regulations, 281–282
  innovation and entrepreneurship, 275–277
  integrating organizational units, 282–283
  leadership, 275
  offshore operations, 282
  organizational readiness, 277–278
  people, 262–264
  policies and procedures, 278–279
  processes, 265–266

Evaluation of decision-making
    performance,
  products and services, 268–269
  purposes, 264–265
  resources, 269–274
  strategic thinking, 266–267
Excellence, 132
The Executive guide to better listening,
  245
Executives
  definition of, 16
  forward-looking, 17
Experience questions, 165
"Expert Choice," 177
External decision drivers, 46–48

Face-to-face communication, 228–229
Failed project, history of, 2–5
  Cooper's studies, 4–5
  Eisenhardt study, 4
  Nutt's research, 3–4
The Fall and Rise of Strategic Planning,
  266
Fast and slow decision-makers, 230
Feedback, as barrier to effective
  communication, 249–250, 257
The Fifth Discipline, 132
Finance, evaluation of decisions related
  to, 274
Financial Times, 195
Ford Motor Co., 47
Foreign-service engineers, 49
Forward thinking, 224
Freedom to act, 268
Frustration costs, 110
The Functions of the Executive,
  219
The Future of Management, 17

Going global, evaluation of decisions
  related to, 280–281
Good to Great, 144
Gouter, 97
Government regulations evaluation of
  decisions related to, 281–282

Grouches, 246
Groups, communicating in, 229

Hiring
  of experienced specialist, 122–124
  practices, 120
The Homework Beyond Teamwork, 102,
  130
Human resource department (HR),
  energizing, 118–120

IBM Global CEO Study 2006, 63
IBM Rochester (IBMR)
  ambitious goals of, 177–180
    Council of Customers, 179
    IBMR culture, 178–179
    Migration Invitational, 179–180
  birth of, 170–171
  competition with others, 171
  Fort Knox project, 171
  Furey's questions, 173–177
    agreement on specifications, 175
    communication of plan, 174
    low end model, 176
    market focus, 175–176
    organizational structure, 174
    resources allocation, 177
  launch of Silverlake, 180–181
  lessons learned, 181–187
    Fort Knox Project period, 182–183
    Pre–Fort Knox project period, 182
    Silverlake Project period, 183–187
  market challenges, 172
  new directions for, 172–173
  overview, 169–170
IBMR. *See* IBM Rochester (IBMR)
Idea/concept stage, 222–224
IEEE Code of Ethics, 253
Innovation and entrepreneurship, 30–31
  external obstacles to, 63
  evaluation of decisions related to,
    269–270
  internal obstacles to, 63
  organizational challenges in, 62
  promotion of, 61–65

requirement for, 63–64
task not to do for, 64–65
Innovation by Design, 5, 63
Innovation Prevention Department, 5
In Search of Excellence, 61
Intellectual property, access to,
evaluation of decisions related to,
269–270
Investment
in new technologies, 57–59
in new-to-the-market product or
service, 55–57
Irrelevant information, 238–239
IT projects
causes for failure of, 99
improving performance, 98–101
Standish Group report, 98–100

Judgment, as barrier to effective
communication, 248–249, 257
Justice Rule, 254

Knowledge chain, 44–46
discipline specialists, 45
executives in all areas, 45
managers at all levels, 45
staff executives, 44
Knowledge management (KM), 35
Knowledge questions, 164–165

Language, as barrier to effective
communication, 235–238, 256
Leadership, 28–30
evaluation of decisions related to,
275
Learning to make decisions, 148–151
clear presentation of issues,
148–149
creating debate, 149
decisions by consensus, 150–151
intentional dissonance, creation of,
149–150
timely decision, 150
Limited Scope project, product
modifications in, 81–82

Listeners
bad, 246
good, 246–247
Listening, as barrier to effective
communication, 245–248,
256–257
Literacy, 32–33
Location of business operations, 65–66

Macro decisions
describing problem or opportunity,
97–98
execution of, 92–93
improving IT project performance,
98–101
overview, 91–92
using tools and techniques, 93–96
Management by Objectives (MBO), 185
Management by walking around, 108
Management of technology (MOT), 36
Managers, 19–23
administrative work, 21
appointment of, 36–37
dealing with people issues, 21
focusing on business, 22
project, 25–27
providing direction, 21
resolving high anxiety issues, 22
responsibilities of, 21–23
taking action, 21–22
transition from specialist to, 136–137
Marketing and sales, evaluation of
decisions related to, 270–271
Market segmentation, 175
MBO. *See* Management by Objectives
(MBO)
Migration Invitational, 179–180
Mobilizing Minds, 17
Moral Rights Rule, 254
MOT. *See* Management of technology
(MOT)

The Nature of Technology, 236
New market, decision for entering, 59–60
New technologies, investment in, 57–59

New-to-the-market product, 221–226
  idea/concept stage, 222–224
  marketplace execution stage, 225–226
  pre-project stage, 224–225
  project stage, 225
New-to-the-market product, investment
        in, 55–57
  determining idea viability, 56
  project development, 56
  project execution, 56–57
Noise, as barrier to effective
        communication, 238–245
  elimination of, 256
  environment, 244–245
  irrelevant information, 238–239
  opinions instead of facts, 240–243
  unnecessary interruptions, 243–244

Offshore operations, evaluation of, 282
Opinionator, 246
Organizational decision-making, 9–11
  approval process and, 10–11
  corporate level, 10
  functions and, 10
Organizational decisions, 70–72
  approaches for, 70
  current business to new business unit
        continuum, 78–79
  current business unit to new-game
        continuum, 79–80
  functional unit, decisions in, 80–81
  governance decisions, 72
  investment decisions, 70–71
  knockouts, 83–84
  limited scope to expanded scope
        continuum, 81–82
  low cost to high cost continuum, 75
  low impact to high impact continuum,
        73
  low risk to high risk continuum, 75–77
  operational decisions, 71
  operations issue and, 86–87
  organizational growth decisions, 72
  simple to complex continuum, 74–75
  strategic to operational continuum,
        82–83

  thinking process, 84–89
  upgrade to innovative continuum,
        77–78
Organizational discipline, 5–7
Organizational functions, principal,
        14
Organizational governance283–284. *See
        also* Project governance,
        evaluating decisions related to
Organizational management
  engineers and other discipline
        specialists in, 23–25
  executives in, 15–16
  management model for, 14–15
  managers, 19–23
    administrative work, 21
    dealing with people issues, 21
    focusing on business, 22
    providing direction, 21
    resolving high anxiety issues, 22
    responsibilities of, 21–23
    taking action, 21–22
  new management paradigm and,
        16–19
  organization's requirements, from
        management and staff, 27–39
    appointing managers, 36–37
    implementing decision, 35
    innovation, 30–31
    introducing change, 32
    leadership, 28–30
    literacy, 32–33
    project management, 33–34
    project team members, selection of,
        37
    rationalizing silos, 34
    return on investment, 38–39
    rewarding performance, 37–38
    single-issue management, 35–36
    vision or purpose, 28
  overview, 13–14
  project managers, 25–27
Organizational proprietary technologies,
        evaluation of, 270
Organizational readiness, evaluation of
        decisions related to, 277–278

Organizational requirements, from management and staff, 27–39
  appointing managers, 36–37
  implementing decision, 35
  innovation, 30–31
  introducing change, 32
  leadership, 28–30
  literacy, 32–33
  project management, 33–34
  project team members, selection of, 37
  rationalizing silos, 34
  return on investment, 38–39
  rewarding performance, 37–38
  single-issue management, 35–36
  vision or purpose, 28
Organizational restructuring, decision-making in, 52–54
  legitimate reasons for, 53
  Sloan model of, 53–54
Organizational units, integration of, evaluation of, 282–283
Organization's purposes, evaluation of decisions related to, 264–265

People decision-making
  appointments, 128–130
  assigning work, 135–136
  college recruitment programs, 120–122
  direction and style, setting, 131–134
  employee performance, evaluation of, 124–126
  employee potential, assessment of, 126–127
  hiring
    of experienced specialist, 122–124
    practices, 120
  HR department, energizing, 118–120
  overview, 117–118
  question to ask, 127–128
  selection
    of right people, 134–135
    of team members, 130–131

  specialist to manager, transition from, 136–137
  succession competence, building, 140–141
  unlearning, 139–140
People, evaluation of decisions related to, 262–264
Perseverators, 246
Policies and Procedures (P&Ps), evaluation of decisions related to, 278–279
Practical Rule, 254
Preambler, 246
Pretender, 246
Problem-solving sessions, 244
Processes, evaluation of decisions related to, 265–266
Product line, discontinuation of, 60–61
Production capability, evaluation of decisions related to, 273–274
Products and services, evaluation of decisions related to, 268–269
Project cycle time, management of, 105–111
  cycle duration, management of, 109–111
  new technology and, 110–111
  new-to-the-market product, introduction of, 109–110
  production facilities and, 111
  System Cycle Time Management, 105–106
  time management, 106–107
Project governance, evaluating decisions related to, 284
  alignment, 284
  authority formal, 284
  authority informal, 284–285
  boundaries of operation, 285
  bureaucracy, 285–286
  community participation, 286
  competitive business model, 286
  decision rights, 286–287
  employment contracts, 287
  organizational structure, 288–289
Project launch, 225

Project management, 25–27, 33–34
  adequate reporting project data,
      ensuring, 104–105
  adjustment approach, 105
  avoid competition with team, 102–103
  gaining management support, 101–102
  job essentials, focus on, 103
  knowing project team, 102
  learn to say no, 103
  manage change control, 103–104
  project cycle time. *See* Project cycle
      time, management of
  project success measurement, 101
  support for offsite teams, 104
  systems perspective and, 111–113
Project Management Institute (PMI), 225
Project managers, 25–27
Project objectives, 161
Project review meetings, 229
Project scope, 161
Project staffing, 161–162
Project team members, selection of, 37
Promotions, 128–130
  approaches need to consider for, 128

Reinventing Project Management, 25
Resources, evaluation of decisions
      related to, 269
  access to intellectual property,
      269–270
  customers, 272–273
  distribution, 272
  finance, 274
  managing technology, 270
  marketing and sales, 270–271
  production capability, 273–274
  suppliers, 273
  time, 271–272
Return on investment (ROI), 38–39
Rewards, for performance, 37–38
Rise and Fall of Strategic Planning, 266
ROI. *See* Return on investment (ROI)

Salary schedules, 138
SCTM. *See* System Cycle Time
      Management (SCTM)
Selection
  of right people, 134–135
  of team members, 130–131
Silverlake Project, 169
  benefits of, 176
  Furey's vision on, 173
  launch of, 180–181
  period of, 183–187
Single-issue management, 35–36
Skilled incompetence, 132
Skills questions, 165
Standish Group, 4–5
Standish Group report, 98–100
Strategic discussions, 239
Strategic thinking, evaluation of
      decisions related to, 266–267
Succession planning, 140–141
Suppliers, evaluation of decisions related
      to, 273
System Cycle Time Management
      (SCTM), 105–106

Technology, as barrier to effective
      communication, 250, 257
3M culture, 232–233
Time-to-decision, 271–272
Top-down strategy, 231–232

Unlearning, 139–140
Unnecessary interruptions, 243–244
Up–down–lateral continuum,
      information from, 229–230
Up-front work, 222
Utilitarian Rule, 254

The Wall Street Journal, 38, 108, 140,
      195, 237
Worldwide operations, expansion of,
      48–49